The Pyramid Approach to Education,

2nd Edition

Andy Bondy, Ph.D.

Pyramid Educational Consultants, Inc.

www.pecs.com

Copyright, 2011, by Andy Bondy

ISBN-13: 978-1-907857-02-7

Published in 2011 in the United States by

Pyramid EducationalConsultants Inc.

13 Garfield Way, Newark, DE 19713.

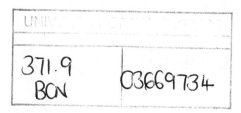

Table of Contents

1 The Pyramid Approach to Education 15

Features of the Pyramid Approach to Education. 18

The Base of the Pyramid 19

    The *Why* of Behavior: The Science of Learning 19

    Firming the Foundation: The *What* of Teaching 19

The Top of the Pyramid 22

    Getting There: The *How* of Teaching 22

Assessing and Evaluating: Collecting and Analyzing Data . .22

Putting it All Together .23

Summary 23

Chapter 1 Resources 25

2 The *Why* of Behaving: The Science of Behavior . . 27

Science and Human Behavior 28

Learning About Teaching and Learning 30

How Does Learning Come About? 32

Operant Conditioning. 33

The A-B-Cs of Behavior Change 37

    Context. 37

    Antecedents 37

    Consequences 38

Behavioral Procedures. 43

The Three-Term Contingency 44

Complex Learning. 45

Limitations on Our Teaching 46

Summary 48

Chapter 2 Resources 50

3 What to Teach: Functional Objectives 52

Deciding *What* to Teach. 52

The Long Range Goals of Education. 53

    Getting a Job. 53

    Living Independently 53

    Being Happy 53

Choosing Objectives 54

    Select Developmentally Appropriate Objectives 54

    Identify Areas of Strengths and Weaknesses 55

    Promote Pivotal Developmental Skills 55

    Consider a Learner's Chronological Age When Choosing
        Instructional Objectives 56

Choosing Functional Objectives 58

    Deciding Whether a Goal is Functional or Not: "If the learner
        doesn't do it, who will?" 58

Using Functional Activities as Vehicles for Teaching Other Skills
   59

Functional Skills within the School 60

Functional Skills within the Home. 60

Functional Skills within the Community 61

Functional Job Skills. .63

Generic Work Skills 63

Recreational and Leisure Skills. 65

Social and Communicative Objectives. 66

General Considerations in Using Functional Objectives. 67

    What Materials Should We Use? 67

    Preparing for Generalization and Discrimination. 69

    Goal Selection and Generalization 69

Criteria of the Next Environment. 70

Summary 71

Chapter 3 Resources 72

4 Powerful Reinforcement Systems 74

Accentuating Positive Reinforcement 75

Identifying Learner-Centered Reinforcers 75

    A Natural Solution. 75

    Reinforcers Incidental to Activities of Daily Living 76

    High Rate Behaviors. 76

    Locating Functional Reinforcers 77

    Inquire 78

    Observing Direct Interaction 78

    Offer Choices. 78

Making the Most of Reinforcers 79

    The Origins of Reinforcers 79

    Reinforcers are Relative. 80

    Establishing Events 81

    Timing of Reinforcement 82

    Other Strategies to Boost Reinforcer Effectiveness. 83

Using Powerful Reinforcers to Promote Learning 84

    Frequency and Distribution of Reinforcers: Learning versus
        Sustaining Change 84

    Teaching without Prompting - The Joy of Shaping! 86

    Differential Reinforcement - A Little Here Means a Lot There! 87

    Helping Teachers to Make the Most of Reinforcement 89

    Putting it all together - Let's make a deal! 89

Summary 93

Chapter 4 Resources 94

5 Communication and Social Skills: Functional Communication 96

What is Communication? 96

Why Do We Communicate? 99

Choosing Communicative Skills to Teach 100

   Communication is Bi-directional. 101

   Is Talking Always Communicative? 102

   Don't Just Hope For, Teach For, Generalization. 102

   Choose a Communicative Modality. 103

   What is PECS?. 104

Select Critical Communication Skills. 106

   Critical Productive Skills. 106

      Asking for help. 107

      Asking for a break 108

      Accepting or rejecting 108

   Critical Receptive Skills. 108

      Following Directions 109

      Transitioning from One Activity to Another 110

      Waiting Patiently. 111

      Following a Schedule 113

Communicating About Emotions 114

Communicating Skillfully in Social Circumstances 115

      Eye Contact. 116

      Greetings 116

      Communicating within Social Interactions 116

Assessing Your Learner's Most Critical Communication Needs 117

Play 119

Summary 122

Chapter 5 Resources 122

6 Preventing and ReducingContextually Inappropriate Behaviors 126

General Precautions 127

Promoting the Well-being of Learners with Special Needs . . 127

Assessing the Function of the CIB 129

Identifying Functionally Equivalent Alternative Behaviors (FEABs)
. . . . 130

Manipulating Antecedents 134

Differentially Reinforcing Acceptable Behaviors 135

Advantages and Disadvantages of Differential Reinforcement 138

Practical Hints for Using Differential Reinforcement 138

Reacting to Contextually Inappropriate Behavior 139

Summary 141

Chapter 6 Resources 143

7 Generalization 145

Why Discuss Generalization So Early? 147

Types of Generalization 148

Promoting Stimulus Generalization 149

Promoting Response Generalization. 152

Summary 157

Chapter 7 Resources 158

8 Designing Effective Lessons 162

Preparatory Steps 162

Review Objectives 163

Match Lessons to the Objective. 163

Plan Ways to Incorporate and Apply Laws of Learning and
Behavior Change 164

Antecedents and Consequences 165

Different Kinds of Antecedents 165

Consequences 165

Control by Discriminative Stimuli 166

Antecedent Stimuli and Lesson Planning 166

Teaching Scientifically 167

Teach by Trial and Success 167

Prompt for Success 169

Cues versus Prompts 170

Formal Lesson Design 171

Discrete Trial Lessons 171

What is a Discrete Trial? 171

Objectives Suited to Discrete-Trial Lessons 172

Assuring Learner Attending 172

Presenting Instructions 173

Presenting Consequences 173

Using Prompts if Necessary 173

How many prompts should be used? 174

Providing Opportunities for Repetition of the Correct Response
. . . . 174

Frequently Posed Questions about Discrete Trial Teaching . . 174

Sequential Lessons 177

Designing Effective Task Analyses 177

Task Analyses and Behavioral Chains 178

Initiating the Sequence 180

Reinforcement during Sequential Lessons 180

Learner Initiated Lessons 183

Summary 186

Chapter 8 Resources 188

9 Specific Teaching Strategies 190

Prompting 192

   Types of Prompts 192

   Prompts versus Natural Cues 193

   How to Identify Natural Cues 194

Prompting Strategies 196

   Selecting Prompts 196

   Eliminating Prompts 198

      Fading Prompts 198

      Fading Spoken Prompts 198

      Fading Physical Prompts 198

      Fading Gestural Prompts 199

      Fading Model Prompts 199

      Fading Augmented Stimuli 199

   Prompt Hierarchies 202

      Least-to-Most Prompt Hierarchies 202

      Most-to-Least Prompt Hierarchies 203

   Delayed Prompting 204

   Be Careful with Your Prompts! 206

How to Teach Sequential Lessons 206

   Whole or Partial Task 206

   Forward or Backward Chaining 207

Summary 209

10 Minimizing and Correcting Errors 211

Errorless Learning 212

How Do We Design Errorless Lessons? 213

Teaching for "Errorless Learning." 214

Fading *color* cues 216

Fading *size* cues 216

But Suppose Learners Do Make Mistakes? Coping With Errors
. . . . 218

Discrete Trials: The 4-step Error Correction Sequence 219

What Happens if the Learner Continues to Make Errors? . . 221

Correcting Errors in Sequential Tasks 221

Backstepping 221

Anticipatory Prompting 223

Commonalties Among Error-Correction Strategies 224

Summary 225

Chapters 9 and 10 Resources 226

11 Collecting and Analyzing Data: 227

Why Collect Educational Data? 228

Designing and Changing Lesson Strategies 228

Analyzing the Environment 229

Who Collects Data? 230

Qualities of Useful Data 230

Validity 231

Reliability 231

What Learner Data to Collect 232

Types of Data to Collect 233

Form of the Behavior 233

Form versus Function 233

Frequency 234

Rate 234

Duration 235

Intensity 235

Latency. 236

Behavioral Recording Procedures 236

Getting Started 236

Crucial Identifying Information. 237

Observational Recording 237

Continuous Observation. 238

Behavior Sampling 239

Recording Results of Behavior 239

Making Use of Data 240

Assessing the Function of a Behavior 241

Assessing Learner Progress 243

Analyzing Instructional Methods 244

Making a Case for Special Placement or Supplemental
    Resources 245

Dealing with Limited Resources 246

Who Else's Behavior is Assessed? 247

Assessing Costs and Benefits Associated with Taking Data. . 247

Getting the Most from Your Data 248

Graphing Data 248

Data as a Reinforcing Tool 249

The Data Collection Plan 250

Summary 250

Chapter 11 Resources 252

**12 A Day in the Life: Practical Application of the
Pyramid Approach to Education** **253**

Miss Mindy's Preschool Class. 255

Ms. Beal's Middle School Class 258

Mr. Manuel's High School Class 261

Arrival – Miss Mindy. 264

Arrival - Ms. Beal 268

Arrival - Mr. Manuel 272

Midday - Miss Mindy 275

Midday - Ms. Beal 283

Midday - Mr. Manuel. 286

Afternoon - Miss Mindy 291

Afternoon - Ms. Beal 295

Afternoon - Mr. Manuel 298

Evening - Ezra's Home 301

Late Afternoon and Evening - Rose's Group Home. 304

Summary 309

Foreward

This book is an invaluable resource to teachers who seek to provide state-of-the-art effective intervention to learners with autism and to parents who wish to understand effective instruction. The Pyramid Approach provides an excellent framework for comprehensive service delivery to learners with autism. The author cites as a goal "active engagement in meaningful learning." This is a laudable, functional and relevant goal for all individuals with autism, and this book provides a road map for achieving that goal.

The Pyramid provides the specifics on the Whys, Whats, and Hows of teaching. The focus on functional objectives and on ultimate outcomes is the perfect framework for the remainder of the book. The author emphasizes the importance of understanding functionality in the context of the environment – of home, school, and community. He also delineates important aspects of tasks that are relevant to functionality, such as duration, social/communicative element, and supervisory conditions. He emphasizes the need to evaluate many dimensions of tasks and skills, and prepare the learner for the context in which skills need to be demonstrated.

In addition, the author helps to focus us as educators and parents on analysis at the level of the INDIVIDUAL. What are this person's preferences, strengths, weaknesses? Which skills are most pivotal for his or her success? In communication, he focuses our attention on skills involving the individual as a speaker, as an initiator. His discussion of communication modalities and of critical communication skills is superb. Naturally, the use of PECS and its utility for learners with limited vocal communication is clear and cogent. The comprehensive nature of PECS as a system of social communication is elucidated perfectly. But the discussion is broader than modality, and reflects the author's sophisticated understanding of verbal behavior, functionality, and socio-communicative response classes.

In teaching core skills across areas of the curriculum, the author notes that there is a critical need to balance responsivity training with initiation training, and the author highlights best practices to facilitate both classes of behavior. The chapter on generalization is an elegant analysis of how to teach to promote real world application. The emphasis on natural reinforcers is excellent. In addition, the tips on teaching loosely and spot checking for maintenance are important and noteworthy.

The chapters on effective lessons and teaching strategies highlight again the importance of individualization as the key to programming successfully. The distinction between cues and prompts will be incredibly useful to teachers and parents alike. Examples of natural environmental cues and of intrinsic natural rewards really illustrate how functional programming is achieved, and how such skills are maintained.

The author gives extremely specific examples of how errors can be addressed to increase the effectiveness of teaching. Given the importance of errorless teaching, and given the propensity of learners with autism to repeat errors, these clear guidelines are invaluable. The suggestions for data collection are equally helpful. There are many options for data collection offered, to match every possible skill, behavior, and environment. In addition, the author discusses the importance of collecting data on others in the environment as well.

This broadening of the lens is a refreshing theme throughout the book. A comprehensive focus on programming within a behavior analytic framework is rare. Often, resources help to address aspects of assessment or intervention, or focus on an area of the curriculum. This book provides the full and complete road map. It answers the question, "What is effective intervention for autism?" It answers that question on two fundamental and essential levels – through science, and at the level of the individual. The recommendations given are clear and unambiguous and clinically sound, and they are derived from the science of behavior. The author recommends empirically validated strategies and evidence-based treatments. Most importantly, there is an emphasis on applying such interventions to the individual – incorporating their strengths, preferences, and skills into programming in maximally effective and naturally sustaining ways.

This book fills a tremendous hole in available literature. It provides teachers and parents with more than a how-to guide. It provides them with a why, what, where, when, and how-to guide. It is not just individuals with autism who have trouble answering WH questions. When it comes to autism treatment, parents and educators have sought answers to the WH questions associated with effective intervention as well. Now, they have their answers in this wonderful resource.

Dr. Mary Jane Weiss

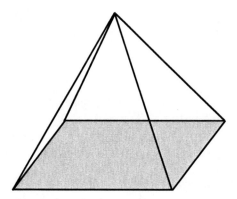

1
The Pyramid Approach to Education

A little girl with a head full of soft blond curls lisps, "It's your turn." Her tongue pokes into the space where her new front tooth is just breaking through the gum line. A boy, a bit taller, pulls his gaze away from his flicking fingers, looks at the girl and spins the spinner. "Where do you have to go?" the girl asks. The boy points to a box on the board depicting a cookie. "Yes, you can go to the cookie square," and he moves his marker to the correct spot.

In another classroom, a teacher is seated with three children. They read their primers in unison, "Billy and Tommy are sailing their boats." "Put your finger on Billy's boat. Good Carlo. Good Heather. Uh oh, Victor. You've found Tommy's boat." The boy quickly switches his finger over to the other object. They practice pointing to different objects, switching ultimately back to Billy's boat. This time Victor gets it right. "Okay. Now each of you gets an ice-cream cone token." The children each take a foam-rubber trinket and place it onto their token boards. "Just one more for each of you and we can go for our ice-cream."

In another school, a group is working in a middle-school science laboratory. The learners are drawing pictures of the algae they have scraped from the side of a fish tank and viewed under a microscope. They are preparing reports to present orally for grading. One boy renders an almost photographic facsimile of the specimen, but when an aide asks him the name of his drawing, he does not say the term aloud. Instead he writes it down.

The last setting is a residence for eight young adults. Posted on the wall is the schedule for the day, a set of pictures and words fastened to a Velcro® strip. A tall young man has just moved a picture of a toothbrush into the upper portion of the schedule board to indicate it is time to progress to the next activity. Now he, another youth, and a more mature woman, the group-home manager, stand before a washing machine. "How much soap powder do we need?" "A half cup," the two boys answer. "Okay. Go ahead." One of the boys reaches for the measuring cup, using it to extract just the right amount and pours the powder into the tub, then turns on the machine. "Good for you," says the woman, "You figured it out all by yourself."

What is so remarkable about these events? After all, kindergartners play board games, youngsters in primary grades learn to read, middle-schoolers participate in science lab, and most young adults operate washing machines, don't they? Suppose we were to tell you that all but the little girl playing the board game and the group-home manager have been diagnosed with autism or another developmental disability. Yet this scenario is exactly the sort of thing you will see in educational programs operating according to the precepts of the *Pyramid Approach to Education*.

Notice that each of the learners is actively engaged in a meaningful learning experience, each is the recipient of powerfully motivating rewards, and none are misbehaving nor totally tuning out. Those major accomplishments have resulted from a long history of effective teamwork among staff performing at the highest quality level, and cooperative parents. And each of these elements involves cornerstones within the broad field of applied behavior analysis.

Unfortunately, while success stories like these are becoming more familiar, they are not as widespread as they might be. Many people still regard good teaching as an inborn trait, incapable of being improved. As a case in point, a few years ago, a principal of a local school rebuffed an offer of staff-development services from the author. "Son, it's really simple, good teachers just are born that way." Apparently, once they stepped foot into the classroom, according to that principal, it was already too late.

Others fail to recognize the universality of laws of learning. An elementary teacher asked for help in managing a particularly active learner. When the conversation veered in the direction of effective instructional strategies, the teacher asserted flat out, "Look, you teach him how to sit in that chair and I'll teach him how to read!" "But," the consultant wondered to himself, "if she truly knew how to teach him to read well, wouldn't she also know how to teach him to sit?"

Perhaps the situation is somewhat more complex. Is it possible that the principles of learning associated with reading are distinct from those associated with sitting? We assume something far simpler - had she used good practices to teach reading, she could have used similar methods to promote his remaining seated. Unfortunately, many educators appear to make a sharp distinction between misbehavior and skill acquisition. One of the main reasons we have written this book is to dispel this line of belief. We hope to share with you, our reader, what we have learned about how to successfully apply established learning principles to teach many different things: academic concepts and skills; effectively communicating and otherwise interacting socially; remaining safe and healthy; becoming physically adept and emotionally controlled. As a result, you should design more effective educational environments anywhere, regardless of whether the setting is regular or special education, or your learners are infants, children, youth, or adults with specialized or typical needs. While the main focus here will be on learners with autism and related disabilities, we hope you will see the breadth of its application. We also will stress that the orientation and strategies offered within this book can be useful to classroom teachers, paraprofessionals, behavior analysts, speech-language pathologists, occupational and physical therapists, parents and other care-givers as well. Anyone in a 'teaching' position relative to someone else can benefit from using the *Pyramid Approach* to better accomplish their goals.

We don't suggest that becoming an excellent teacher is a simple matter. If it were, deficiencies in academic performance and conduct wouldn't be as widespread as they are today. It takes little exposure to the classroom for most teachers to realize that, like so many other deceptively simple approaches, effective teaching demands well-honed skills. Good results depend on teachers who choose, organize, and sequence optimal instructional experiences, reinforcing learner progress along the way. Each of these skill sets will need to be applied, regardless of the nature of the learners.

We share considerable experience as teachers and performance managers. We have taught just about every category of learner: business executives and managers, school administrators, professional and research psychologists, health and human services providers, teachers, economically and culturally advantaged and disadvantaged children, those with special talents, and those with educational and developmental delays. We have found that, indeed, the fundamental principles of effective education and training apply universally. It is only in the specifics of the execution that differences arise - in selecting what to teach - where, when, and how, in particular.

To illustrate, while serving as head administrator of a statewide public school program for children and adolescents with autism, the author joined his colleagues in devising a powerful staff-development and training system. In general, staff, parents and other family members working with children, adolescents, and adults with various types of developmental disabilities learned to apply those methods in different types of settings - classrooms, the gymnasium, the lunchroom, job sites, workshops, group and private homes, and elsewhere. Soon, learners were making major improvements academically, socially, and otherwise, to the extent that the state education department no longer sent learners to out of state to residential treatment facilities[1].

Objective assessment of learner and teacher progress has demonstrated that applying solidly established principles of learning in manageable ways has produced impressive results across the gamut of learner conditions[2]. In the *Pyramid Approach to Education*, we describe the practices we and our colleagues have found most effective and user-friendly for educating learners with special needs like autism. Our intention in the pages to follow is to elaborate on the approach in order to enable teachers and other educators[3] to do the best job they can and derive pleasure from the process.

Features of the Pyramid Approach to Education

Relatives and professionals ("teachers") responsible for teaching individuals with autism or related disorders[4], and those training and/or supervising those teachers, seek effective, user-friendly methods. An organized, manageable educational design based on solidly established principles of learning and behavior is just the thing, especially when paired with the tools allowing them to determine if their methods are having their intended effects.

---

1   See two book chapters describing the application of this model within a public school program: Bondy, A. & Battaglini, K. (2006). Application of the Pyramid Approach to Education Model in a Public School Setting. In J. Handleman & S. Harris (Eds.) *School-age education programs for children with autism* (pp. 163-193). Austin: TX. Pro-Ed Inc. and Bondy, A. & Battaglini, K. (2007). Application of the Pyramid Approach to Education Model in a Preschool School Setting" In J. Handleman & S. Harris (Eds.) *Pre-school education programs for children with autism 3rd Edition).* (pp. 283-308). Austin: TX. Pro-Ed Inc.
2   See two volumes of collected papers published by the *Journal of Applied Behavior Analysis,* one on behavior analysis and developmental disabilities, the other on behavior analysis and education in general.
3   Throughout this book, we use the term *teacher* to refer not only to certified classroom teachers but also to anyone (including parents, siblings, speech-language pathologists, psychologists, paraprofessionals, classroom teachers, consultants and so on) engaged in the activity of promoting learning.
4   Henceforth, for the sake of brevity, we use the term "autism" to include that condition as well other related disorders.

You might wonder why we use a complicated symbol like a pyramid, instead of a simpler design, like a straight line, to describe our system. We believe that the three-dimensional qualities of a pyramid help remind us that effective teaching demands we attend to a number of factors at the same time: *why, what*, and *how* we are doing things the way we do, and how well those efforts are paying off (see Figure 1-1). A visual image of a system like this also should help you recall its critical parts.

The Base of the Pyramid

The *Why* of Behavior: The Science of Learning

Remember, the pyramid is one of the most stable geometric forms known to humanity. While the forces of nature may cause palaces, office buildings, factories, and homes to crumble, the pyramids of the Pharaohs still remain intact after thousands of years. As they did, we must begin with a solid base before constructing the main body of the full pyramidal structure. We will use this same analogy to present a sequence of critical educational issues to address, beginning with its firm foundation.

Of what is this base composed? The science of learning and behavior. This science has produced enough evidence to spawn many general laws of learning. These laws explain much about why people do what they do[5]. The fruit of these efforts is a set of principles or rules of behavior change that we can use to teach successfully. As implied earlier, this knowledge base is our reason for choosing the science of behavior as the foundation upon which to erect the Pyramid. Chapter 2 elaborates on this fundamental concept of *The Why of Behavior*.

Firming the Foundation: The *What* of Teaching

Once we begin to understand why people do what they do, we next need to consider *what to teach*. We reason that when we want to teach learners something, we want to change the things they say or do - their behavior. Two areas of behavior generally demand the attention of those working and living with learners with autism and other special needs.

1. The presence of challenging behaviors (referred to as 'behavior excesses' by Martin & Pear, 2011). The list is large and includes hitting, screaming, tantruming, biting, spitting, throwing objects large and small, run-

---

5   Biomedical researchers are beginning to discover factors related to malfunctioning of the central nervous system among people with autism and related disabilities. As is becoming standard practice in the treatment of true attention deficit/hyperactivity disorders, ultimately we may find ways optimally to combine medical and behavioral interventions to minimize the damaging effects of these conditions. Because this book is directed toward the teaching role, we restrict our discussion to the areas in which it is appropriate for teachers and parents to intervene.

ning around at amazing speeds all day, self-stimulating at high rates (rocking, finger-flicking, or spinning objects and so on), echolalia or repetitive speech, and countless other upsetting actions.

2.   The absence of important key behaviors (commonly referred to as 'skill deficits') such as functional communication (whether via speech or other modalities), eye-contact and other orienting reactions (like looking in the direction of a teacher's pointing finger), appropriate toy play, social skills involving adults or peers, staying in an assigned area, attending to a group task, and many related deficits.

We plan our lessons to enable learners to do something differently afterwards than they could do before the lesson. That is, our lessons are aimed at reducing the acts in the first category and increasing those in the second. But which should we address first?

Problem behaviors like those in the first category seem to demand instant relief. Think about your last conversation about your job with someone close to you. Were you more likely to have reported, "You know, 73% of the time, he independently followed 17 steps in the right order to tie his shoes," or "He scratched me again. Look!"? It is those bothersome behaviors that tend to command our attention and gain us sympathy. That is why many choose to begin by eliminating the problem behaviors: stop the learner from self-stimulating, running, hitting and so on, as a way to get him "ready to learn." As we soon will see, this tactic is a mistake. We should note that we will discuss situations that require 'crisis management,' but those strategies are not designed for long term behavior change.

First of all, this commonly used phrase - ready to learn - concerns us greatly because it seems to imply that the learner is not yet capable of learning. Everything we know on the subject, however, suggests that learners can and do learn, even under all sorts of conditions, and at various times and places. It is not necessary for them to be sitting quietly in a chair with their hands in their laps for 10 seconds before responding to a teacher's single instruction. They can learn while sitting on the floor, running around the room, or playing with dirt on the playground. To us, the more critical question should be, "Is the teacher ready to teach?"

Another broad concern about beginning by attempting to eliminate behaviors is that unless certain things are in place, our efforts will not pay off. Numerous research studies have shown that some learners hurt themselves, by scratching or biting, as a way to gain attention. Let us assume that certain methods allow us to stop a learner from doing that. However, when the learner sits motionless, what is she now lacking? Right, attention! Maybe we have taken away her only means of getting it. That outcome would be unusually harsh for someone so dependent on others for her wants and needs. Furthermore, we should hardly be surprised when she reverts to scratching herself, or devises on her own a different, possibly more damaging technique, like hitting her head, or hurting others. If a learner is not likely to generate an effective new solution - a new way to cope with the situation - it is up to us to teach one. Now we begin to see that a better place to start is by building new effective, and presumably healthier, attention-seeking skills. For, unless we pair a *constructive functional skill* with our efforts to eradicate inappropriate behaviors, the intervention will not succeed.

Building skills, then, is the primary emphasis of Chapter 3, *Functional Objectives*, our first chapter in the *what* category. That does not mean we intend to ignore dealing with disruptive, damaging, and dangerous behaviors; only that we postpone the topic until we have provided teachers with the means to devise constructive alternative objectives. Choosing optimal functional objectives is not always easy, though. The chapter will help you out by offering a set of guidelines for generating instructional objectives that are developmentally appropriate and useful to the learner in various ways.

People learn for a reason, usually because it does, or promises to provide, something people want or need to know, or get, or rid them of something they don't. The material in Chapter 4, *Powerful Reinforcement Systems*, describes ways to encourage people to keep trying. In that chapter you will find out how to enrich the environment by providing many opportunities for learners to experience reinforcement as a result of their efforts. When you use these tactics to optimal advantage, any necessity to resort to coercion will be minimized.

Learning not only addresses interactions with the physical environment - tying shoes, drinking from a cup, catching a ball, and so on - but also those within the social environment. People must learn to communicate and interact effectively with others. Chapter 5, *Functional Communication and Social Skills*, addresses appropriate goals and procedures for teaching toward those skills. The last element of the base of the Pyramid concerns itself with those remaining behaviors that interfere with one's own, or others', learning and well-being. Chapter 6, *Preventing and Reducing Contextually Inappropriate Behavior*, describes ways to reduce those troublesome behaviors that remain following the implementation of the first three elements of the Pyramid.

Teaching teams often are composed of staff with different levels of expertise. Despite any such differences, though, all members should find that the chapters in this *What to Teach* section provide them with some valuable problem solving tools. It is hoped that the material will counter the team's general tendency to want to assign a new learner's disruptive actions top priority. Instead, if any effective long-term solution is to be found, we urge teachers to take the *Pyramid Approach* by first putting in place the other elements of the base: functional objectives, powerful reinforcement systems, and functional communication skills.

The Top of the Pyramid

Getting There: The *How* of Teaching

Once we have addressed why people behave the way they do and what to teach, we are ready to consider the question of *How to Teach*. By reviewing how to achieve our teaching aims, this third section is the one that transforms the Pyramid into its full three-dimensional structure. The strategy involves asking very broad questions before narrowing in on more specific topics. Therefore, before we begin to teach a lesson, we should be clear about where it eventually leads. That is, we need to remind ourselves what should take place, where, and when, by the end of the lesson. It is not enough to teach a learner to do something with a particular object only for a teacher in a classroom or a parent at home. The usual intention is broader than that - extending the skill beyond, to other times and places, and with different people. Consequently, from the very start, we will need to build into our methods strategies to promote *Generalization*, the subject of Chapter 7.

Once we understand the full nature of the lesson we want to teach, it is time to attend to broad guidelines for *Designing Effective Lessons* (*Chapter 8*). Chapter 9, *Specific Teaching Strategies*, describes the type of temporary help teachers can provide learners, and how best to withdraw that assistance. Furthermore, while our general approach will always be to try to minimize errors, we must have specific lesson plans for responding to them when they do occur. These issues are detailed in Chapter 10, *Minimizing and Correcting Errors*.

Assessing and Evaluating: Collecting and Analyzing Data

Finally, everything that we do in our attempt to understand our learners and ourselves, to set worthy objectives, and to design and implement effective lessons, requires careful assessment and evaluation. We need to know what conditions are supporting behaviors of concern, and which ones have been interfering with learning. We have to develop useful methods for finding out if our efforts are working or not, and whether we need to consider making some changes. Therefore, the *Pyramid Approach* requires that we collect, summarize, and analyze data to be certain that our methods are having the intended positive effect. In essence, data ties to every element of the Pyramid: the principles of learning on which it is founded, what we teach, and how we choose what to teach, and the way we go about teaching. Strategies for collecting and analyzing data are reviewed in the Chapter 11, *Collecting and Analyzing Data*.

Putting it All Together

At this point, you may be feeling overwhelmed, wondering how all the pieces of the pyramid puzzle join together and operate. A teacher, Anne Overcash, implementing the *Pyramid Approach to Education* understands your concern. She, like the rest of us, has had to work hard to learn to apply the *Pyramid Approach* effectively in her own classroom. So, in Chapter 12, she describes the practical application of the *Pyramid Approach* in several different settings with several different learners. Invisibly cloaked, so as not to disturb the routine, you can watch and listen to what happens from the moment the learners arrive until they depart. You can read the chapter first to gain a sense of the Pyramid reality. Then, later, review it to identify each of the elements of the Pyramid. That will help you to begin to fashion your own school - or home - based instructional design, then conduct and assess progress. While there is no guarantee your learners will progress through school unassisted, we can promise that if you learn, and abide by, the principles and practices suggested in this book, you will see considerable improvement in your learners' progress.

Summary

Today, thanks to the field of applied behavior analysis, individuals with autism and related developmental disabilities have made greater strides than anyone might have imagined just a few decades ago. They enter and succeed in school, care for themselves at home, become gainfully employed, and function effectively in social and community situations. This encouraging state of affairs has resulted from the recognition that the laws of learning can be applied to change the behavior of anyone, as long as the specific procedures stemming from those laws are optimally arranged within a supportive environment to suit the learner's current set of skills.

The *Pyramid Approach to Education* describes the most fundamental of those laws of learning and related procedures, and describes how to apply them effectively. In systematic fashion, the book will teach you to plan *what* to teach by setting functional educational objectives, and ways to organize a reinforcing environment, promote effective communication skills, and minimize behaviors inappropriate in particular contexts. Then it will guide you through the process of selecting and applying methods for achieving those aims. You begin by organizing for generalization from the onset, designing and carrying out specific lesson plans accordingly. Assessing and evaluating your choice of procedures and their effectiveness will allow your instruction to be self-correcting. If progress is in the direction and at the rate anticipated, you continue on course. Otherwise you try another approach, saving precious time and other resources in the process. In essence, we are trying to guide you to ask the right questions, rather than try to imply simple answers to every situation. If you ask the right questions, we trust your answers - as well as your ability to test whether those answers are in fact good ones.

The book contains many concepts and guidelines. The last chapter permits you to see several cases of how everything fits together. That should give you some ideas for adjusting the *Pyramid Approach* to your own particular situation. Learn your lessons thoroughly, apply them with care, and watch the progress!

Figure 1-1

The Pyramid Model

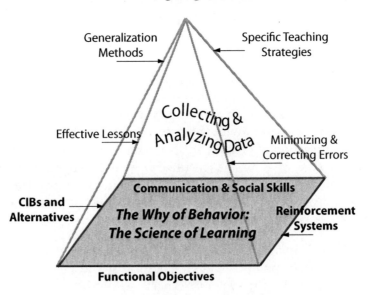

Chapter 1 Resources

The Pyramid Approach to Education

To	Read
Share one family's experience in coping successfully with their children's autism.	Maurice, C. (1993). *Let me hear your voice: A family's triumph over autism*, New York, NY: Ballantine Books.
Gain a layperson/parent's perspective about the value of an applied behavior analytic approach to intervening with learners with autism.	Catherine Maurice. Why this manual. In Maurice, C., Green, G. & Luce, S., (Eds.) *Behavioral intervention for young children with autism.* pp 3-12. Austin, TX: Pro-Ed.
Become informed consumers of treatment for your child.	Harris, S. L., & Weiss, M.J. (1998). *Right from the start: Behavioral interventions for young children with autism: A guide for parents and professionals.* Bethesda, MD: Woodbine House.
Find out the answers to questions parents commonly ask about early intervention with children with autism.	Luce, S. & Dyer, K. Answers to commonly asked questions. In Maurice, C., Green, G. & Luce, S., (Eds.) *Behavioral intervention for young children with autism.* pp. 345-358. Austin, TX: Pro-Ed.
Find information related to applied behavior analysis, key terms, and principles.	Martin, G.L. & Pear, J. (2011). *Behavior Modification: What it is and how to do it, 9th Edition.* Columbus, OH: Pearson Cooper, J.O., Heron, T.E., & Heward, W.L. (2007). *Applied Behavior Analysis, 2nd Edition.* Columbus, OH: Merrill.

To	View
Watch children with autism, and their families, experience intensive early intervention education.	Groden, J., Spratt, R.J., Fiske, P. & Weisberg, P. (1998). *Breaking the barriers III. Intensive early intervention and beyond: A school-based inclusion program.* Champaign, IL: Research Press

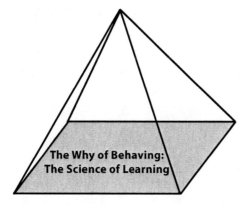

The Why of Behaving:
The Science of Learning

2

The *Why* of Behaving:
The Science of Behavior

"This time it's going to be different," we vow to ourselves on New Year's Day. "I'm going to exercise and eat healthy food; get enough sleep." We stick to this regimen for a week or two, and then begin to slack off. Eventually we are right back where we were, gobbling down fatty fast foods; convincing ourselves that we're too busy to exercise; absolutely having to check out what our favorite late-night talk-show host has to say, or surf to just one more web-site. Periodically we scold ourselves, "Why, why don't I have more will power?"

We pose these same sorts of questions about other people too: Why does a person commit a given act of evil or heroism? Where do qualities like dependability, persistence, disloyalty or impulsiveness come from? Why is it that some people seem to take everything at face value, while others catch subtler meanings? All these illustrate things people *do* that many of us find confusing.

Those of us living and working with individuals with special needs continuously find ourselves trying to understand their odd behavior. Why does Louis, a four-year-old diagnosed with autism, scream when a detour sign forces his Mom to take a different route to school, or when she brings his sandwich wrapped with any but yellow paper? Why does he rock in his chair endlessly or arch away from anyone who tries to hug him? Are those acts determined by forces from without or within, or do they just happen?

An even more important question for many who have daily contact with youngsters with special needs is, "Given the situation, is there anything that can be done to change it? If so, what?"

Science and Human Behavior

Humans have been pondering questions like those for a long time. Now, at the dawn of a new millennium, many scientists are bringing us ever closer to finding the answers. Neuroscientists are discovering more about how the brain is structured and what physiological changes occur during learning. Behavioral scientists are describing patterns of behavior and how they relate to social, genetic, and other factors. *Behavior analysts* also are among these groups of scientists. These specialists continue to make important discoveries about the relationship between people's environments (what occurs inside and outside their bodies) and their actions.

It is this last focus, the science of behavior analysis, which forms the basis for our *Pyramid Approach to Education*. Why? Because, as we soon will discover in this chapter, behavior analysis helps explain the two things we want most to understand about ourselves and others:

1. **How people learn: why they do what they do, when they do it.**

2. **How to teach: how to alter aspects of the environment that relate to when, where, and how people act.**

The foundation of all science is that the events under study are observable by everyone in the community. If I let go of an apple several feet above the floor, everyone watching will agree that the apple went *down*. Only after we all agree that this event took place can we study why it happened and consider other aspects of falling objects. For a behavior analyst, the same conditions are true - we can only study in a scientific manner things that everyone agrees took place. This does not deny that there are 'private events' - things that only one person is aware of - but it does limit how we can use science to study these.

Notice that our main focus in studying learning and teaching is on what people do: where, when, and how a person shouts, rocks, laughs, cries, reads, or reasons aloud in some particular way, and what *conditions* are influencing the way it happens. When we discover events that consistently affect the behavior, often we can do something about those events, thus influencing the behavior in question. After all, changing behavior is what teaching - and preaching, training, managing, counseling, and therapy - is all about. The person shouts or rocks *less*; reads *more* of certain things, reasons in a *more* logical fashion, communicates for the first time, laughs or cries *sometimes but not others*, according to socially acceptable norms.

Note also, we do not place our main focus on people's thoughts, impulses, or feelings. There's a good reason for this. It is only by analyzing people's actions or behaviors[1] directly that we can discover what factors are regulating or "controlling" those behaviors, and then, possibly do something to alter the situation. Again, it is most helpful to view 'thoughts' and the like as behaviors themselves, not something that is of a distinct and unique nature.

How, then, can we find out what those controlling events are? We need to detect them in some unbiased way. Similarly, we need to measure objectively how those events relate to the behaviors of concern. Louis' mother wants the flexibility of picking up his lunch from several fast-food restaurants, not just one. Yet Louis only smiles and eats his sandwich when it is wrapped in a familiar yellow wrapper. He cries and pushes the food away if it is wrapped in white. We know this because we have observed and counted laughing, crying, eating, and pushing the food away according to whether the wrappers were yellow or white. If there were no objective ways to observe and measure any change in those behaviors when we try to teach him to act differently, it would have become a guessing game. That is why thoughts, feelings, and impulses are not our main focal point.

Does that mean that we consider "internal events" unimportant? Not at all. Surely people think and have feelings, and we assume these are affected by the same principles as any behavior. The difference is that because we cannot detect thinking and feeling directly, we can only guess what is happening based on what our own senses tell us, including what people say about themselves. Whether what they say matches exactly what is happening within them is not possible to determine. Although changing what people report can be the main focus, as in many forms of psychotherapy, probably readers of this book are more concerned with actions than words. When, for instance, we are trying to find out what a girl really likes to do, we can monitor:

- How long she stays with a particular activity.

- Whether she attempts to escape from the situation.

- How frequently she selects or rejects it when given a choice.

---

1   We use the term *behavior* to describe anything the person *does* or *says*, good, bad or indifferent.

- Whether she smiles, laughs, frowns, or cries while involved in a certain situation.

Assume we already had run that kind of test with Louis and found out that indeed he accepted yellow-wrapped, and rejected white-wrapped, sandwiches. Now, suppose we want to see if we can help him by eliminating his unpleasant reactions to sandwiches wrapped in white. We locate wrapping paper in varying hues from deep yellow, to lighter and lighter yellow, to white. Then every five days or so, we wrap the lunch sandwich in a slightly lighter wrapper. To find out if this tactic works we measure how Louis responds during the process (Figure 2-1). We are convinced that this "fading"[2] method is effective because while we are introducing the white wrapper, Louis nearly always continues to accept and eat his food at school, at home, and even at local fast-food restaurants, without crying. Unable to see inside his head and locate his likes and dislikes, we are doing the best available thing - watching his behavior.[3] Had we not continued to observe carefully, we might have been tempted to give up the one time, part way through, when Louis pushed his lunch away, or the two times he cried. After the full lesson is complete, we keep count of Louis' reactions for a few more weeks. To everyone's delight, as Figure 2-2 shows, Louis no longer seems to care about whether his sandwich wrappers are yellow or white.

In the previous example, we portrayed both learning and teaching. Where does it all begin? From infancy onward, how we react to events - in a broad sense, our *behaviors* - are continually changing. When those behavioral changes are relatively long lasting, we say we are *learning*. Moving from being fed to preparing one's own meals; from not using money to determining the amount of money to pay for something; from being frightened when setting foot into a strange classroom to entering the place with confidence - all exemplify learning. Each example focuses on changes in what someone does. At all levels of learning, from childhood through adulthood, we will emphasize that 'you must show what you know.' The methods of change, a *fading* procedure in Louis' case, illustrate *teaching*. The changes in the rate or form of his various behaviors demonstrate *learning*.

Learning About Teaching and Learning

For many years, behavior analysts have been studying how learning occurs by systematically measuring changes in behavior in relation to

---

2   This method is described in greater detail later in the section on prompting (Chapter 10)

3   Today, sophisticated instruments can detect things happening in areas within the brain, even groups of neurons firing. No one, though, claims to be able to decipher the "content" of these events.

events that come before (antecedents) and after (consequences) the action. Whenever they find that certain arrangements of consequences and/or antecedents produce consistent results across species, locations, individuals, and so on, that is cause for excitement. The discovered rules describing the nature of these relationships are called *principles of behavior*[4] and form the basis of the field of experimental behavior analysis.

The heart of this book consists of a description of practices based on well-established behavioral principles. We illustrate how they have been applied, especially to teach learners with various kinds of developmental challenges, and suggest how you in your role as an educator or parent can make use of these techniques. The principles hold true for everyone: You; us; children developing typically; those experiencing developmental challenges; rocket scientists; people living in poverty; bankers; professors; construction workers; migrant laborers; the aged and infirm; star ball players; and they apply to non-human animals such as cats, dogs, and parrots. Differences may crop up in the individual's *rate of learning*, the *form* or *medium* of the response (most people and some parrots speak; toddlers and some children and adults communicate primarily by means of gestures; other children and adults use pictures and other icons to communicate); how broadly they apply what they've learned; how long the new learning lasts; and the resources necessary to achieve the best possible results. Knowing basic principles of behavior empowers us because we then can use this knowledge to better understand the critical issues and thus more effectively design opportunities to learn. Let us, therefore, begin by exploring how learning occurs.

Figure 2-1

Louis' Response to Sandwiches Wrapped with Yellow and White Wrappers before Any Systematic Teaching

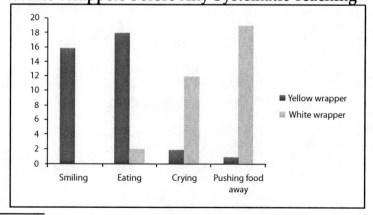

---

4   Behavior principles, when applied toward promoting particular objectives, are called behavioral procedures.

Figure 2-2
Louis' Reactions to Sandwiches Wrapped in White
Before and After

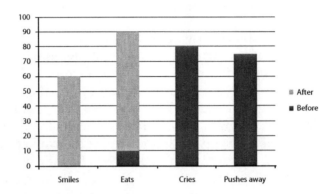

How Does Learning Come About?

The systematic behavior change we call *learning* can be simple in nature, or more and more complicated. One of the most basic forms of learning is called "classical conditioning." Here is a general way to describe how classical conditioning takes place: Just about every complex individual organism (animal or person) is born with a tendency to respond to certain events in predictable ways. When there is a loud sound, a baby responds with a startle. A puff of wind or a sudden bright light before her eyes causes her to blink. Pavlov's dogs salivated when meat powder was placed into their mouths. We call the events that *elicit* the responses *stimuli*, abbreviated as S. When the stimulus (S) is seen to produce or *elicit* the behavior or *response* (R) just about every time, independent of the individual having any particular experiences related to the response, we call that eliciting stimulus, an *unconditioned stimulus* (UCS) and the reaction an *unconditioned response* (UCR). Figure 2-3 shows the series of events in this kind of *classical conditioning*:

Figure 2-3
Unconditioned Response

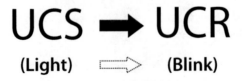

UCS ➡ UCR
(Light)   ⇢   **(Blink)**

So far, no learning has occurred. In fact the "unconditioned" (*U*) in *UCR* and *UCS* is the same as "not learned." We say this because infants blink the very first time a light flashes before their eyes. Now, let's add something to the situation. Mommy reliably touches the light switch just before the bright light comes on. For Pavlov, he reliably rang a bell just before giving the dog food. Over a series of pairings between the two stimuli, learning is demonstrated when the child blinks when the light is touched, or the dog salivates when the bell is rung. Note that the response to this new stimulus (i.e., touching the light or ringing the bell) is the same form as the response to the UCS (i.e., the bright light or the food). Because they are paired closely in time, now baby blinks when mom touches the light switch, and Pavlov's dog salivates when the bell rings. The new working stimulus is called a *conditioned stimulus* (CS) and the response it produces, one almost identical to the unconditioned response, is called a *conditioned response* (CR) (See Figure 2-4). The entire arrangement is called *Classical Conditioning*. When our mouths begin to water at the smell of fresh bread, or we feel nauseated by the sight of a particular food that previously made us sick, classical conditioning is responsible. *Learning* best describes these kinds of changes in patterns of behaving.

Figure 2-4

Classical Conditioning

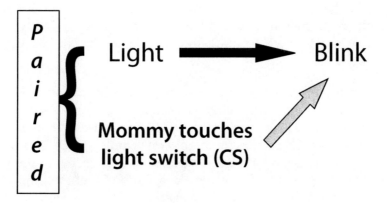

Operant Conditioning

Most parents and educators of students with special challenges are less interested in the kinds of teaching just described and more concerned about schooling of a different variety.[5] B.F. Skinner introduced the term *operant conditioning* to describe the type of learning most commonly of interest to educators and parents. He selected that term because the type of behaviors of interest here are those that "operate on the environment." Operant behaviors are those whose occurrence/rate is highly influenced by ensuing changes in the environment - the consequences. A specific antecedent stimulus is not essential to operant behavior. At various times, a baby smiles, moves his hands or feet, opens his mouth - all without any clear connection to an antecedent stimulus. Each is an *operant behavior* (B). Learning occurs when that operant produces a dependable effect or *consequence*. When the response increases in rate that consequence is *reinforcing* (abbreviated R+) (See Figure 2-5).

Figure 2-5
Operant Conditioning

$$\text{B} \longrightarrow \text{R+} \Longrightarrow \text{B}$$

waves   "Good boy"   waves again

So, when baby smiles and mommy routinely picks him up and feeds or hugs him, he is more likely to smile. Daddy heralds baby's first hand wave with an enthusiastic, "Good boy! You're waving to daddy." Guess what? Baby begins to wave more often, especially when he sees his daddy (Figure 2-6).

This increase in behavior (B), especially when certain antecedent cues (As) are present, is primarily what we seek as educators. As you will see later, many of our teaching objectives involve increases in some aspect of a behavior, such as its rate: in the number of words spoken, read, spelled or written; in the variety of job tasks performed correctly; in the number of children with whom a youngster plays, or the number of minutes she sticks to a task. In essence, *rapidly promoting enduring learning of functional objectives* is what quality education is all about.

---

5   We are not suggesting that classical conditioning should be ignored. In fact, some critical behaviors for everyone involve this type of learning, as we will see when we discuss challenging behaviors in Chapter 6.

Figure 2-6
Operant Conditioning

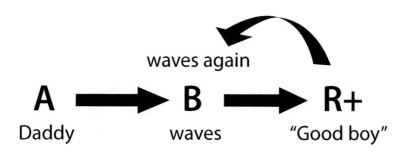

How do we accomplish this purpose, though, especially with individuals who learn slowly, for whatever reason? They have so much catching up to do - so many new challenges facing them. Despite these factors, we can count ourselves fortunate thanks to thousands of operant learning experiments from which we have learned many dependable principles of behavior. These principles provide us with teaching tools in the form of behavioral procedures for delivering a high quality education to anyone.

Take the fictitious example we offered above, the one in which Louis was taught to "tolerate" a white wrapping on his sandwich. How did that relate to operant learning research? In many ways. Embedded in the procedure are the essentials:

- the *reinforcer* - food that Louis enjoyed

- the *behavior* - consuming the food

But the connection between the two was blocked by Louis' emotional response to the antecedent stimulus, the unfamiliar color. The teacher's task was to teach Louis to accept a wrapping of a different color, minus the interfering response. Here was the dilemma (Figure 2-7):

Figure 2-7
Louis' Original and Changed Reactions to White Wrap

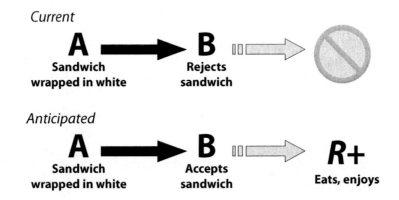

Current

A ➡️ **B** ⇨ 🚫

Sandwich   Rejects
wrapped in white sandwich

Anticipated

A ➡️ **B** ⇨ **R+**

Sandwich   Accepts   Eats, enjoys
wrapped in white sandwich

The teacher turned to related research showing that errors, which typically provoke unpleasant emotional reactions, could be avoided. The change was accomplished by means of an "errorless learning"[6] method, first found to be successful with pigeons, and now known to be as effective with people.
This strategy consisted of:

1. Starting with an effectively working A-B-R+ connection (here, where A = yellow paper and the behavior, B = accepting, and the consequence, R+ = consuming and enjoying the reinforcer).

2. Very gradually introducing hardly noticeable differences in the A.

3. Obtaining the same results (consuming/enjoying) as before.

4. Gradually continuing the very slight adjustments in A until it was really quite different from the starting point, in this case white.

We are not implying that we know how to teach everyone everything, but it does mean that, regardless of developmental barriers, if we understand how to support behavior change, we can make the most of our efforts. When we see what conditions reliably influence behavior, we can use that information to broaden our knowledge and hone our skills as educators. The outcome is that we teachers, administrators, supervisors, parents, coaches, communication specialists, and other professionals can help our learners make the most of their capabilities.

---

6 Terrace, H.S. (1963). Discriminative learning with and without errors. *Journal of the Experimental Analysis of Behavior, 6,* 1-27.

The A-B-Cs of Behavior Change

As you now see, discoveries about the nature and history of the relationships between a particular behavior and what came before and after it may enable us to design powerful instructional methods. These associations are the reason that it pays for us to get a better handle on what these relationships are all about. For instance, we know that particular events like reinforcers (R+s), or other *consequences* (Cs), that follow a behavior may influence the way that behavior is repeated later on. We also saw an illustration of how *antecedents*, the things that happened before the behavior of interest - such as Daddy's presence - affected the outcome. Let's look more closely at how these relationships happen, and how one might arrange antecedents and consequences to promote meaningful change in the behavior of interest. We shall begin with context, move on to prompts and cues, then shift over to the powerful role consequences play in this drama.

Context

Learning happens somewhere, in a *context* or setting that can influence the rate of change. Just as a field of grain needs to be plowed and fertilized to nurture optimal crop growth and yield, teaching contexts must be prepared to support productive change in the behavior of concern. Supportive contexts can help learners and teachers focus upon the task at hand in order to put out their best effort. Different contexts may alter the relation between the behavior and its consequences. The very same behavior, say, yelling and screaming, might be reinforced within the context of a soccer game but punished within the context of a wedding ceremony. The context produced by eating a great deal of salted popcorn will increase the reinforcing value of drinking fluids.

It would be wonderful if there were one ideal context for learning but, sadly, that is not so. Some learners learn better in an environment free of distractions; others when they can observe their peers engaged in work, or see items or activities they would like to have or do. The different sounds and sights to which learners attend also can vary. Some want to touch certain objects; interact with particular people; watch or participate in given activities. Others might be repelled by those stimuli. Time of day, weather conditions, noise, minutes since one's last meal, and health status (yes, contexts can be internal too) also may influence what happens.

Antecedents

Antecedents are events that *precede* the behavior of interest more immediately. Those stimuli are especially important when they are related to specific consequences. Prompts and cues like hints, gestures, rules, oral and written instructions, signs, pictures, symbols, sounds, or the behavior of others serve this purpose in educational settings. They signal to the person the chances a particular behavior has of being reinforced. We saw how Daddy's presence eventually became a signal for baby to wave. Daddy's being there made it more likely that he would wave back, smile, talk to baby, and so on. After all, if he or anyone else weren't there, waving would produce little. "Time for snack. Let's clean up," signals that the behavior of cleaning up will lead to getting a snack - especially if it has previously.

Have you noticed that, contrary to popular belief, these stimuli do not guarantee the response we would like to see? They only alter the probability that the behavior of concern will follow. We may consider these antecedents "suggestions" because they do not make the response occur. Getting the response depends on the individual's *learning history*, particularly the frequency and regularity with which the behavior has resulted in reinforcing consequences in the presence of that *particular stimulus*. We could 'make' someone do something - raise an arm, perhaps - even while that person was sleeping, but 'raising the arm' in that situation would not be considered 'a behavior' and thus no learning should be expected.

Threats and promises are good examples of this point. A promise is only as good as its history of being reliable in the past. If a parent promises a child a preferred treat after he cleans his room, but then regularly fails to deliver, eventually the promise will have little effect on how often he cleans his room. But if the promise is always kept, and the treat remains a powerful incentive, the child will begin to "trust" the promise and act accordingly. If the child listens to his parent's promise, it is because of the history associated with that promise - not the future treat that has yet to occur.

We adults respond no differently. Recall your own driving patterns, say, when the posted speed limit is 55 miles per hour. If you typically drive faster than 55 MPH in a particular region, and the result is neither directly nor indirectly unpleasant, there is a good chance you will continue to speed there despite the posted or signaled limit. Instead, if you have seen others detained by the police, or you yourself have received speeding tickets when exceeding the limit in that area, you probably slow down there.

Consequences

Later, when we go into the details of successful instruction, we shall talk about how to manage prompts and cues effectively. For the moment, let's concentrate on the most essential element of the learning process, the consequences (Cs) of the behavior of interest. Types of consequences are defined by how they influence behaviors they reliably follow.

- If a consequence to a specific behavior results in an increase in the rate of that behavior (i.e., we see more and more of that behavior over time), that *consequence* is called a positive reinforcer (R+). Colloquially, we would say that the person does the action more often because he wants or likes the outcome. The *process* by which the rate of the behavior *increases* or persists at a high level is called reinforcement.

> **How do we know a consequence is a *reinforcer*?**
>
> The only way to know if a consequence is functioning as a *reinforcer* - either positive or negative - is to see if the rate of the individual's behavior *increases* when it leads fairly regularly to that consequence. That is, if the behavior tends to be repeated more often after it has resulted in, or been instrumental in, producing or removing that consequence.

Realize, though, that what is a "wanted consequence" for one individual at one time may mean nothing for that person at a different time, or nothing or even the opposite to a different person. We return to this point in Chapter 4.

Examples

Harry hits himself in the chest (the behavior). His mom looks at him for a moment (the consequence: getting attention, something Harry "wants"). Over time, Harry hits himself again and again (the result: increase in behavior following receipt of the consequence).

Sally says "milk" (the behavior). Her mom gives her a little milk (the consequence: getting what she wants). Over time, Sally says "milk" again (the result: increase in behavior following receipt of the consequence).

- If a consequence to a specific behavior results in a decrease in the rate of that behavior (i.e., we see fewer and fewer responses over time), that *consequence* is called a punisher (The punisher itself is often referred to as an aversive stimulus). When the rate of a behavior *decreases* as a result of a specific consequence the *process* is called punishment (*not* negative reinforcement).

> **How do we know if a consequence is a punisher?**
>
> The way to know if a consequence is functioning as a *punisher* is to see if the rate of a particular behavior *decreases* when followed regularly by that consequence.

Examples

Harry hits himself in the chest (the behavior). His mom shouts, "Stop hitting yourself" (the consequence of yelling provides something aversive). Over time, Harry stops hitting himself (the result: decrease in behavior following receipt of the consequence).

Sally runs toward the street (the behavior). Her mom yells, "Sally, No!" (the aversive consequence). Sally no longer runs toward the street (the result: decrease in the rate of the behavior following receipt of the consequence).

- The removal of a consequence to a specific behavior may result in an increase in the rate of that behavior. In such cases, we would say that the *consequence* the behavior is avoiding or escaping from is a punisher (or an aversive stimulus). The *process* by which a behavior increases when a consequence is avoided or escaped is called negative reinforcement (*negative* because something is *subtracted or removed; reinforcement* because the preceding behavior increases). Note that this is not punishment because here the rate of the behavior increases.

Examples

Harry hits himself in the chest (the behavior). His mom stops nagging him to eat his vegetables (the consequence: takes away something aversive). Next time his mom nags him to eat his vegetables; Harry hits himself over and over (Harry's self-hitting increases). Over time, his behavior has been negatively reinforced (the result: increase in behavior following removal of the consequence).

Sally is seated in the circle with the other children. The others begin to sing a song. Sally asks for a break (the behavior). The teacher guides her to a quieter spot (the consequence: takes away something aversive – the other children singing). Next time the children sing, Sally asks for a break (the result: increase in behavior following removal of the consequence).

- The removal of a consequence to a specific behavior may result in a decrease in the rate of that behavior. In such cases, we would say that the *consequence* that is removed is a reinforcer (or appetitive stimulus). The process by which a behavior decreases following the removal of a consequence is called *response cost* (or it may be termed *negative punishment*). When we remove the opportunity to continue to engage in a reinforcing activity, the descriptor timeout often is used.

Examples

Harry has been earning stars he can exchange for his favorite orange juice when he does his lessons without hitting himself in the chest. When he hits himself in the chest (the behavior), his teacher takes a star away (response cost). Harry hits himself less frequently over time while doing his lessons (the result: decrease in behavior following removal of the consequence).

*Harry hits himself in the chest (the behavior). His mom turns off the TV program he was watching for five minutes (response cost). He stops hitting himself. His behavior **decreases** as a function of the **cost** of the response - the removal of, or timeout from, the opportunity to watch something he enjoys.*

Sally is seated in the circle with the other children who begin to sing a song Sally especially enjoys. Sally starts to scream the words (the behavior). The teacher has everyone stop singing (response cost). Sally stops screaming. They all start to sing again and this time Sally does not scream (the result: decrease in behavior following removal of the consequence).

Sally jumps up and down so forcefully (the behavior) while the group is singing her favorite song that the other children become upset. The teacher removes Sally to a quiet place for a few minutes (timeout). When Sally rejoins the group, she does not jump up and down again (the result: decrease in behavior following removal of the consequence).

Behavior rates also may change as a result of a new pattern between the behavior and the consequence. Two general cases will be illustrated.

• When a punisher for a specific behavior is no longer presented, that behavior is likely to return to its previous (i.e., pre-punishment) *higher* rate. The term for this process is recovery.

*Harry has been hitting himself (the behavior) less and less frequently after his mom began to shout at him every time he did that. Now his mom has stopped shouting at him when he hits himself. Within short order, Harry is back to hitting himself as often as he formerly did (the behavior **recovers** its former rate).*

*When Sally disturbs the group by jumping up and down loudly while they are singing her favorite song, no one removes Sally to a quiet place for a few minutes. Sally's rate of jumping up and down **recovers** to its original level.*

- When a reinforcer for a specific behavior is no longer presented, that behavior is likely to eventually return to its previous (i.e., pre-reinforcement) *lower* rate. The term for this *process* is called *extinction*. It should be noted that the immediate reaction to the sudden withdrawal of a reinforcer is likely to result in a sudden, short-term increase in the rate of the behaivor, followed by a gradual reduction in the rate. The sudden increase in the rate of the behavior is termed an *extinction burst*. We should be careful not to say that we have extinguished the behavior (nor the behaver!).

Examples

> *Harry hits himself (the behavior), although the action does not result in serious harm nor damage. While his mom has generally paid attention to this behavior, now she stops doing that. At first, Harry hits himself harder but mom continues to pay no attention to his behavior. After a while, Harry hits himself less frequently (behavior decreases).*

> *When the children start to sing, Sally asks for a break. Her request repeatedly is ignored. At first, Sally screams, "Break!" Gradually, Sally stops asking for a break.*

Table 2-1 summarizes these behavioral processes, describing the effect on the behavior as a function of the consequences operating on it.

Table 2-1
Terms for Processes
Based on the Relation between the Response
and its Consequences

Operation			
Nature of behavior change	Behavior leads to something added	Behavior leads to something subtracted	Behavior leads to something no longer added or subtracted
Increases	Positive reinforcement	Negative reinforcement	Recovery
Decreases	Punishment (positive)	Response Cost/ Timeout (negative punishment)	Extinction

Behavioral Procedures

It is important to notice that terms are defined by their relation to changes in behavior, not to the feelings of the one behaving. That is, to merely say we 'like reinforcers' and 'dislike punishers' will not allow us to define reinforcers or punishers. To take on the learner's perspective, we may notice that Johnny claps his hands loudly and his teacher routinely yells, "Stop!" - and yet his clapping continues and even increases. If we asked him whether he 'likes' to be yelled at by the teacher, he says, "No!" - and yet the yelling is functioning as a reinforcer. Phyllis does a nice job on her math work and her teacher publicly praises her. However, that very praise leads to a gradual reduction in the number of math sheets Phyllis completes. Phyllis may even say that she likes to get attention from the teacher but, in effect, the public praise is functioning as a punisher.

As a teacher, maybe you have already noticed that these *processes* can operate without regard to your intentions; that each of these processes is identified by the actual changes in a learner's behavior, rather than in your intended change. The true change in a behavior can only be determined after observing many opportunities, not just one episode. From a single occurrence of an action, we cannot determine its rate. For example, we may scold a child for running around the room and notice that the child immediately sits down. From this single interaction, we may conclude that scolding is a punisher - it seems to have resulted in reducing the child's running. However, when we monitor what happens over the course of the entire day, we see that the rate of running around is quite high and sustained. In this case, our interaction with the child, although we scolded his action, actually provided something reinforcing (most likely our attention) because the behavior of running was maintained or even strengthened over time. We might test this guess that attention is the reinforcer by withholding that consequence. That is, we stop scolding the child when we see him run. If, over time, he runs less and less, then we would feel more comfortable concluding that scolding was a reinforcer because withholding it (i.e., putting the behavior on *extinction*) led to a reduction in that behavior.

You also may have noticed that there are *several* procedures that result in increases or decreases in the strength of a behavior. In other words, there is always more than one way to change a behavior, whether we are trying to increase or decrease its strength. This diversity of options is very important to remember with your learners. To decrease a behavior, you do not have to resort to punishment. You may choose instead to reinforce some alternative action. Likewise, you may want to use extinction to reduce the rate of some behavior but realize that you do not control the effective reinforcer - perhaps the reinforcers are provided by peers. In such a case, you may opt to use a response cost strategy involving a point system that you have established. In each case, there are many strategies that you can choose to use.

The Three-Term Contingency

Figure 2-8 is a picture of the *three-term*, or A-B-C, contingency set within its context. Notice how the consequence, C, influences B over and over. As we now know, if the consequence is a reinforcer, the rate of the behavior it follows will increase. We also have just seen that other consequences can have different but similarly powerful influences.

Figure 2-8

The Three-term Contingency Set in its Context

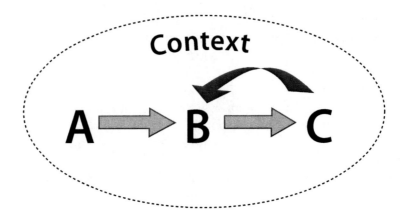

These concepts are straightforward and, thus, one may think they should be easy to apply. But that is not necessarily so. For one thing, each person has a unique and distinct learning history; for another, how much a person wants to have something or avoid something may change from circumstance to circumstance. We must understand and adjust for these complexities if we are to teach effectively.

Many consequences, like food for the hungry, rest for the weary, and money for the poor are almost universally reinforcing. However, as we have hinted, *many consequences are specific to the person within a given context*. While lots of people seek and enjoy companionship and affection, others may not. Viewing a football game may appeal to one audience; an opera to a different one. If you are fortunate, your closest companions enjoy providing pleasure and support; but have you ever heard of someone who seems to delight in inflicting or receiving discomfort? We all have our likes and dislikes in food, jobs, and recreational activities.

Complex Learning

So far, we've talked about the simpler processes of behavior change. As you might have suspected, though, that certainly is not all that there is. Learning is not only about increases and decreases in behavior. Among others, learning also may involve:

- The behavior taking place under one set of circumstances and not under a different set of circumstances, as in dressing for the cold only in winter. The name for this type of learning is a *simple discrimination*.

- One behavior occurring under one set of circumstances while another behavior occurs under a different set of circumstances: dressing for the cold when it is snowy; dressing for the heat when it is warm and sunny. Because each behavior is dependent upon one of two or more antecedent conditions, this type of learning is termed a *conditional discrimination*.

- Practicing the same behavior across differing circumstances: being polite at home, in school, and at work, as well as with authority figures. Behavior analysts call this broadening of behavior *generalization*.

- Continuing the behavior over time, for example, speaking French now as well as you did in school twenty years ago. *Maintenance* is the term behavior analysts use here.

- Numerous other categories[7].

Each of these more complex forms of learning will be included later, where they seem especially relevant. In the chapter on generalization you will learn more about broadening the circumstances under which a behavior occurs, as well as broadening aspects of the behavior itself, and in the chapters on teaching strategies, we will discuss strategies resulting in narrowing the circumstances for behaving in given ways (*discrimination learning*). Beforehand, though, we begin by helping you decide *what* to teach, and elaborate on how reinforcement can be integrated within systems to produce powerful teaching and learning of productive, functional activities as well as contextually appropriate communicative and social skills.

Were you to survey the field of "behavioral education," you would discover a huge and ever-expanding number of examples of effective teaching

---

7 For a more thorough, technical treatment of this subject refer to Sulzer-Azaroff & Mayer (1986) *Achieving Educational Excellence*; or (1991), *Behavior Analysis for Lasting Change*.

strategies based on principles of behavior. You might see how the standardized test scores of students in the ghetto have surpassed those of many in the wealthier suburbs; young children have mastered calculus and can perform intricate jobs that many adults find challenging. Learners have included just about every category, from infants to golden-agers, those with developmental delays, business managers and executives, school administrators, scientists, teachers, parents and regular pre-school through post graduate learners. Curricula have covered training in just about every imaginable academic, social, personal and vocational skill area. Increases in classroom academic performance, self-help, vocational, interpersonal, leadership and many, many other skill categories have been the happy outcome[8].

Limitations on Our Teaching

Before going any further, notice we do not promise you the ability to teach successfully each and every learner all that you would like them to learn. First of all, individuals have their own *physical limitations*. No more than we can spread our wings and fly like a bird, or become Olympic gold medalists in the broad-jump if our legs are short, neither can we expect to teach people who lack the essential physical attributes to learn and perform exactly as their more fit peers do. Performance is always a result of a genetic endowment and a history of interacting with the environment.

That is the bad news. The good news, though, is that physical abilities, as well as brain functioning, can improve as a result of intensive training and experience, especially in the early years. Therefore, just as anyone can improve the distance of her broad jump through training, given rich educational experiences, so children with delays of various kinds can increase the length and number of their academic, social, emotional, and physical strides. Furthermore, adults can continue to acquire and sharpen skills, even if not at the same rate as much younger individuals.

More good news is that, in the same way humans have discovered they can fly with the help of an airplane, people with physical limitations can make use of technological supports to assist their performance: walkers or wheelchairs to help them go from place to place; glasses and hearing aides to improve the way they see or hear; picture systems or electronic communication boards to support their ability to interact with others. These and other compensatory interventions may not result in learning new skills and yet do result in better performance. For example, those who need to use glasses do not 'learn' to do so, but their vision improves which may

---

8   Check out the educational pages and links of the Cambridge Center for Behavioral Studies' web site (http:\ \www.behavior.org) for sources.

influence much that they do. We need to include optimal use of aides or alternatives like these within the learner's list of high priority objectives.

The second important constraint is that *many aspects of the environment are not under our control*. If these events are tied to the behavior of concern, and we cannot manage them, we will not change the behavior. Among others, these limitations could include:

- Lacking sufficient tangible resources like funds, space, equipment, staffing, and supplies.

- Lacking intangible resources like sufficient energy, patience, knowledge, and skills.

- Internal events, unpleasant ones the person would try to avoid or end, like hunger pangs, aches and pains, or pleasant ones such as the satisfaction a person derives from moving his body in a particular way.

- The actions of others - groups of strangers, friends, family, community members, supervisors, and peers.

If we find ourselves unable to continue along a path for the reasons just stated, we have a few choices: push harder, give up, or find another way. Pushing harder actually is a fairly common response. It worked before, why not now? When we insert money in the soft-drink dispenser and it fails to deliver, we push the lever or button harder and faster. When a learner fails to repeat a phrase he said last week, we prompt him again and again and again. Had we successfully taught Kevin, Gloria, and Elvis to operate the washing machine, we probably would repeat the same technique to teach Erica. When she fails to master the skill, we repeat those methods over and over and over, and often all we accomplish is wearing ourselves out. Ultimately, we give up. Then, in our frustration, instead of assigning the responsibility to the teaching technique, where it rightfully belongs, we are tempted to blame the learner or some other outside cause. "She is a poor learner." "Her disability is at fault." "What would you expect with parents like hers?"

Giving up, also not unusual under the circumstances, sounds like copping out. Indeed, maybe it is. But often there is another, better way. Good teachers seek to change how they teach by using different tools and new approaches. It may just take stepping back, reviewing the situation, and using a different approach. We might, for instance, break the teaching steps down into much smaller parts, or use pictures or diagrams to prompt what is to come next. We could even work backwards, instead

> **We only can change what we can manage.**

of forwards[9], completing all steps ourselves except for the last - pushing in the dial - which we leave for Erica. Assuming she is successful there, next we would omit the last two steps: turning the dial to the proper position, until she mastered that; and the process would continue in that way until she could complete the entire sequence on her own.

Sometimes, though, a particular alternate way may not be the wisest approach. We need to ask ourselves if the extra effort, time, materials, and other resources would justify the results. Do the costs of achieving this objective warrant the benefits? Using the elaborate method we described to teach Erica to operate the washing machine might take more time than we can spare currently. Perhaps it would make more sense for the present to teach her how to bundle her dirty laundry for us to wash for her. Would it be more advisable to remove the white wrapping from Louis' sandwiches and substitute it with a yellow one? Could the time be used more wisely to teach him how to communicate his wants and needs more effectively? Later, in the chapter on selecting objectives, we shall return to this point. For now, we need to realize that sometimes, *instead of changing the behavior, it would be wiser to change the instructional objective.* Nonetheless, setbacks of this type do not mean that the laws of behavior are at fault; rather, it is a particular set of circumstances beyond our control that limits us.

The good news here, though, is that the behavioral approach to education can also empower learners, parents, educators, friends, companions, and so on. For they can learn to apply these principles to manage their own behavior, as well as that of others. Teach your learners or yourself to smile or comment positively about how good it makes you feel when someone compliments you or does you a favor, and you will probably find that the number of those agreeable experiences will increase[10]. When a person who craves attention says something you would just as soon not hear too often, such as complaints and fault finding, direct your notice elsewhere, and after a while those irritating comments may well begin to diminish.

Summary

The *Pyramid Approach* treats teaching as a technology for promoting be-

---

9   The technical term for this procedure is "backward chaining."

10   These examples, though common, are not universal. Later you will learn that not everyone responds identically to the same events. The behavior of many people with autism is not reinforced by compliments or attention, so applying them systematically may not work for you in the beginning. Yet you can teach these learners to use those tactics to teach their parents, teachers, and others to do more or less of what they like or dislike.

havior change. Through the use of the Pyramid, we seek to create effective educational environments. Like any effective technology, the principles of behavior we apply are founded on scientific discoveries. At the most fundamental level is laws of classical and operant conditioning. All other assessment and instructional strategies flow from those laws, including the way we 1) analyze and understand the conditions currently controlling given behaviors, and 2) adjust the educational context of the behavior of interest, and specifically modify its antecedents and consequences. The broad application of such methods has produced a tremendous number of success stories, empowering educators, parents, and the learners themselves. The behavioral approach to teaching does not promise miracles, especially when we are bound by circumstances over which we have no control. Our best alternative then, is to re-think what and how we teach. The main focus of the next chapter will be on what to teach.

Chapter 2 Resources

The Why of Behaving: The Science of Behavior

To	Read
Discover what the research has to say about early behavioral intervention with children with autism.	Green, G. (1996). Early behavioral intervention for autism: What does the research tell us? In C. Maurice, G. Green, & S. Luce (Eds.), *Behavioral intervention for young children with autism* (pp.29-44). Austin, TX: Pro-Ed. Harris, S. L., & Weiss, M. J. (1998). Does early intensive behavioral intervention work? In S. L. Harris, & M. J. Weiss (Eds.), *Right from the start: Behavioral interventions for young children with autism: A guide for parents and professionals.* Bethesda, MD: Woodbine House.
Survey, from a behavior analytic perspective, the current research and issues in the field of autism.	Frea, W.D., & Vittimberga, G.L. (2000). Behavioral interventions for children with autism. In J. Austin & J.E. Carr (Eds.), *Handbook of applied behavior analysis* (pp. 247-273). Reno, NV: Context Press.
Find out about characteristics, definitions and basic principles of behavior.	Michael, J.L. (1993). *Concepts and principles of behavior analysis.* Kalamazoo, MI: SABA
Learn generally, and in depth, about applied behavior analysis.	Cooper, J.O., Heron, T. E., & Heward, W.L. (2007). *Applied behavior analysis: 2nd Edition.* Englewood Cliffs, NJ: Prentice-Hall. Sulzer-Azaroff, B., & Mayer, G.R. (1991). *Behavior analysis for lasting change.* Atlanta, GA: Wadsworth Group; Thompson .
Review general inferences based on a survey of basic learning experiments.	Catania, A.C., (1992). *Learning, 3rd Edition.* Englewood Cliffs, NJ: Prentice-Hall.
To	**Read**
Survey learning from a bio-behavioral perspective.	Donahoe, J.W., & Palmer, D.C. (1994). *Learning and complex behavior.* Needham Heights, MA: Allyn & Bacon.

Learn the characteristics, definitions and basic principles of behavior, and their relation to social and cultural issues.	Skinner, B.F. (1974). *About behaviorism.* New York, NY: Knopf.
Become familiar with science in autism treatment.	*Science in Autism Treatment.* Association for Science in Autism Treatment. 175 Great Neck Rd., Suite 406, Great Neck, NY 11021
To	**View**
See behavior principles in action.	Videos by E.P. Reese. Can be obtained via www.behavior.org
To	**Attend**
Hear about the latest in research, theory and issues in behavior analytic approaches to education and treatment of people with autism.	The Association for Behavior Analysis state, regional, national and international conventions. The International Conference on Science in Autism Treatment. The PECS Forum.

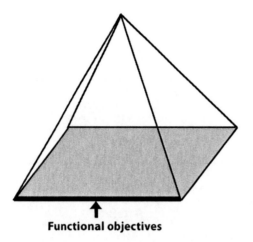

Functional objectives

3

What to Teach:
Functional Objectives

Kelly, a seven-year old learner with autism, has just been assigned to your class. From your earlier observations of Kelly in her previous class and at home, you recognize that she faces many challenges. You try to learn everything you possibly can about Kelly by reading records, meeting with the family, talking to the teachers, professionals, and paraprofessionals familiar with her, and participating in an Individual Educational Plan (IEP) meeting with all concerned. Overwhelmed by the length of the journey you and Kelly must take together, you realize you need to make some important decisions: The first is *What to Teach*.

Deciding *What* to Teach

You may wonder what you should teach on Monday morning. There are so many choices! Consider how we would plan a vacation - we wouldn't start with where we will be moments after we begin the trip - we would first pick out our long term destination. Once we've picked our long term destination, then we can decide how to get from here to there. Similarly, the *Pyramid Approach* reminds us that our initial step in educational planning is to choose our destination. What will the situation be like once all of our teaching goals have been reached? It helps for us to step back and pose this kind of long range question before trying to answer for the here and now.

The Long Range Goals of Education

One good way to begin is by asking ourselves, "Why do schools exist in the first place? What is the purpose of public education? What does Kelly need to learn before her educational support runs out, generally at age 21?"

Getting a Job

Often we hear that learners should become contributing members of our society. For that, they typically need to be employed (or be included in the family business). Consequently, we teach skills to learners while they are in school to improve their chances of getting and keeping a good job after graduating. We do not teach reading and math simply to say that a child can read and compute at a particular grade level, but because these skills eventually should, in part, help lead to successful employment. That is, achieving a high school level of reading skills should result in greater job opportunities than reading at the second grade level.

Living Independently

What else do parents typically anticipate once their children reach 21 or so? We have asked this question of hundreds of parents everywhere. The resounding answer is that their children live elsewhere independently! In other words, parents hope schools will provide their children with the skills that will enable them to live outside their parents' home by the time they are adults.

The long-term goals of education for learners with autism or other severe developmental disabilities are no different from those for all learners: helping them get a good job and live away from their parents. The *Pyramid Approach* shares the same long-range goals for those it reaches. It is not any specific reading, writing, or mathematical level learners might achieve, but whether their skills are sufficient to help them become, and remain, as independent as possible.

Being Happy

While many would not necessarily consider this an educational goal, parents also want their children to be happy. Typically, this area involves a set of social and communication skills, as well as recreational skills, both interactive and personal. We should be sure to include such targets in all situations.

Choosing Objectives

Having reminded ourselves of the long-range perspective, now the question becomes, "How do we get from here to there?" We will focus in on the stepping-stones along the way. As we will see, more than one path can get us there.

Select Developmentally Appropriate Objectives

A common goal-setting strategy begins by comparing the current abilities of the learner against skills mastered by typical age-mates (i.e., a norm-referenced group). Selection begins with those skills that are missing, or significantly delayed, relative to peers. This developmental perspective suggests that if a child is five years old, but does things more characteristic of a three-year-old, then one should begin teaching typical four-year-old skills.

Making reasonable choices depends on whether we are well-informed. Therefore, one of the first things to do is to find out about what typically developing children of the same age can and cannot achieve. Such information is very valuable. It can help guide what is and is not reasonable to expect of a child. For example, how would you respond to someone who says the he wants his three-year-old, developmentally-delayed son to independently select his own clothes each day, to dress alone, and put his soiled clothes into the hamper? Just about everyone one would point out that this expectation is far too high for any three-year-old.

This developmental perspective also encourages teachers and parents to be familiar with characteristic sequences in skill development in broad areas such as fine and gross motor skills, communication, conceptual (problem solving), social, affective, sensory, and other areas. Such information will be useful as general guidelines, but not necessarily as the sole basis for choosing curriculum content items, because we realize it is unsuitable to try to teach every age-appropriate skill to a learner deficient in many areas.

Being informed about the usual sequence in which skills develop within a particular area also may guide our goal selection. Children at very young ages pick up and hold items differently from the way they do once they gain certain digital strength and coordination. We would not view a two-year-old clenching a spoon in his fist as an error, but would expect a ten-year-old's fingering position to be more age-appropriate.

Identify Areas of Strengths and Weaknesses

Use a checklist to inventory each learner's performance across key areas. The developmental profiles of many children with disabilities are relatively 'flat' across skill areas. That is, a child with a one year delay in communication frequently will show a similar one year delay in other ability areas. Such patterns tempt us to conclude that a learner's performance in one area reflects his performance in other areas. However, learners with autism or related pervasive developmental disabilities often display a different pattern. Their developmental profiles often show sharp peaks and valleys across skill areas. While their average delay may be substantial in some areas, say in subtle social skills, in others like art, reading, or music, they may display skills comparable to, or even beyond, those of their peers. Therefore, assessing abilities in each general skill area is important for every learner.

When you look across performance areas, identify relative strengths and weaknesses. That is, although compared to peers, a learner may show delays in all areas, and each individual is likely to be more proficient in some areas than in others. Be sure that some of your targets involve the learner's strengths and avoid focusing all attention on weaknesses. Obvious weaknesses readily lead us to choose objectives in areas where the learner's delays are most severe. By also focusing attention upon a learner's relative strengths, you can minimize the ongoing sense of failure the learner would experience were instructional efforts limited only to critical weaknesses. Building on strengths leads to high rates of success and reinforcement. In fact, while you may be tempted to begin instruction with the next level, an effective strategy is to drop back a level or two, where success is virtually guaranteed. The momentum of doing well and receiving appropriate reinforcement will carry both learner and teacher along, readying them for greater challenges beyond. Furthermore, your focus on strengths is likely to coincide with activities the learner enjoys, providing a motivational avenue to new skills. If your learner has a "talent" for drawing, begin with a drawing exercise, and then gradually shift it over to a writing task. Other learners may have different strengths, such as singing, physical skills, or the ability to use pictorial representations drawn by others. The point is, knowing a learner's relative strengths allows you to take advantage of these strengths to teach for success.

Promote Pivotal Developmental Skills

Teaching learners with special needs is always a contest in efficiency, balancing what needs to be accomplished with what time and resources are available. From the infinite number of possible instructional objectives, we need to choose those that will give us the "biggest bang for the buck." Certain clusters of "pivotal" skills serve as tools for mastering many other objectives. You could teach a child to clap his hands, or to touch his nose, or to tap his head, as if these were three separate lessons. More effective would be to teach the child to imitate simple body actions, imitate object selection, and imitate object use. Then you would have a powerful strategy – *imitation* – to rapidly develop new skills. Thus, generalized imitation functions as a pivotal skill. Other such skills could include attending to general instructional cues, orienting to one's name, effectively reaching for and picking up objects, and requesting desired items. Children who lack these kinds of pivotal skills are at a great disadvantage when it comes to more advanced learning.

Consider a Learner's Chronological Age When Choosing Instructional Objectives

Applying a developmental perspective intuitively makes a great deal of sense but, sometimes, as the gap between the learner's age and developmental level increases, we need to consider other factors. For example, if our learner is 18-years-old but is assessed as performing similarly to typically developing 3-year-olds, then a strict adherence to the developmental model would suggest we should work on skills appropriate for 3-year-olds. Such reasoning easily can lead to providing this teenager with the kinds of activities and materials preschoolers enjoy. If you ever have watched a teenager or adult playing with pegboards or stringing large wooden beads, however, you probably have felt as uneasy as we have. In responding to this concern, many practitioners maintain that we should use age-appropriate materials in our teaching. The materials (including toys) that teenagers and adults use should be the same as those used by typically developing peers. What may be modified are the skills associated with these materials, as well as the level of support the learner may initially need to use them effectively.

One difficulty here lies in locating age-appropriate materials the learner can successfully manipulate or play with. Another issue is that, while we may succeed in locating such articles - maybe chess pieces instead of pegs, a basketball rather than a large rubber ball - we have to ask ourselves just how functional the activity is for the learner, especially given time constraints.

Given that the learner's skills are already delayed, time becomes an important issue. We need to begin to make some difficult choices, selecting the most critical goals from the large pool of possible instructional objectives. Should we concentrate on teaching age-appropriate social skills to a fifteen-year-old, or do we need to focus on enabling him to develop skills that will benefit him in an adult-oriented world? An example may help clarify this point. People often have expressed to us their desire to teach their high-school aged learners with severe challenges to join their age-mates for lunch in the cafeteria. Suppose, though, a particular learner seems frightened in crowded situations. How necessary would it be to teach this learner the skills to eat his meals in a large communal setting? To decide, you might ask yourself, "When I have traveled to another city, have I ever asked a friend to take me out to the local high school for lunch?" Let's face it - after we graduate high school, most of us would be delighted never to have to eat in a school cafeteria again! Apparently, that skill is of time-limited value[1]. If we consider future needs, it is preferable to teach our fifteen-year-old to eat lunch in a break area among a small group of adults. That skill is likely to serve him throughout his working life.

Another concern about using a strictly developmental approach is that chronological age may be used inappropriately to explain behavior. "Oh, he's just in that stage, you know, the terrible twos!" In this case, the age of the child is viewed as a cause of his actions. Still one more issue is that teachers and parents may over-rely on age to choose objectives. Perhaps we think: "If I want to choose a skill to teach my 3-year old, I simply have to look at what other three-year-olds are doing and teach these same skills. If my learner acquires the skill (e.g., coloring, watching a video), then he is 'acting' like a three-year-old." This type of reasoning risks overlooking the behavioral sequences that a developing child learns along the way, depending too heavily on the age at which certain behaviors typically appear.

For example, you're working with a six-year-old child who knows about 100 spoken words. Use of a checklist indicates that the child cannot name several convenience stores. Therefore, you set up a lesson to teach the child to appropriately respond to the direction to, "Name some convenience stores." After many trials, the child learns to respond, "7-Eleven, Wawa, MiniMarket." It seems that she's learned the lesson. But then you ask, "What's a store?" and the child simply repeats the list. This child has never bought anything in a convenience store, and the only time she needs to respond to the word 'store' is within this lesson in the classroom environment. In this case, a skill was taught that actually is functional only if other skills are present - skills related to shopping, familiarity with one's

---

1   It should be noted that our culture sets the context for how appropriate and time-related a particular skill is. For example, in many a kibbutz in Israel, the full community does eat main meals together. Thus, in such a setting, learning to eat cafeteria-style would be viewed as a life-long skill.

neighborhood, etc. These related skills, in part, depend upon exposure to the natural situations. Developing meaningful, practical skills depends in large part on the presence of other skills the learner has learned previously, rather than strictly on age.

When teachers select objectives solely on the basis of a developmental assessment or some other inventory (i.e., "knows own address," "names 5 items to eat") in essence, they are "teaching to the test." A teacher may notice that a child cannot respond to a particular test question and then decide to teach the answer to that particular test item. However, items in developmental assessment tests are designed to *sample* from a much larger array of children's skills, because it would be impractical to probe for every one of them. By limiting teaching to just that one test skill, a teacher would be violating the very basis upon which the test was created. Furthermore, the test question was part of the assessment precisely because we assume that children are not drilled to learn the answer.

Choosing Functional Objectives

Is there another perspective beyond the developmental one that will help us select objectives? One alternative is to focus attention upon skills a person needs to function in our society. So, how can we identify what is functional?

Earlier, we noted that the long-term goal of an education was to enable learners to be successfully employed and live as independently as feasible. Therefore, even though we provide educational services within a school or classroom setting, part of our ultimate goal involves skills that must be applied outside of the school - in the community and home settings. Therefore, the objectives we select also need to reflect the paths we wish to take in those directions. Objectives need to be *functional* to fulfill these important purposes; purposes that will afford learners timely, frequent re-inforcement here and now, as well as later in their future jobs and homes.

Deciding Whether a Goal is Functional or Not: "If the learner doesn't do it, who will?"

This question is one that Lou Brown and his colleagues[2] pose when they want to decide whether an objective is functional or not. Brown noted an important difference between activities begun by learners that we adults would be compelled to complete for them, versus those not essential for

---

2   Brown, L., Nietupski, J., & HamreNietupski, S. (1976). The criterion of ultimate functioning and public school services for severely handicapped learners. In M. Thomas (Ed.), *Hey, don't forget about me: Education's investment in the severely, profoundly, and multiply handicapped* (pp. 215). Reston, VA: Council for Exceptional Children.

the learner's progress. For example, if a girl cannot feed herself, will someone else feed her? Of course. If a young boy cannot dress himself, someone surely will do that for him. Notice that there are many auxiliary skills associated with these important ones. Eating cannot happen unless someone buys the food, unpacks it, and prepares it. Then someone needs to set the table, clean up the dishes, and so forth. These activities would all be viewed as functional because either the person learns to accomplish these independently, or someone else will need to do it for her. Similarly, dressing appropriately requires that someone will buy, clean, and put the clothes away.

Contrast these types of activities with an objective such as teaching size, shape, or color by enabling a learner to fit items into their proper slots in a form-board. If a learner did not fit in all the pieces into a four-shape form-board by the end of lesson time, how essential would it be for the teacher to replace all the pieces before progressing on to the next activity? Is this the most functional way to teach such skills? Furthermore, what happens to the materials once they are placed into the form-board? Right, we remove them so that the learner can put them in all over again.

Using Functional Activities as Vehicles for Teaching Other Skills

An especially meaningful way to teach learners to build their physical, cognitive, and communicative skills while interacting with others is to set instruction within a functional context. So, rather than instructing a learner about colors and shapes solely by using colored circles and blocks, we would find more meaningful materials and activities in the learner's current environments. In the process of organizing the clean laundry to put it away, we might teach a learner to sort different items of clothing - shirts, socks, pants, or underwear - by what they are used for, or their color or shape. Or, you might teach him to separate the light from the dark clothes, or group them by type of fabric, in preparation for washing. While learning to put away toys, a child can be guided to arrange them by use, color, form, size, or number. It should be noted that we know of no research that suggests it is more effective to teach about colors using pieces of paper than with clothing, toothbrushes, or other common objects. We will return to this point shortly. Later, in *The How of Teaching* we present various techniques for carrying out this instruction.

How can we assure ourselves that we are covering the full range of necessary functional skills for any given learner? In contrast with the developmental approach, where we looked for 'underlying' skills and partitioned our objectives according to their form ('cognitive' versus motor skills; gross or fine motor), here we stress the importance of functional activities. We organize our objectives by asking what the learner will need to do within the various facets of daily life, and classifying them into *environmental* or *skill-based domains* according to their common function[3]. Critical environments include areas associated with living at home, school, in the community, and at work. Critical broad skills that may be needed across environments include recreation and leisure skills, as well as social and communication skills. First we address issues connected with environmental domains.

Functional Skills within the School

Within a school setting, we are used to planning to teach academic skills. Federal, state, and local educational agencies are responsible for specifying curriculum content that learners are supposed to learn through elementary, middle, and high school years. In general, such curriculum content emphasizes reading, writing, and arithmetic, along with specific factual information, such as history, art and music appreciation, and so on. Why have these skills been selected? Do we teach these skills merely to say, "Johnny can read at a 4th grade level?" No, it is because for the great majority of learners, progress in these skills will contribute significantly to their success in earning a living and living as independently as possible. It will be possible for some learners with special-needs to participate in exactly the same curriculum as that designed for the general population. However, if it is not reasonable to aim to teach a learner the same curriculum content, we must still keep in mind that our lessons ultimately should help each learner function more successfully in the world beyond school.

When we consider the skills learners need to succeed in school, we quickly see that academic tasks are only part of the story. Learners with special needs are expected to engage in the same categories of activities as those within regular education settings. These include following individual and group instructions, taking turns, moving around the classroom and the school (i.e., going to gym, the nurse's office, the main office, the art room, and elsewhere); also, when appropriate, to remain within identified areas (i.e., a play area, a classroom, a line, and so forth). Note that while regular academic objectives can be included within this domain, they are not the only focus. Rather, we consider all skills learners need to successfully manage themselves in school.

Functional Skills within the Home

The skills everyone needs to live successfully in a home environment can be clustered within a 'domestic domain.' Functional skills within this

3   See Snell, M. (1987). *Systematic instruction of persons with severe handicaps*. Columbus, OH: Merrill.

domain would include activities related to eating (e.g., storing, preparing food, eating, cleaning up, washing dishes, putting away utensils), dressing (e.g., getting dressed, washing, sorting clothes, folding and putting away clothes), grooming (e.g., washing, combing and/or brushing, brushing teeth), cleaning (e.g., sweeping, mopping, vacuuming, dusting), and recreation/leisure (e.g., playing with toys and games, watching TV, listening to music).

Why should a classroom teacher be concerned about the skills learners need to learn to use at home? Take the parents' perspective. Would you as a parent be pleased to learn that your child had learned to read and write but could only do so within the confines of the classroom? Undoubtedly not. Therefore, skills taught in the classroom must be used within the home. Similarly, unless learners learn skills for living successfully outside of the parents' home, they will not fully participate in our society. Although parents will have more natural opportunities to teach their children domestic skills, teachers and other educational professionals tend to have more instructional expertise for accomplishing this long-term goal. Of course, parents can learn the same teaching tools as used by successful teachers!

As we noted earlier, the age of the learner will impact upon the degree of independence we may reasonably expect. For example, we can anticipate that a four-year-old boy can learn to help set the table, but with materials such as plastic cups and napkins instead of the full set of fine china, in deference to his age. Subsequently, we will discuss how important it is to teach even young children to be actively involved in many routines within the home - in part because the more they can accomplish, the greater the opportunity for setting a variety of communication goals. Similarly for adults, if they are not expected to participate in many routines, then their communication skills will remain limited.

Functional Skills within the Community

Assuming learners are to function effectively within their local and wider communities, teachers within the regular education system focus considerable effort on teaching learners about the 'real world' - the world beyond the classroom. The same is true of learners with special needs. We may need to modify our methods for our special learners, but not that long-term objective. Because most schools lack sufficient resources to bring their learners in contact with the broader experiences the world might offer, teachers arrange instead to convey the world to the learners through media like books, newspapers, magazines, films, videos, slide shows, computers, the Internet, and so on.

Where does "the community" begin? Fundamentally, the learner's community is everywhere he might spend time now or later outside his home or primary classroom. Children need initially to learn to move around all areas of the school, and later to function effectively in parks, playgrounds, shops, libraries, health care settings, on transportation, and at the many other places youngsters make use of outside of school.

Even very young learners, including preschoolers[4], need community-based training. Even if teachers routinely do not take preschoolers out of the school building, such training is warranted with children with special needs because parents often face problems with these children when they venture outside their homes. For instance, many parents of preschool children with autism have reported difficulties when attempting to take their child to the store, medical or dental offices, places of worship, or the homes of neighbors, friends, or relatives. One family we know reported they went shopping at 2:00am because previous attempts to take their son into super-markets at more usual hours had proven embarrassing and futile. Two in the morning was the only time they could be assured their child would be asleep. The boy's school team decided that teaching this 3-year-old to use socially acceptable manners while visiting common community settings would relieve the entire family and permit them a more normal life-style.

Safe pedestrian and transportation skills also fall within community-based domains. Most children will need to learn how to wait for the green light, use a cross-walk, and behave appropriately in a car (i.e., use seat belts, and operate windows and doors properly). Different rules apply to riding on a school bus; others to using public transportation like buses, subways, or trains. In these latter cases, socially acceptable ways of interacting with other travelers become especially critical.

Community recreational settings offer important opportunities for skill development. Whether at a sports event, film, picnic, or other amusement, learners need to be prepared to participate in such activities without interfering with the enjoyment of others. Explore your community to see what recreational facilities are available and tie some objectives to those.

Are there ways we can sub-divide the potentially vast realm of the community? One is to look at how we interact with its various elements[5]. For example, we act as consumers of products in some locations, such as stores,

---

4   Bondy, A. & Battaglini, K. (2007). Application of the Pyramid Approach to Education Model in a Preschool School Setting" In J. Handleman & S. Harris (Eds.) *Pre-school education programs for children with autism, 3rd Edition*, pp. 283-308. Austin, TX: Pro-Ed Inc.

5   Squittiere, D. and Bondy, A. (1988, May) Autistic learners as consumers and providers of community service: Implementing community-based training within a public school system. Association for Behavior Analysis Convention, Philadelphia, PA.

restaurants, and recreational facilities, while in other locations we are assisted by different service providers (e.g., banks, post offices, libraries, movie theatres, sporting events). Quite different types of objectives need to be set for those two different categories.

Finally, when selecting a community-based objective, we need to consider our main purpose. Is it to teach the learner a set of skills, or to meet our own needs as consumers? If our goal is to teach a community skill, then we should not simultaneously plan to use the setting for our own personal needs. That is, if the teacher's or parent's aim is to teach a child to shop in a grocery store, then the adults should not plan to do their own shopping at the same time. Should a temper tantrum suddenly erupt, they would want the freedom to leave, not feel bound to remain because they haven't finished purchasing all the items on their list[6]. When they indeed need to shop, they should cope in the best way possible, understanding that teaching is not likely to progress in such situations.

Functional Job Skills

One of a school's principal functions is to help learners develop and practice job skills to enable them to obtain and retain satisfactory employment. Thus, many decisions must be made about what objectives to set, as well as when, where, and how these will be taught. Many of the general developmentally- and functionally-related objectives, such as core academic subjects, social skills, and so on, can be tied to eventual successful employment. Additionally, there are those particular to specific jobs, including using tools and materials, and performing tasks correctly in their appropriate sequence. Every trade involves acquiring specific skills: an auto-mechanic must know what tool needs to be used, with what parts, in what order; a schoolteacher must handle audio-visual and computer equipment when teaching academic subjects; professional ball players have to handle the ball; and our learners need to master the specifics of their own trades. Still, long before providing work materials to our learners, there are a great many skills that can be addressed involving more age-appropriate materials.

Generic Work Skills

Some features are common to most jobs, despite dissimilarities between particular ones. These general skills include arriving and departing on time, following specific instructions, practicing basic social skills, such as being appropriately attired, meeting fundamental hygienic standards, say-

---

6   Bondy, A.S. & Battaglini, K. (1992). A public school for children with autism and severe handicaps. In S. Christenson & J. Conoley (Eds.) *Home School Collaboration*, pp423-441. Silver Springs, MD: National Association of School Psychologists.

ing "Good morning" and "Good evening," "Please," and "Thank you, " cleaning up one's work space, refraining from distracting others, and so on.

Doing a job *correctly* is of paramount importance. Suppose a candidate for a mail-advertising job folded a brochure neatly sometimes but not every time. His potential employer might insist on no more than a one-percent error rate. She also probably would be interested in the total number of times the applicant were capable of repeating the process within a given time period (its *rate*). For example, filling 100 envelopes *per hour*. What if the worker could meet that standard, but were only capable of doing the job for one hour per day? As his teacher, you might have to refine the objective to include a minimum duration time requirement of six hours per day, five days a week. Finally, we learn that the job requires that the employee work among five other employees, sharing the same supervisor. Working effectively only under one-to-one supervision, with no one else present, would be an unrealistic goal given practical and financial limitations of job support systems. The training objective would need to be clarified to include those kinds of specifications.

The previous example illustrates some of the many potentially important task dimensions that we ought to consider when setting instructional objectives:

1) *Frequency or Number.* A minimum number of work units must be completed.

2) *Rate.* The minimum number of repetitions per time block.

3) *Accuracy.* The minimum proportion of perfect performances to the total number, or the maximum error rate allowed.

4) *Duration.* The minimum length of time the work must continue.

5) *Social/Communicative Elements.* Social standards to be met at work.

6) *Supervisory Conditions.* The ratio of workers to supervisors.

Can we teach these general skills without working on actual vocational materials? That is, must an 18-year-old learner use actual job materials to begin to gain the kinds of skills just listed? Suppose we were to change the situation to a much younger child learning to put away his blocks. Just as filling a single envelope would be unsatisfactory, were this boy to put away one block properly, we hardly would conclude he had mastered the skill. More likely, we would feel content only if he put away many blocks (*number*), within a set amount of time (*rate*), without making too many mistakes, such as putting the square blocks with the round blocks (*accuracy*), throughout the entire cleanup time (*duration*), surrounded by other children (*social/communicative*), and with the teacher standing far from the child and next to the doorway (*supervisory*). As we can see, each of the factors we have identified as important for job success can be identified in teaching younger children far simpler skills. Similarly, wherever possible, we can and should include such elements within activities at school and home (e.g., cleaning one's room, setting the table, doing the laundry).

Within the *Pyramid Approach*, we promote working on these general vocational skills long before beginning to teach a learner how to manipulate real work materials. Furthermore, it is important to recognize that these changes will gradually accumulate over a number of years. Therefore, good record keeping, in the form of carefully documented changes in these various facets of doing a good job, is very important. Such information will permit new annual teaching teams (whether IEP or vocational) to set realistic goals based on prior learner progress. Now, we turn to critical skill clusters that often cross environmental domains.

Recreational and Leisure Skills

Leisure and recreational skills form a domain that spans multiple activities and environments. Although the particular recreation/leisure activities in which we engage at home often differ from those in community settings, presumably both are fun (i.e., reinforcing), relaxing, and socially acceptable. For example, in our home, recreation or leisure activities might include watching television, listening to music, reading books and magazines, playing cards and board games, and small-area sports such as Ping-Pong or pool. We may be less concerned with wider social aspects. In the community, different rules apply. How we conduct ourselves while watching a movie may differ from the way we watch television; listening to music at a dance involves different skills from listening to music with a head-set; and playing baseball demands following many more procedural and social rules than playing Ping-Pong.

We need to consider teaching recreation/leisure activities for transition times or long waiting periods, because those times are especially challenging. Remember that we all tend to self-stimulate more when we have nothing to do - biting our nails, bouncing our legs, or playing with our hair. In fact, in our culture, under circumstances when waiting often is necessary, books, magazines, music, video displays, and other stimuli often are supplied. When visiting the doctor's or the dentist's office, many of us anticipate the possibility of a delay and make adequate provision by bringing along something to do in the interim - a book to read, or our laptop computer to operate. Similarly, we must make certain that our learners can entertain themselves in socially acceptable ways while waiting for the next activity, or en route to their destinations. Being capable of reading a magazine, playing with an electronic or hand-held toy, listening to music over a personal stereo player, or similar skills, will serve our learners well while using public transportation to travel about the community. We should help our learners - both child and adult - by anticipating their need to bring along simple 'filler' materials to support appropriate choices of actions to engage in while needing to wait in various home and community settings.

Solo and group, simple and complex, brief and extended recreational and leisure activities are essential aspects of everyone's lives - young children, adolescents, and adults. Our learners need to learn and practice these skills at home, at school, during breaks on the job, and while being transported about, and making use of services and facilities in, the community.

Social and Communicative Objectives

We need to consider the characteristic social and communicative difficulties of learners with autism and related conditions when designing objectives. Instructional teams need to identify not only which skills should be taught, but also the conditions under which these skills should and should not be displayed. For example, because Kelly does not greet people appropriately, the team stipulates that skill as an important instructional objective. "Greeting people," though, is stated too vaguely because social convention dictates when, where, and how greeting others is acceptable or unacceptable. The team needs to determine the way Kelly's peers hail one another or adults, in school, and elsewhere. They discover they say, "Hi," or some equivalent, in different ways:

- At *school*, when their classmates enter a room, join others at the cafeteria table, or in other informal groupings.

- When other children or adults say "Hi" to each other.

- They *do not* respond to another's greetings while the teacher or another person in authority is addressing the class.

- In the *community*, when a shopkeeper, sales person, receptionist, or person in charge (e.g., doctor, bus driver) greets them first. They do not initiate or respond to greetings from strangers in malls, parks, movie theaters, and other public areas.

- And there are others. Can you add a few?

In this realm we see how important it is to specify objectives in sufficient detail that all the crucial conditions and restrictions are included. Clustering these skills within an IEP may be helpful to the team members as a way of assuring that all critical skills are addressed. However, although these skills may be combined within the same IEP domain, we should not assume they all would be taught the same way.

General Considerations in Using Functional Objectives

Before finalizing a set of functional objectives, you need to take stock of the resources that are, or will be, available to you for achieving each. Consider how suitably they lend themselves to generalization or transfer across situations or responses, and how useful they will be as conduits to other skill categories.

What Materials Should We Use?

Detailing the various times, places, and other conditions in our objectives can help us select instructional materials wisely. That is, when we construct our lesson, we should consider the long-term use of the skill, including generalization across time, place, people and materials. Many teachers err by choosing their instructional materials prematurely.

Here is an example: Assume that an assessment has indicated that a 4-year learner does not 'know' her colors. Based on this, the teacher writes an objective: "Mary will learn to identify five colors." Because the teacher has not considered the long-range purpose of knowing colors, she chooses colored paper circles (or blocks, or similar simple objects). She conducts all lessons individually with Mary at a small desk. Maybe the teacher places the circles before the child and, using a prompting strategy, instructs her to "touch RED." However, at another time of day, this teacher may be instructing the youngster in the bathroom how to brush her teeth. Because eight similar soft-bristle toothbrushes of different colors hang on the wall, the best cue for the child to distinguish her own toothbrush from the others is by its color. Yet, despite learning to distinguish paper circles by their color, Mary never uses the 'color' skill in the bathroom. Here, many would be tempted to ascribe the problem to the child: "Mary has failed to generalize her color skills to toothbrushes," when in reality the instruction was less than optimal.

Now the teacher will have to teach the entire lesson over with the toothbrushes, because brushing one's teeth is an essential functional activity, while correctly choosing the colored paper served purely to teach that les-

son and no other purpose. Would the quality of the child's life change markedly if she were unable to touch the red paper circle, but could pick her own toothbrush from the group? Had future needs been considered and detailed in the objective, such extra effort could have been avoided. (Our section on Generalization contains helpful information on how to design lessons to promote transfer of skills from function to function, time to time, place to place and material to material.)

Why do so many of us choose to start a lesson on colors labeling colored paper shapes? Most likely it is because it is easy for the teacher to prepare such materials. While that certainly is understandable, within the *Pyramid Approach,* we hope to challenge teachers to consider their choices of materials with care, basing them on their likely effectiveness with regard to learning the target skill, rather than on how easy they are to obtain or prepare. One way to avoid this kind of trap is to ask questions like, "Who benefits from the lesson?" or "How has the learner benefited from this lesson?" Such questions will help you choose which objectives to teach first. In the lesson involving teaching the child to respond to "Touch RED," what is the outcome from the child's point of view? When the child responds correctly, we will praise the child, "Good job! Way to go! Nice touching red!" Is such praise truly reinforcing to all learners? We could try to boost the power of the reinforcer by using some type of token-reward system, but we are still the one arranging to provide some reward for appropriate performance. Are there other types of reinforcers that can be more effectively integrated into this lesson? That is, are there lessons or activities associated with color in which the reward is currently operational?

What we can see in these examples is that when we want to teach a skill, such as 'colors,' we should *first* determine how color is (or should be) important to the learner in the immediate or next environment. This determination may take some time, as different learners will have different preferences. We may decide to create situations in which color is important as in teaching a child to find his favorite toy hidden inside a RED box. When we think about Mary as a four-year-old, we can consider where color is important to children of this age. Notice that some lessons may not be age-appropriate, as in teaching her to walk vs. stop at green vs. red traffic lights. That is, we do not expect any four-year-old to walk around the neighborhood independently. In searching for important items for four-year-olds associated with color, we may find that, besides candy, various toys, clothes, drinks, utensils, etc. are relevant. What we must now do is find materials for which color is important, but is also the only distinguishing feature. That is, we could not effectively teach Mary to request a red ball from a blue ball if the red ball is also bigger than the blue ball (or striped differently, etc.). Obviously, gathering such materials will involve more effort than simply cutting out circles of colored paper, but our increased initial effort will more than pay off by reducing the total amount of time we will spend on teaching this lesson. In part, this issue is associated with selecting effective reinforcers, but it also is pertinent to the topic of which lessons we should begin to teach.

In our work with Mary, we've noticed that when offered a handful of Skittles, she always selects the red ones. What is her action telling us? First, it tells us that she 'knows' how to discriminate colors! She is very careful in her selection of the candy. In this situation, her action is governed by color. She may not use any color words or respond when you say a color but what she does - in this case selecting candy - is sensitive to the color of the candies. Second, we now know that 'red' is associated with a powerful reinforcer. Can this information influence how we teach this lesson? We can teach her to request her favorite candy (via speech, PECS, or some other modality). When she requests 'RED candy' what will be the reinforcer? Of course, it is simply the candy, though we will be sure to add our praise as well! Which lesson will the learner find more interesting - "touch RED" or getting something important? Of course, other learners may be more interested in their favorite red toy, shirt, ball, or whatever. Thus, we are likely to need different materials to teach different learners about colors.

Preparing for Generalization and Discrimination

When choosing objectives, being very precise and detailed about our instructional goals helps us to avoid falling into a couple of common traps. One is assuming that when we teach learners something at one time and place they will naturally transfer that skill to other relevant times or places (technically, the assumption is that the behavior will *generalize* spontaneously). For instance, if Mary learns how to ask to join in a circle game in the playground at school, she will use the same skills to ask to join other children playing in the park. The second assumption is that the learner will not automatically transfer the skill when circumstances dictate otherwise (technically, *discriminate*). Although Mary has learned to accompany her to a different part of the school at the invitation of the communication specialist, she will not go along with just any stranger who approaches her in the mall. Like so many other situations in life, investing up front, in this case by being as detailed as necessary about specifying instructional objectives, will pay off in the future.

Goal Selection and Generalization

Later, we will review in depth various methods for promoting generalization of skills. At this point, however, we wish to emphasize that your

plans for generalization need to be taken into account while you are selecting and planning curriculum. Choosing single skills without regard
to how they relate to other skills, settings, people, and so on, is neither
very effective nor efficient in the long term, because you would have to re-
teach the skill under each of those other circumstances. Planning teams,
therefore, should map the various forms they hope generalization will take
before they begin to train any specific skills. This is why we caution you to
include long-term planning in the very earliest stages of identifying what
to teach.

Criteria of the Next Environment

Typically, we tend to focus on the present when considering what is
functional for children or adults to learn - where they go to school, where
they live, where in the community they go, and so on. As noted, keeping
the big picture in view, by asking what our learners will need to do when
they leave school, is very important. Is there an intermediate point between our hopes for the future and our lessons for today? That is, what are
our next steps and how large should they be?

One tactic is to investigate the learner's next environment and match
it against what we know about his present environment. For example, if
a child currently were in kindergarten, it would be helpful to know what
is expected of typical first-graders. Will the children be expected to sit in
chairs at individual desks quite different from the classroom arrangement
for kindergarten? What songs does the first-grade teacher usually teach
the children to sing? Must the children line up at the doorway and wait for
several minutes? Although these routines may not currently be expected of
the kindergarten class, rather than waiting for the child to enter first grade,
it may be possible to begin teaching the necessary skills before the end of
kindergarten. Here, though, we want to be cautious about stretching the
steps too far because that could lead to the child becoming confused, or the
teacher wasting her efforts by teaching meaningless lessons. Attempting to
teach a kindergartner second-grade skills can be an exercise in futility for
the child and a waste of time for the teacher.

The same concept of planning for the next environment also needs to
be considered for adolescents and adults. For example, if we are informed
about the location of a job-training site for a trainee, it would be very helpful to find out about typical routines, such as where employees take a
break or eat lunch, which employees typically meet and interact during
the workday, and other routines specific to that job site. We have found
that some work locations have break areas very different from any available in a school. By knowing the configuration of the work site break area,

we can simulate the break area within the school or current vocational setting. Trainees then practice taking a break or eating lunch in the type of environment into which they will soon move. When trainees are already familiar with the expectations and routines associated with the new work place, their transition from school to work is likely to go smoothly.

Summary

As so often happens, advance planning really pays off when it comes to instruction. Yet, deciding what to teach *our* learners is no easy matter because there is so much for them to learn and the time available to teach them is finite. Planning ahead by choosing those instructional objectives of greatest importance for our learners is the most reasonable way to proceed. If we remind ourselves that the long-range goals of education are to enable the learner to get a job and live independently, we can match any tentative objective against those outcomes.

Whenever possible, objectives should be as *developmentally appropriate* as feasible, especially those pivotal to learning other related skills. Most critically, the academic, personal, communicative, and social skills we hope to teach in school, at home, on the job, and in the community need to be as *functional* as possible. These skills then have a better chance of maintaining over time and fulfilling important purposes in the person's life.

When we select and detail our objectives, considering in advance how the skill is to generalize will prove most cost-effective because it will allow us to avoid re-teaching the skill from scratch under varied circumstances. Beyond obtaining essential materials, referring to the circumstances of next environment into which the learner will progress as a guidepost also should enable an efficient and smooth transition.

Chapter 3 Resources

What to Teach: Functional Objectives

To	Read
Develop an effective *Individualized Educational Plan (IEP)*.	Chapter 8, Develop a Balanced Program. In J.E. Janzen, (1996). *Understanding the nature of autism.* San Antonio, TX: Therapy Skill Builders: A division of The Psychological Corporation.
Select teaching programs to match chosen objectives.	Taylor, B.S. & McDonough, K.A. (1996) Selecting teaching programs. In C. Maurice, G. Green, & S. Luce. (Eds.) *Behavioral intervention for young children with autism.* Austin, TX: Pro-Ed Inc.
Decide what to teach and how to teach it.	Harris, S.L. & Weiss, M.J. (1998). What to teach and how to teach it. In S. L. Harris. & M. J. Weiss. *Right from the start: Behavioral interventions for young children with autism: A guide for parents and professionals.* Bethesda, MD: Woodbine House.
Choose what to teach and how to teach it; an older version.	Lovaas, O.I. (1981). *Teaching developmentally disabled children: The Me Book.* Austin, TX: Pro-Ed Inc.
Select targets for change.	Chapter 3; Cooper, J.O., Heron, T. E., & Heward, W.L. (1987). *Applied behavior analysis.* Englewood Cliffs, NJ: Prentice-Hall. Mager, R.F. (1975). *Preparing instructional objectives, 2nd Edition.* Belmont, CA: Pitman.

Ethically decide whether and how to select goals and objectives.	Chapters 2, 3 & 4 in Sulzer-Azaroff, B. & Mayer, G.R. (1991). *Behavior analysis for lasting change.* Atlanta, GA: Wadsworth Group: Thompson. Sulzer-Azaroff, B. & Reese, E.P. (1982). *Applying behavior analysis.* New York, NY: Holt, Rinehart & Winston.
Write lesson plans for teaching functional skills.	Bondy, A.S. (2002). *Lesson plans for young children: Volume 1.* Newark, DE: Pyramid Educational Consultants.

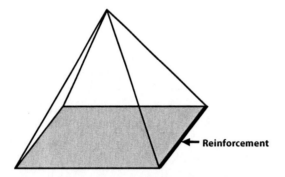

Reinforcement

Powerful Reinforcement Systems

Holding a favorite juice box in one hand and a thin straw in the other, Stacey tries to push the straw through the small circle of aluminum foil on the top. Finally, she succeeds and gleefully starts to drink the juice. Tony has a puzzle before him and is holding the last piece in his hands. He manipulates the puzzle piece and it finally falls into place. He beams proudly as he shows the finished puzzle to his teacher, who pats him on his shoulder saying, "Well done, Tony!" Charlotte goes outside for a walk with her umbrella tucked under her arm. Within minutes, it begins to rain. She opens up her umbrella and continues her walk. What does each of these scenarios have in common? They all demonstrate reinforcement at work.

In Chapter 2, we reviewed the basic principles of applied behavior analysis and described the way in which behavior analysts study how both antecedents and consequences influence particular actions. Stacey's handling of the straw led to the consequence of her drinking the juice. She's now more likely to repeat the technique of inserting straws into other juice boxes. Manipulating the puzzle piece led Tony's teacher to provide the social attention he treasures - virtually assuring that he will try to put more puzzle pieces into puzzles. Raising her umbrella kept the rain from soaking Charlotte's hair, increasing the prospect that she would take her umbrella with her in similar situations. In each case, the consequences of an action resulted in a greater probability of the individual repeating the same action. We now know that these types of consequences are called *reinforcers*.

In these examples, we can see the two main types of reinforcers - *positive*, like receiving *added* juice or praise, and *negative* (removed or subtracted) as in stopping rain from soaking our heads, the sound of the alarm clock buzzer, or a baby crying.

Accentuating Positive Reinforcement

Although both applying and removing certain consequences can reinforce the actions that lead to these changes, choosing positive over negative consequences is more ethically defensible and effective in the long run. Yes, in teaching a lesson we could encourage a learner to work harder to avoid our scolding, but that is using coercion, not education, as a teaching process.[1] Although any instructional procedure, including positive reinforcement, can produce some unwanted side effects, it is best whenever possible to minimize the use of negative reinforcement, punishment, and extinction. These latter methods tend to evoke aggression, escape, and a variety of other reactions that can get in the way of productive learning. Therefore, in this chapter we emphasize the whys and hows of using positive reinforcement effectively.

Identifying Learner-Centered Reinforcers

The consequences that will operate as powerful reinforcers to motivate learning vary from person to person. Doing your homework on this subject will be worth the investment because you will see your learners acquire better, faster, and more durable skills as a result of connecting with a broad range of reinforcers. Let's describe several ways we can go about conducting effective reinforcer assessments.

A Natural Solution

Many of our own actions are part of a natural sequence or *chain* of events. We prepare our food, then eat; groom and dress ourselves, then go out; turn the key in the ignition, put the car into gear, press the accelerator and go, eventually reaching our destination; we open a door and go outside; go to the refrigerator and get something we like to eat. Similarly, many actions of our learners result in changes that appear as natural aspects of their surroundings. That is, no one has to arrange anything special for the learner in order that a reinforcing consequence occurs. These natural consequences provide an excellent teaching opportunity. When you block access to that event temporarily, you now can teach the next essential element of the sequence. Marcus runs to the door but his teacher

---

1   Sidman (1989) discusses this topic in, *Coercion and Its Fallout*, Boston, MA: Authors Cooperative Inc.

blocks the doorway and uses the incident as an opportunity to teach Mark to request opening the door. When Mark makes the request, his reinforcer is getting to go outside. In this type of situation, there is no need to add candy or even tokens - going outside is powerful enough for Mark.

Let us look at another example. Suppose young Anna has learned to dress herself. Now you want to teach her to tie her shoelaces. For most youngsters this skill is very difficult[2], requiring strong motivation. You know that powerful reinforcers will be essential. You have a choice: Anna loves M&Ms and she also enjoys going out to the playground, especially when she's told that you are going to push her on the swing. Which would you choose?

If you seek a natural solution, you will take the latter course of action. Why? M&Ms are artificial - they typically have nothing to do with shoelaces or going outside - and thus are not always around. Furthermore, Anna's efforts might become dependent upon your presence and seeing M&Ms. The candy also might lose its appeal after a while and Anna's efforts will diminish. You want to resort to those contrived reinforcers only when strong natural consequences are unavailable.

Reinforcers Incidental to Activities of Daily Living

A person's day is full of *incidental teaching* opportunities. Eating food right away naturally reinforces setting the table or making sandwiches. Communication, in any modality, could function in a similar way. Place the peanut butter jar just out of reach so the learner must request it. If number concepts are of concern, place the napkins on a shelf and ask the learner to say or show the number she needs. We might say that these consequences fit the context of the lesson.

High Rate Behaviors

In the event that you are having a difficult time identifying sufficient reinforcing opportunities of this kind for someone (yourself included), observe the individual throughout the day. Take note of the things he or she approaches, requests, or spends lots of time doing. Is it watching TV, leafing through magazines, running around, playing with or holding a favored object or socializing? Interpose instruction at a point just prior to those preferred or high rate activities. You will be capitalizing on a behavioral principle, known as the *Premack Principle*, which states that *access to*

---

2   In Chapter 7 we discuss keeping the size of the teaching objective sufficiently challenging to encourage progress but small or simple enough so it can be fairly readily achieved.

high frequency behaviors can serve as reinforcers for lower frequency behaviors. The emphasis here is to consider behaviors as reinforcers, not just material or social outcomes.

Locating Functional Reinforcers

A reinforcer is functionally defined - it increases the rate of the behavior it follows. Most of the time, the reinforcers maintaining a behavior seem fairly apparent. We shop for food to have the ingredients to prepare, then eat; work at our jobs to earn money allowing us to buy food and other necessary, or optional, items; we work out to stay in shape, to be healthy and attractive to others and ourselves.

Sometimes, though, the reinforcers supporting a behavior are difficult to figure out. Why does Aunt Cora complain so much? Is it because complaining gets a reaction and any attention is better than none? Perhaps you have a learner with a history of displaying dangerous behaviors, such as severe aggression or self-injury. Maybe you have attempted to determine the function that those behaviors serve for the learner. Do they allow escape from the task or produce assistance, affection, or attention? Whichever is the case; those very same consequences have a good chance of being effective when used as consequences for learning productively. Give the learner a way to request those items via any effective modality and deliver the requested item following successful progress in the task at hand.

When we observe behaviors that are very persistent, even in the face of our best efforts to eliminate them, you can bet that some very powerful motivators are at work. In our chapter on changing *Contextually Inappropriate Behaviors* (Chapter 6), you will see that the most effective interventions begin by determining the functional control of the behavior. That is, by asking why the learner is engaging in this action. As with any behavior, reinforcing consequences play a major role, now or in the past. Some learners hit their heads for attention, or to obtain help or gain access to something they want. Others may hit their heads to get away from hard work or noisy environments. These same consequences can be used for educational purposes - to teach more socially acceptable tactics, like calmly requesting attention or help, or asking for a break or for a moment of peace and quiet. How such lessons can be incorporated into a plan to deal with problem behaviors will be clarified in that later chapter. For now, let's review some common strategies aimed at determining what is most reinforcing for a learner's actions.

Inquire

If your learner has well established communication skills and you are searching for powerful reinforcers to apply in a particular teaching situation, don't overlook the obvious. *Ask your learners to say or signal what they like or want*, either directly or by means of a survey, questionnaire, or checklist. In cases where a person has limited communication skills, teachers can interview parents or other teachers for this kind of information. Frequently, but not always, the answer will be accurate. Sometimes a learner may find something reinforcing at home but show no interest in the same item at school. What do we do, though, when our learners say they want to do or have something, but then fail to work hard enough for it? In such cases, we should trust their actions over their words. Therefore, whatever we are told about a learner's preferences, to verify our hunches we must move to the next strategy - direct observation.

Observing Direct Interaction

A simple way to find reinforcers is to give the individual free access to an array of items, including toys, snacks and other readily available materials. Which ones does he pick up first? Which ones does she play with the longest? Observe closely the individual's reaction when you try to take the item away. If he doesn't seem to care, then the item is not likely a powerful reinforcer at that particular time. If you have a wrestling match, then it is! Sometimes, you arrange what's offered, but at other times you may take advantage of naturally occurring opportunities, as when you take a child to the toy store and simply watch what happens. Perhaps you cannot afford a particular item but you may still figure out what is so appealing about it. Does it light up, does it make sounds, or does it vibrate? Occupational therapists may be a great resource in many situations - they typically have a host of items that involve all sensory systems, and you definitely want to go beyond simple things to touch, eat or drink.

Offer Choices

Similar to open observation is to assess for reinforcers by offering choices. It is preferable to use real items but, for some, you may present pictures or other representations of potential reinforcers. Present two objects, such as two toys, sets of materials, or activities. See which one the learner reaches for or points to first. Allow the learner to briefly enjoy that reinforcer, then say, "My turn." Remember your goal here is to get the item so that you can continue with the reinforcer assessment. It is not the right situation to teach, "Give it to me." Remove that item and present two other choices, and repeat as before. Continue this process several times until you now have a set of preferred objects, or symbols. Eliminate those not chosen and now pair two of the formerly preferred items. See which one of the new pairs the learner now prefers. Repeat with the other selected items, each time eliminating the one that was not chosen this time. By this process of elimination, ultimately you will have discovered the learner's number one choice[3]. By this process you also should establish a reinforcer hierarchy from most preferred, to reasonably liked, all the way down to non-preferred or avoided items. As a bonus, you also may find that learners who have the opportunity to choose their own reinforcers engage in fewer problem behaviors. Another added advantage is that the items found to be non-preferred will be necessary to help teach communication skills such as "No thanks" or "I don't like broccoli!" For learners with reliable picture or symbol selection skills, you may want to use such symbols to offer the choices. Furthermore, remember that when offering choices - either of items or symbols - preferences may change frequently. Therefore, all types of reinforcer assessment strategies must be considered an ongoing, never-ending process.

Making the Most of Reinforcers

There are reinforcers and there are reinforcers. In any given situation, some may work more powerfully than others. Scientists have invested a good deal of effort over the years in attempting to unravel the mystery of what accounts for these differences. Today we know that a person's history of learning, or *conditioning*, has much to do with the relative effectiveness of specific reinforcers. What happens when those historical experiences blend with current circumstances also is becoming clearer. The more teachers understand the way people learn and change, the better they can maximize the power of reinforcers and, as a consequence, the outcome of the lesson.

The Origins of Reinforcers

Some reinforcers are tied to the person's physical survival, such as food, fluids, and warmth. These *primary*, or *unconditioned*, reinforcers are effective without parents or teachers needing to take any special actions. They appear to work the first time the individual encounters them. Other events become effective reinforcers only due to occurring close together in time with established reinforcers: sunshine and a blue sky signifies an absence of rain; a smile on Daddy's face often is followed by a treat or pleasurable event like being hoisted on his shoulders and being paraded around the room. Parents or teachers often arrange these kinds of pair-

---

3   See Dyer, K., Dunlap, G. & Winterling, V. (1990). Effects of choice-making on the serious problem behaviors of students with severe handicaps. *Journal of Applied Behavior Analysis, 23,* 515-524.

ings as an aspect of their formal teaching: a good paper earns the learner a star and praise from teacher and parents. These *secondary*, *learned*, or *conditioned reinforcers*, such as praise and money, are effective only because they were paired in time with a reinforcer already powerful for the person. We work hard for money because of all the reinforcing items we can buy.

At any given time, circumstances like deprivation and satiation can influence the effectiveness of both primary and secondary reinforcers. A learner who has not eaten all day is likely to be highly motivated to learn how to make a pizza. However, a learner who has just eaten a few slices of pizza probably will feel relatively sated with food. He then may put out less effort to learn a new set of words during the pizza preparation activity. Deprivation can even make a difference with conditioned reinforcers, though perhaps to a lesser extent. Anna probably would work harder on her shoe tying if she had been cooped up in the house for a couple of days and really wanted to go outside. Fortunately, people do not *satiate* as rapidly on recreational activities, social events, praise, recognition, affection, and other sorts of secondary reinforcers. That is why frequently praising progress can be helpful.

Reinforcers are Relative

Do you recall your own childhood experiences of going to a toy or candy store where so many options were offered that you were unable to settle on a satisfactory choice? How about the three- or five-ring circus? Where did you concentrate your attention? You would hardly notice, and certainly not make any concerted effort to pay attention to, still one more option. By contrast, remember days when it was so unpleasant outside that you began to feel stir crazy? Almost any novel event would have been appealing.

To make the most of a potential reinforcer, then, evaluate its *relative* value at that time and place. The effectiveness of any one reinforcer relates to the availability of other reinforcers. A cookie is relatively attractive next to a tiny piece of pretzel, but it is hardly of value compared to a huge slice of cake. An offer to help fill the last two envelopes with a flyer is less important to me than your offer to help with the several hundred I have to complete. In both situations, the reinforcer - the cookie or the offer to help – doesn't change. It's what else is happening at that time that partially determines how strongly it will serve as a reward. Therefore, to increase the effectiveness of a reinforcer you have two choices. You can boost the power of the reinforcer, or minimize the availability of alternatives. For some learners, a significant reduction in environmental distractions might boost the value of the current reinforcers. Another way to boost attending to the task at hand is to boost the value of the reinforcers associated with task completion. Make sure that the reinforcers you do use are sufficiently powerful - whether natural or contrived - to retain their potency during the instructional sequence, or be prepared with a sufficient array of different reinforcers to support continued effort.

Establishing Events

As in the case of the relative number of available reinforcing opportunities, special events may change the value of the very same item or event (or even tilt it toward serving as a punisher). Your first candy bar or favorite beverage may taste terrific, but the tenth could make you ill. We already have seen instances of *establishing events*[4] or operations. When the person was deprived of a given reinforcer for a time, it became more powerful. When it was freely available for a long time, or other stronger reinforcing opportunities were available, it became less potent. Other examples of establishing operations might include:

- Providing salty food or encouraging vigorous exercise changes the value of liquids.

- Providing brief access to items or activities, or the opportunity to watch someone else enjoy that item or activity, may increase the potency of the item or activity as a reinforcer.

- Exposing someone to a rhythmic beat in the background may enhance the likelihood of dancing.

- Allowing an enticing aroma to waft into the room may enhance a food's attraction.

You even can transform a potentially unpleasant event into a reinforcer by applying these strategies. For example, Harry often gets very upset when the gym period is over and he must return to his classroom. To avoid his frequent tantrums, his teacher comes up with a clever solution. Before she announces the end of gym, she asks Harry, who enjoys listening to music, which one of his favorite CDs he would like to listen to back in the classroom. Being aware that he will listen to his preferred CD now establishes leaving the gym as a major signal to the availability of a reinforcer. His teacher has changed the focus from a negative one (i.e., what he's about to *lose* - gym) to a positive one (i.e., what he's about to *gain* - music).

---

4   In 1982, Jack Michael used the term "establishing operation" while elaborating on the distinction between discriminative and motivational functions of stimuli. *Journal of the Experimental Analysis of Behavior, 37,* 149-155.

Timing of Reinforcement

The sooner reinforcement happens following a behavior, the more powerful the effect. We adults appreciate getting the good things in life as rapidly as possible and the same is true of learners. Wouldn't you like your next raise right now rather than having to wait until the next calendar year? Don't you wish you could attend right away that basketball, football, or soccer game, or the play or movie now scheduled for a month away?

The issue, though, is not only one of preference. It is one of instructional effectiveness. Behavioral scientists have found that immediate reinforcement is much more powerful than delayed. In fact, delay reinforcement too long and learning can be severely jeopardized. What is too long a delay? Surprisingly, especially for new skills, delays more than even ½ a second can substantially reduce the effectiveness of the reinforcer. Thus, whenever you are teaching a new skill, try to follow this 'half-second rule.' For actions that are established, we will try to stretch the time between the behavior and the outcome - but not at the start of the lesson!

How can teachers assure that a reinforcer can be provided that quickly? We might be tempted to put food or drink directly into the learner's mouth. However, not only does this look unappealing; it also is not as effective as other strategies. Fortunately we need not be limited to providing only primary reinforcers within the critical ½ second. As an alternative, we can use secondary reinforcers such as praise (e.g., "Way to go!" "Great!" "Yes!"), or even the *tone of voice* you have used whenever providing rewards instead. Of course, if you want to use such consequences, you must be sure they are truly reinforcing before you start the lesson.

"Certainly," you might reasonably protest, "we do learn to wait for our reinforcers: we save our money, put our children's needs ahead of our own; avoid getting trapped into enticing entanglements; schedule and plan." But that takes the right kind of reinforcement history: one in which we have learned to tolerate longer and longer delays in order to benefit the most in the long run. Youngsters, and people faced with special challenges, typically lack that sort of fortunate history. When they begin to learn a new skill, they must attain their reinforcers immediately after each successful effort. Over time, to achieve greater independence, we may gradually increase the time between completing the step and getting the reward.

You also can rearrange materials to assure speedy reinforcement. To help a child discriminate between colors, for example, you could hide a favorite snack under an inverted blue cup, while leaving nothing under the red one. As soon as the child lifts the blue cup, she sees the snack, even before you get to provide praise. Of course, you'll move the snack so that she can track the color of the cup. The point here is to focus on how quickly we have arranged for the reinforcer.

Earlier, we noted a preference for tasks that have natural consequences like peeling a banana, then eating the inside. In such lessons, *task completion* results in immediate access to the reinforcer. Not every activity has a naturally reinforcing consequence, though. When we are hired to wash dishes in the restaurant, we get paid when we've finished our job. However, while a learner is learning to wash dishes there are many steps to be acquired before mastering the entire sequence. What reinforcers should teachers provide while the lesson is taking place? That is, *within the task*? Along with social reinforcers, they can use a variety of other more concrete secondary reinforcers, such as points or tokens, to mark progress through the task. Over time, all within-task secondary reinforcers should be removed, while natural reinforcers for completing the task are left intact.

As we recognized earlier, learning to tolerate reinforcement delay is essential to socially acceptable behavior. Given a gradual increase in the level or complexity of the instructional objective, this will occur as a matter of course. Alternatively, consider introducing gradually longer and longer delays between the response and the more powerful reinforcement. In the meantime, substitute weaker, more natural social consequences, such as praise, recognition, and feedback, to bridge the gap and assist the learner to tolerate the delay.

Other Strategies to Boost Reinforcer Effectiveness

Many factors can influence the reinforcing effectiveness or potency of an item or event. *Novelty* itself can be reinforcing for some individuals: seeing a new toy in the classroom, being offered a new candy, having a new shirt to wear. It may help to limit access to certain toys or games for planned periods so their re-introduction (on that 'rainy day') gains the learner's immediate attention. Don't offer everything you have at once. Reinforcer *variation* can be a powerful tool to heighten reinforcer effectiveness. Plan to create variation, and even novelty, by mixing and rotating toys, treats, books, and other interesting items. Offer a variety of types of reinforcers - ones that play upon all the senses. Providing the same reinforcer constantly and rapidly often leads to satiation. *Choice* and *control* over reinforcer selection can raise the value of rewards selected. Giving individuals control over choosing may be an indirect way of influencing their actions. You may say to your child, "It's bed time! Do you want a glass of juice or water?" The child can choose what to drink, but not whether or not to go to bed. That is not an option. So, too, in the classroom you might offer a choice of books to read, or even the choice of doing math or spelling. If the learner picks math first, he'll still do spelling later. In a home, offer the choice of making the bed first or vacuuming the floor. Here too, though, both will eventually be completed.

Using Powerful Reinforcers to Promote Learning

When, where, how and how many rewards of what kind you arrange for your learners to receive can affect how rapidly they learn and how long lasting their learning is. Teachers need to be clear about the purpose of their lessons so they can make the most suitable plans.

Frequency and Distribution of Reinforcers: Learning versus Sustaining Change

Is it best for teachers to deliver a reinforcer immediately following every single appropriate response, or to limit the number of reinforcers they distribute? That depends. If learners are trying to learn to do something new and especially challenging, the more frequently they receive reinforcers, the better. For new, challenging tasks, initially arrange things so that every single successful effort results in a rich and powerful reinforcer. The pattern between the occurrences of the behavior and its consequence is known as the *schedule of reinforcement*. When reinforcers are scheduled to occur every time a behavior is emitted, we use the technical label, *continuous schedule of reinforcement* (abbreviated *CRF*).

You may be concerned, and rightly so, that continually receiving a reinforcer will cause it to begin to lose its value. Certainly, this would happen if the reinforcer were food, like fruit or candy, or an activity that involved much time or effort, such as shooting baskets in the gym. Fortunately, a few options are available to avoid such satiation. You can:

- Begin to limit the size or amount of each individual reinforcer to just enough to sustain the learner's continued effort. For example, one or two raisins instead of a handful, or a short section of a CD instead of the whole song.

- Offer choices and switch to a different reinforcer.

- Begin *gradually* to reduce how often you deliver the reinforcer (*thin* the schedule), so instead of *continuous*, it now is *intermittent*.

One of the most effective schedules is one that varies about a given average number of occurrences, such as roughly every three times. The technical term for this sort of schedule is *variable ratio* (abbreviated *VR*). VR schedules tend to promote high, steady performance rates, as the example in Box 4-1 below indicates. At times, it may be easier to arrange for reinforcement based on time - or the *interval* between reinforcers. A *variable interval* (abbreviated *IR*) schedule also sustains behaviors at steady rates, as when we praise a learner for remaining on task about every five minutes (with individual intervals varying from one to 10 minutes).

Box 4-1

Intermittent Schedules and the Real World

With an intermittent schedule, only some, not all, of the responses of concern are reinforced. This strategy may sound complicated but it is also one of the oldest strategies around. Gambling relies upon this principle and those who run casinos are masters at controlling *variable ratio reinforcement schedules*. If you want to watch the impact that such schedules have on persistent behavior, just watch people operating a slot machine for hours on end.

The thing to avoid in using intermittent schedules is thinning them too rapidly. When the learner's efforts begin to pale, immediately begin to suspect that the schedule needs to be adjusted back to a richer level. Otherwise, change the activity, the reinforcer, or the schedule.

If the learner is tiring of the activity, before ending it, present a previously mastered task and heavily reinforce its successful completion. That enables you and the learner to end on a successful note and makes returning to the task later on more appealing. Other strategies include:

- Substituting a token instead. A token is like an IOU. It can be exchanged for the actual reinforcer at a later time. Most of us are familiar with bus or subway tokens. Money is a token, as is a check or certificate exchangeable for a prize[5]. If the learner does not understand the 'value' of the token, be sure to teach that using skills already in the repertoire. Then, once he knows that tokens are valuable, you'll use them to help motivation in new or harder tasks.

- Gradually matching the schedule of reinforcement to that of the real world. If the task is doing an assembly or service job, for example, aim toward the standard compensation for that task. In assessing natural community settings, consider multiple sources of reinforcement. For example, in addition to working for our paychecks, we all take a break

---

[5]   Pyramid offers as a product a token system appropriate for learners with delayed development, and an iPhone/iPad (Working4™) app that serves the same purpose.

every couple of hours and find something to drink or snack on. So, too, should our learners have the same opportunities for the types of rewards we all seek. If an academic response, try to approximate the requirements of a regular classroom (e.g., 10 spelling words for the test).

• Pairing natural consequences with the currently effective reinforcers, gradually thinning the latter while retaining the former. Similarly, if learners are to succeed in a broader environment, their behavior must ultimately be controlled by natural consequences. Social behaviors tend to elicit reciprocal responses: A "Hi" for a "Hi"; a "Bye" for a "Bye." Classroom learning leads to comments from the teacher, grades, and report cards.

Teaching without Prompting - The Joy of Shaping!

Most of us think of teaching as giving clear instructions to learners. Is it possible to teach without the use of instructions, guidance, or prompts? To help isolate this issue, let's consider the dilemma of someone given a very different type of responsibility - teaching a pet pigeon or porpoise to perform a trick. We cannot tell the pet what to do. Physical assistance may be impossible. Imagine trying to take the head of a pigeon and pushing it to peck a small disc on a panel. Would the pigeon tolerate this? If we want to teach a porpoise to jump several feet out of the water, it won't help to try to model the trick either! When watching people who are highly skilled at this type of problem, we see that reinforcement is the best tool available when they want to teach new actions. With the porpoise, the instructor often uses a conditioned reinforcer, such as a clicker or whistle, to reward any movement out of the water[6.] Gradually, the porpoise will need to jump higher and higher to earn the reinforcer. This process starts with what the learner currently can do and rewarding small changes in the direction of the action we are trying to develop - a process known as *shaping*. In more technical terms, shaping is reinforcing successive approximations toward the ultimate behavior.

Of course, although our learners are not pets, and we won't treat them as such, we do face a similar problem in that our instructions and attempts to assist may be meaningless to the individual when we start to teach. The systematic use of reinforcers will permit us to shape behaviors toward more useful and functional skills, even as we develop more traditional instructional strategies. Remember the simple game of 'hide and seek' from elementary school? No help was offered, not even a touch, other than say-

---

6   For numerous other examples read Karen Pryor's 1999 book *"Don't Shoot the Dog!"* New York, NY: Bantam Books.

ing 'hot' for responses closer to the hidden item or 'cold' for choices in the wrong direction (i.e., reinforcing or punishing).

In addition to shaping new forms of behaviors, we can alter the form of existing behaviors via the same process. Joe can reliably throw a ball three feet. His teacher now stands three-and-a-half feet from Joe and patiently waits for a throw long enough to reach him. When the ball does reach him, he praises Joe excitedly and profusely! Over the next several trials, Joe routinely throws the ball all the way. Now his teacher once more stretches things by standing four feet away. Some of Joe's throws fall short but some reach him and these are followed by enthusiastic praise. The teacher is using reinforcement to shape Joe's throwing over greater and greater distances.

Sometimes a learning objective is so complicated that we are forced to delay reinforcement to such an extent that it loses its effectiveness. Try teaching a three-year-old to tie her shoe, or a non-speaking child to make a request in a full spoken sentence, or most of us to embroider a tablecloth. Success is so remote as to make it virtually unattainable. The opportunity for reinforcement is lost and effort ceases. The solution is to break the task down into *achievable* yet *challenging* parts. In such tasks, provided the segment is *achievable*, reinforcement can be immediate as well as frequent. *Challenging* implies that because the person has not yet fully mastered the task, room for progress remains. Once the part is close to being fully mastered, the response requirement can be adjusted by increasing its complexity or difficulty via shaping.

Differential Reinforcement - A Little Here Means a Lot There!

Patience is an important aspect of shaping. When Joe's teacher used shaping to increase the distance Joe threw the ball he had a difficult choice: How much farther should he move away? The lesson began with Joe throwing the ball three feet and then his teacher moved six inches farther. What now was the consequence to throws that only went three feet? While they used to result in reinforcement, now they only bounced at the teacher's feet. In order to promote new behavior, the teacher had to withhold reinforcing the behaviors that Joe could already accomplish and wait to see if the new criteria could be met.

Figure 4-1

Differentially Reinforcing Increasingly Longer Throws

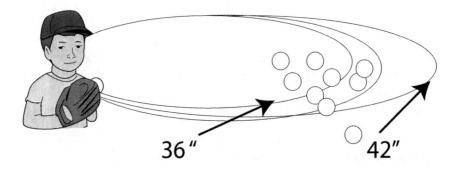

It is impossible to say precisely how far Joe's teacher should move. We know if he jumped 25 feet away, none of Joe's throws would ever reach him. Yet, if he moved only one millimeter, stretching the throw by one foot would almost take forever. Therefore, the key is making a change in the reinforcer criterion that is likely to occur *within the natural variation in all the actions of concern.* Suppose Joe threw the ball the designated distance of three feet when he and his teacher were that far apart, but some of the throws fell short and some landed further away. When they stood 42 inches apart, Joe succeeded more than he failed, but he did better at 40 inches. His teacher would have the choice of dropping back to a 40 inch distance or keeping at the same level until successes were more consistent. No one does *exactly* the same thing over and over - that is precisely why learning is possible. Patience will be required of Joe's teacher while waiting for that slightly longer throw. Withholding reinforcement from one behavior in reserve for another is called *differential reinforcement.*

Differential reinforcement can be part of a strategy in which the learner cannot lose! For example, Sarah wants Sean to expand upon his skill at constructing picture-based phrases within the Picture Exchange Communication System (PECS). Currently, when he asks for something, he creates, "I want cookie." Now Sarah is trying to teach Sean to be very specific about the person he asks by adding a picture representing their name at the start of the sentence. If Sean constructs, "I want cookie," Sarah will reinforce with only a small piece of a cookie. But if he constructs, "Sarah, I want cookie," not only will he get a full cookie but she will heap praise upon him and may even give him several cookies! Both statements work to get Sean a cookie, but one earns him more (i.e., a *different* quantity of reinforcers).

Helping Teachers to Make the Most of Reinforcement

Effective teaching requires providing high rates of reinforcement to each learner. Teachers are reinforcing new skills, new combinations, and some alternatives to problematic actions such as, "I like how you raised your hand instead of calling out!" The necessary level of reinforcement is related to how often both new actions and problematic behaviors are occurring. It would not be unusual in a preschool classroom for the children to need a reinforcer every minute or so to promote adequate learning. In light of all the other things that must take place, the reality of life in the classroom makes it remarkably difficult for teachers to attend to the need to deliver high and sustained rates of reinforcement. Teachers are taking data, consulting with other staff, dealing with immediate crises, responding to the demands of administrators, and so on. It is not practical to expect them to remember to look up at the wall clock every minute or so. How can a teacher set a minimum rate of reinforcement for all learners and stick to it?

One solution is to help teachers with one of several automatic reminders. For example, they can set a timer and each time it rings, praise those learners engaged in appropriate actions. A more sophisticated system involves the use of CDs (or audiotapes) that contain a set of tones that sound on a *variable interval* basis around a set period - 1, 2, 3, 5, 7, 9, or 15 minutes for example[7]. These tone systems can be used either continuously, or primarily during busy times when the teacher's attention tends to be required elsewhere, as during chaotic transitions, group time, or even free play. When a two-minute segment is used, it assures that at least every two minutes throughout the activity, teachers will be reminded to scan each learner to see if some action is deserving of reward. Of course teachers can, and frequently should, provide more than the minimum reinforcement! What this type of system assures is that there is a steady 'background' rate of reinforcement that is somewhat independent of the specific behaviors of the learners. In the chapter on *Contextually Inappropriate Behaviors*, we describe the use of such audio tones within an intervention effort.

Putting it all together - Let's make a deal!

Teachers want their learners to learn and, as we have seen, learn-

---

7   Pyramid offers as a product a set of Audio Reinforcer Reminder Tone (ARRT) CDs appropriate for learners with delayed development, and an iPhone/iPad app (R+Remind™) that serves the same purpose.

ing means changing behavior. In our society, learners come to school ... because they have to! These relatively small people come into a situation where more powerful people want something from them. What other relationship does that sound like? Parent and child for one. Boss and employee for another. Our bosses want us to do something - the job - for them. Why should we do the job? Just to please the boss? No, we work for the boss only when we know what we will get for doing the job - the reinforcer for completing our work. We would almost never accept employment in a situation in which we didn't know in advance what we would get from the job. In fact, we diligently prepare a contract containing a great deal of critical information before we start the job. That is, before agreeing to work for our boss, we negotiate a deal!

What does a well-designed deal include? Probably we want to know how much we will get paid and the pay schedule, as well as information about benefits, especially our vacation days! Just about everyone knows about these conditions before accepting a job. Now think about how we often interact with our learners. How many of us greet our learners and then immediately tell them to get to work? We would not tolerate being treated in the same way by any potential boss who pronounced, "I want you to get to work!" and offered nothing more about what you may expect in return later on. Within the *Pyramid Approach*, we believe that we should interact with our learners just as we would like to be treated in a similar situation. What we set up in our interactions with our boss should resemble what we do in our interactions with our learners (even though, here, our relative 'power' position has changed).

Therefore, when a teacher wants a learner to learn something, just as when a boss wants an employee to do a job, the first thing to determine is the reinforcer. What the learner wants to get or do. Once the teacher knows what the learner wants, then the teacher can make a deal in which the learner gets the desired outcome after learning the lesson (i.e., performing the required skill). Furthermore, remember that just as you, even with your accomplished verbal skills, insist on having your reinforcers listed in a written contract. So, too, it is reasonable for every learner to have a *visual* or tangible *representation of the deal* set with his or her teacher.

What information should be part of this deal? The learner should know what the reinforcer is, how much work is needed to earn it, and when, and how many, breaks will be available (just like vacation days). Over time, the nature of the deal may change. The teacher will require more work or more complicated work for the same outcome, but the contract should not disappear. Would you let your boss tear up your contract after a couple of years?

One way to create a visual representation of the reinforcer to come is to use a type of *token system*. Start by finding out what the learner wants in a particular situation. Place a visual symbol, like a three-dimensional object, picture, or written word on a card that represents the contract. For example, initially the card may have "I'm working for..." printed on it. It contains only a single open circle. Ask the learner do a very simple task, one she already has mastered. As soon as she has completed it, immediately give her a token in the form of something small and age-appropriate. Teach her to place the token on the open circle. Since there is only one circle, the deal is now complete. That is, the learner has placed a token on all empty circles. Teach the learner to hand in, or cash in, the tokens and immediately give her the reinforcing item. We would teach her to hand over the tokens rather than the board just as we would give a cashier our money, not our wallet. Over time, gradually add open circles onto the card, until there are five circles. You might include more than five circles with older learners. See Figure 4-2 for an example. Gradually increasing the work the learner is required to do to earn each token is like applying the principle described earlier - thinning the schedule of reinforcement.

This type of visual reinforcement system contains information about what the learner is working for, how much work is needed, and when the reinforcer will be earned. You may want to add a visual symbol for "break" to this system. See the chapter on *Functional Communication* for a description of how to teach this skill. The learner may even want to 'renegotiate' the deal in the midst of a lesson. That is, perhaps she changed her mind about what she really wants!

A second option is for the teacher to use a picture of a ball that a child wants to play with and have the child earn the picture before receiving the ball. Then the teacher can cut the picture into pieces and have the child earn parts of the picture and gradually put it together like a puzzle. When all the parts are earned and the puzzle is complete, the learner trades it in for the corresponding item.

Does every lesson need a token system? No! Every lesson does need a reinforcer but, re-

> ## No Reinforcer, No Lesson!
>
> **What should teachers do when they can't determine an immediate reinforcer for a learner? If the schedule says, "set the table," should the teacher compel the learner to perform the task? The** *Pyramid Approach* **adheres to a simple rule -** *no reinforcer, no lesson*. **If a teacher insists that a learner set the table when no reinforcer is available for the task, the teacher is using his or her size or power to take advantage of the learner. That is coercion, not education.**

member, the best reinforcers are those that are natural to the setting or context. Teachers try to design lessons that are fun to do, or result in a sense of accomplishment for the learner. However, just as many adult jobs require repetition, so do many lessons. In such circumstances, it's easy to forget the point of the task in the absence of visual reminders that goal. Constantly prompting learners to pay attention and get back to work is just a way of nagging - not a well-documented successful teaching strategy! If a learner's attention drifts, reminders about the potential reinforcer should be sufficient to get the individual to attend to how to earn it.

Figure 4-2

Token Boards

When you work with a learner on a token system, you will be very tempted to take away tokens for inappropriate behaviors. Throughout this book, the *Pyramid Approach* always will emphasize using reinforcers to promote positive changes in behavior. If the tokens were earned for learning a skill but an inappropriate behavior arises, develop a separate system to deal with those behaviors you are trying to reduce or eliminate. Chapter 6, *Contextually Inappropriate Behaviors*, provides many potential solutions.

Summary

Reinforcement is essential to learning, and accentuating the positive is the way to go. Finding powerful reinforcers may prove difficult, though. The first and best way is to identify those events and objects natural to the situation, many of which are incidental to the activities of daily living. Asking and offering choices helps determine the more powerful of these. To make the most of reinforcers, consider whether they are primary or conditioned and their relative value at the time. Variety and novelty may improve their value, while delivering them immediately and as often as possible is crucial at first.

When the learner does not engage in the behavior we hope to see strengthened, reinforcement cannot be forthcoming. The way to deal with that situation is to shape the behavior by reinforcing those actions that progress toward the skill of concern and withholding reinforcement from the others. This variation permits progress without undue prompting or correcting. Negotiating clear "deals" with learners in advance permits everyone to be aware of the good that can come from their efforts. These tasks can gradually become more and more challenging - requiring increasing learner effort and "tolerance for delay." Assuring high rates of effort and performance can be better achieved by using a visually mediated reinforcement system, such as a token board, which permits each of the factors that make reinforcement powerful to be included. Everyone wins when reinforcement operates effectively. Learners learn, while teachers, freed from needing to resort to coercion, enjoy the pleasure of witnessing that progress.

Chapter 4 Resources

Powerful Reinforcement Systems

To	Read
Use reinforcement effectively in general.	The sections on increasing and maintaining behavior in: Cooper, J.O., Heron, T.E. & Heward, W.L. (2007). *Applied behavior analysis, 2nd Edition*. Columbus, OH: Merrill. Sulzer-Azaroff, B. & Mayer, G.R. (1991). *Behavior analysis for lasting change*. Atlanta, GA: Wadsworth Group; Thompson.
Apply behavior analysis with children with autism.	Ghezzi, P.M., Williams, W.L. & Carr, J.E. **(1999)**. *Autism: Behavior analytic perspectives*. Reno, NV: Context Press.
Make the most of your reinforcement procedures through variation.	Egel, A.L. (1981). Reinforcer variation: Implications for motivating developmentally disabled children. *Journal of Applied Behavior Analysis, 14*, **345-350.**
Make the most of your reinforcement procedures through choice.	Dyer, K., Dunlap, G. & Winterling, V. (1990). Effects of choice-making on the serious behaviors of students with severe handicaps. *Journal of Applied Behavior Analysis, 23*, **515-524.**
Practice increasing behavior.	Chapter 5: Operant procedures I: Increasing behavior. In Sulzer-Azaroff, B. & Reese, E.P. (1982). *Applying behavior analysis*. New York, NY: Holt, Rinehart & Winston.
Gain an everyday understanding of how to increase and change behavior in general.	Pryor, K. (1999). *Don't shoot the dog*. New York, NY: Bantam Books.

Survey current research on reinforcement in applied settings.	*American Journal on Mental Retardation* *Analysis and Intervention in Developmental Disabilities* *Journal of Abnormal Psychology* *Journal of Autism and Developmental Disorders* *Journal of Applied Behavior Analysis* *Journal of the Association for Persons with Severe Handicaps* *Research in Developmental Disabilities*

To	Do
Use a token system.	Order a Complete Visual Reinforcement Set from Pyramid Educational Consultants at www.pecs.com (or use their display as a guide to developing your own). Buy *Working4*™ for from the iTunes app store.

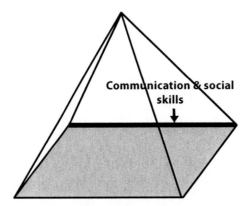

5

Communication and Social Skills:
Functional Communication

A cup of milk tips over. Little Isabella, a typically developing 18-month-old, stops what she's doing, looks at her mother's face, and begins to point back and forth between the spreading pool of milk and her mother. She has not yet learned to talk in whole words but her mother certainly understands what Isabella means! Examples similar to this one remind us that communication does not always involve speaking. Still, the question remains: What is communication? How does it differ from other categories of behavior?

What is Communication?

To help clarify what is unique about communication, consider a situation in which none takes place. Sylvester walks into his kitchen where his father is sitting unnoticed and heads straight to the refrigerator. He opens the door and takes out a can of soda. He pops the lid and drinks it. Is this an example of communication? No. Sylvester simply acted upon objects in the environment (the refrigerator, the soda can, and so on) and a rewarding experience, drinking the soda, followed. These actions would not have changed if his father were absent from the room. That is, getting his reinforcer did not depend upon the help or involvement of another person. Sylvester arranged for his own reinforcer.

Actions directed solely toward the physical environment and leading to rewarding outcomes are not communication. You may feel uncomfortable with this assertion. After all, as the father watches his son, he may well think the boy wants to drink something. By watching what his son does, the father can interpret what those actions may mean (see Figure 5-1). Interpreting, or even explaining, someone else's behavior, though, does not change the nature of that behavior. Because you can interpret someone's behavior does not mean the action is communicative. Something more is required, beyond an action affecting something in the environment, for it to be labeled "communication."

Figure 5-1

Non-Communicative Sequence of Behavior

Now consider a different scenario. A young girl walks into the kitchen, sees her mother and says, "I want soda!" Her mother gets up, walks to the refrigerator, opens the door, takes out a can of soda and hands it to her daughter. The daughter quickly drinks the soda. First, notice that the girl obtains the same thing that the boy did - soda to drink. However, this episode *does* involve communication because the girl acted toward her mother rather than some physical object, like a refrigerator. So, in part, communication requires: 1) at least two people and 2) that one person directs a behavior toward another person. In this case, the girl directed her behavior toward her mother (See Figure 5-2).

Figure 5-2
Communicative Behavior

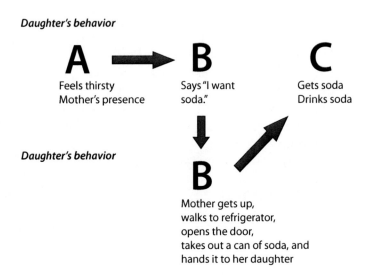

Daughter's behavior

A → B   C

Feels thirsty   Says "I want   Gets soda
Mother's presence   soda."   Drinks soda

Daughter's behavior

B

Mother gets up,
walks to refrigerator,
opens the door,
takes out a can of soda, and
hands it to her daughter

What is the role of the recipient of communication? That is, the audience. In our example, the mother's role was to mediate her daughter's reinforcement by delivering what the child wanted - the soda. The situation illustrates communication because it involves behavior directed to another person, who then provides some reinforcing outcome to the person doing the communicating. In this illustration, since the outcome was something the girl asked for, we will call this form of communication a request[1].

Is there only one type of reward for communication? In our example, the outcome for the girl was something material or concrete. Let's review a different type of outcome by considering a toddler sitting in his high chair in the living room. Looking out the window, suddenly he says to his mother, "Truck! Truck! Truck!" What does he want? Most likely, he doesn't want his mother to go outside and get him the truck. As we continue to observe, his mother replies, "Yes, dear, that's another truck!" Clearly, the boy wants his mother's attention; for her to acknowledge what he is seeing. He is rewarded by the social response from his mother: the attention,

---

1 Skinner (1957, *Verbal behavior*, Englewood Cliffs, NJ: Prentice Hall) termed this type of behavior a *mand* - created from the words *demand* and *command*. For a brief review of the major categories of verbal operants refer to Bondy, A., Tincani, M. & Frost, L. (2004). Multiply Controlled Verbal Operants: An Analysis and Extension to the Picture Exchange Communication System. *The Behavior Analyst, 27,* 247-261.

her praise, her apparent enjoyment in conversing with him. His communication does not get him anything material, like the soda the young girl requested. Instead, he *commented* to his mother who provided him with a social reward[2].

> We can now define functional communication as follows:
>
> ***Functional communication involves behavior (defined in form by the community) directed to another person who in turn provides related direct or social rewards*** (Frost & Bondy, 2002, p. 24).

Why Do We Communicate?

As we see, we can divide these most basic functions of communication into two broad categories: requests and comments. Therefore, when our lesson focuses on communication, our first job is to consider what purpose the communicative act will serve for the learner (i.e., what reinforcer it will produce). Before beginning, we need to know a lot about the learner because this may influence the specific goals and methods of our lesson. For example, if a child has the classic characteristics of autism, we might predict that social rewards would not to be very effective for her. So, initially, she would be better off if we taught her how to request the things we know she likes to do or have, rather than targeting communicative skills that primarily serve a commenting function.

Why should we respond when others try to communicate with us? It may seem that listening is a passive activity - it hardly feels as if we are doing something. However, listening is a skill like any other and it must be learned. Just as we reviewed two primary reasons to communicate - to gain a direct or a social reinforcing outcome - so too are these the primary reasons we respond to someone who is communicating with us. For example, if your learner likes to play with a ball, when you say, "The ball is in the box," he immediately gets the ball if he responds correctly. On the other hand, if you say, "Bring me the tissue," if he responds correctly you would simply provide some praise, as in "Thanks!" Which type of lesson you begin with - listening for direct reinforcement vs. social reinforcement - will relate to how effective these two types of outcomes are for your learner.

---

2   B.F. Skinner (1957) pointed out that the function of this type of comment is *educational*. That is, it is provided to teach the learner the names of various things. His technical name for this category of communicating by labeling is a *tact*.

Choosing Communicative Skills to Teach

Communicating effectively consists of a fairly complicated set of skills. There are several key characteristics of functional communication that we must consider before we start teaching our lessons. Some of these important aspects include:

- The function of the communicative act (i.e., request versus comment).

- Teaching for generalization including the topic, the audience, the complexity of the communication, etc.

- Potentially effective modalities (e.g., speech, pictures, writing, sign, speech generating devices).

- Learning to engage in reciprocal conversations (i.e., responding to what others say rather than only in reaction to things in the environment).

- The language of emotions (i.e., 'talking' about feelings and other types of internal states).

When does communication take place? In our chapter about learning principles, we stressed that we must look at conditions that exist prior to a behavior, as well as its consequences. How, then, do we analyze the A-B-Cs of given communication episodes? That is, how do the conditions just before we communicate influence our behaviors? Consider a common occurrence in a preschool setting. Lori is standing in her classroom waiting for her preschool learners to return from recess. She is eating from a bowl of popcorn. Sarah walks into the room, sees Lori and the popcorn and immediately says, "Popcorn!" Lori gives Sarah some popcorn. Soon, Shawn walks into the room. He walks over to the bowl of popcorn and starts to reach for some. Lori keeps the popcorn out of reach, patiently waiting for him to communicate. He remains silent until she asks, "What do you want?" He immediately says, "Popcorn!" She gives him some popcorn. Nathan walks into the room and goes over to the bowl of popcorn. Silently he reaches for some. When Lori asks him what he wants, he remains silent. She finally directs Nathan to, "Say 'popcorn.'" He immediately says, "Popcorn!" and she gives him some to eat.

If someone were to ask you if each child said, "popcorn" of course you would answer, "Yes." But what if you were asked, "Did each child do the same thing?" Now, you are likely to say, "No!" If this is the case, you are beginning to think (or analyze things) the way a behavior analyst thinks (or analyzes behaviors, including verbal behavior). Sarah *initiated* - she saw something she wanted, she saw someone to communicate with, and she *spontaneously* said "popcorn." Shawn said "popcorn" only after Lori provided a *prompt* or a *cue* - his communication was responsive. And Nathan only spoke the word when Lori provided a specific type of prompt. That is; she *modeled* the word "popcorn," which he then *imitated*.

Why is it so important to make this distinction? If we lived in a world in which we could teach one of these skills - imitation - and the other two showed up for free (i.e., with no further training), we all would be very happy. In reality, though, these are three separate behaviors requiring three distinct lessons. This reality is true for all learners, not just those with significant language problems. Therefore, one of the factors we all must face is which type of communication do we want to teach first? Imitative, responsive, or spontaneous? We will return to this issue later on.

Communication is Bi-directional.

So far, the focus has been on teaching learners to direct communication toward us. However, it also is important to teach learners to understand what we are trying to communicate to them. Teachers often ask simple questions such as, "What's your name?" or "Where is your pencil?", or give instructions such as, "Go to gym!", "Line up!" or "Take out your crayons!" They expect their learners will learn to express themselves and to understand what others are attempting to communicate. Unfortunately, these two skills do not automatically develop hand-in-hand or simultaneously. Just as we ourselves may understand particular "ten-dollar words," but never use them in ordinary conversation, we all have known children who obviously can understand a spoken word but are not capable of saying it. That is, John may respond correctly when told to get a spoon, but when he needs a spoon to eat his ice cream, he cannot say the word. On the other hand, people who study language development have found that very young children who are just beginning to talk may say a particular word, but not respond correctly when that same word is used within an instruction. Therefore, speaking a word and understanding that word when spoken, or used via some other modality, by someone else are learned independently. As typical language develops, children eventually do learn to generalize across these two types of skills but do not do so initially.

To review, before teaching learners to communicate about a particular word or phrase (e.g., the word "popcorn"), we need to identify what functionally controls the word, both in terms of antecedents and consequences. This list could include teaching them to:

- Initiate "popcorn" when they want popcorn, even when no popcorn is around.

- Say "popcorn" spontaneously when they see it, even when they don't want it.

- Imitate the spoken word "popcorn."

- Say "popcorn" in response to questions, as in "What do you want?" "What is this?" "What smells great and makes noise when cooking in a microwave?"

- Get popcorn when presented with an array of food items and an instruction to take some popcorn.

… all these lessons, just for the single word "popcorn"!

Is Talking Always Communicative?

Are there reasons to speak that don't involve communication? Remember, communicative acts must be directed toward another person[3]. We may hear a lovely song and sing it to enjoy its delightful sound. It could even be in a foreign language, so we don't understand its literal meaning. Sometimes we sing in the shower, just for the pleasure of hearing our resonant voices! Singing of that sort would not meet our definition of communicative. It is not uncommon for some individuals with autism and related developmental disabilities to repeat words, phrases, television or radio jingles, or even entire dialogues from DVDs without any apparent understanding of what they're saying. Their words do not appear to be directed toward other people. As likely to repeat the words or phrases alone as in the presence of an audience, these individuals probably derive some reinforcement from their utterances different from what communication typically yields. Therefore, when we assess a learner's ability to communicate, we must go beyond a description of the words the learner can say to analyzing the functions they serve.

Don't Just Hope For, Teach For, Generalization.

Wouldn't it ease our task as teachers if each of these three conditions related to communication, and both types of functions, automatically spread or *generalized* from one to the other? Unfortunately, as research in child development and in learning has shown us, we must not assume such generalization will occur spontaneously. That is, just because a learner can imitate a spoken word, or responds correctly to a prompt, does not guarantee

---

3   We typically separate the roles of *communicator* and *communicative partner*. Skinner (1957) used the terms *speaker* and *listener*, though he made it clear that the terms pertained to any modality of communicative interacting, not just speech. He also pointed out instances in which an individual can perform both roles. That is, in some instances, I can talk to myself just as I would to someone else. However, in this chapter we will keep things simple and separate the two roles.

that he will use that same word spontaneously. Similarly, just because a learner can use a word as a request does not guarantee that she can use it as a comment. In the early stages of language development, all children tend to acquire each of these types of communication skills separately. Eventually, at some later point in their development, most do learn to generalize their new vocabulary across the various skill categories. However, in the early stages of teaching learners with communication deficits, we will have to arrange to teach each of these three classes independently and design specific plans to foster generalization.

Choose a Communicative Modality.

Imagine your mouth taped shut. Would you still be able to communicate? Although speech is impossible, other forms of communication are available to you. For example, you might gesture to get people to understand what you want or what you want them to do. If you knew how to sign, you could communicate effectively with someone else who also understood sign language. Given paper and writing implements, you could write your message to someone who can read. If you were a competent artist, you could draw pictures of objects and actions. And if you couldn't draw but had access to pictures and visual symbols you could manipulate those. Of course, even with all of these options, you still would prefer to reach up and pull off the tape!

Each of these examples illustrates a different communication modality. Each can work effectively alone or in combination with others. In choosing which forms to teach, we need to assess the learner's current skills and different rates of learning via one or more of those modes, along with the comprehension and expressive skills of his or her local and broader audience. It is necessary to consider what a particular audience will understand with respect to the learner's modality of communication. If the learner learns to use gestures to communicate, it is necessary for the audience to understand the gestures. If a young learner writes to communicate, but her peers are not literate, the learner's communication will not be effective with her peers. If the learner speaks English, but his audience speaks Spanish, the communication of the learner will not be effective. This selection process requires a fairly thorough assessment of the individual's communicative skills, as well as looking at other skills such as imitation, how objects are manipulated, etc. Our assessment may reveal that although the learner can imitate certain sounds, she cannot initiate requests. Our primary goal then needs to be to teach her to communicate functionally, while our secondary goal should be to teach her to speak. We recognize that successful communication is a more important initial goal than speaking. Of course, if we can accomplish both, shifting from one mode to the other, all the better.

What is PECS?

The Picture Exchange Communication System (PECS)[4] is a system illustrating the promotion of communication skills independent of speech. The training sequence in PECS begins by teaching learners to initiate communication by giving a communicative partner a picture of something desired that is held by the communicative partner. The system moves through a set sequence of phases to teach simple sentence structure, using attributes within requests, and finally, how to comment. The phases within PECS consist of:

Phase I	Initiating requests
Phase II	Expanding persistence and spontaneity
Phase III	Discrimination of pictures
Phase IV	Sentence structure for requests
Phase V	Responding to "What do you want?"
Phase VI	Commenting in response to questions, and spontaneous comments.

PECS was developed by Lori Frost and Andy Bondy within the Delaware Autistic Program, with the earliest parts of the system in place over 20 years ago. The system aims to teach individuals with communication impairments to rapidly acquire socially initiated, functional communication skills. The system begins by teaching the exchange of single pictures for desired items or activities and proceeds to teach more complex communication structures, as well as additional communicative functions. While PECS was developed with children with autism, it has been effectively used with individuals with a wide array of communicative difficulties[5].

The first phase of training takes advantage of what an individual wants. The training protocol uniquely specifies the use of two trainers - one to entice and the other to physically prompt. This strategy minimizes the chance of the development of prompt dependency. To further ensure spontaneity, no verbal prompts are used during this critical phase. Thus, users of PECS first learn to initiate an approach to someone rather than waiting for a prompt from a communicative partner. As soon as a reliable exchange is evidenced, the user is taught during the second phase to generalize this skill to 1) other people, 2) more motivators, 3) greater distance to communicative partners, including peers and siblings, 4) distance to the pictures,

---

4   Bondy, A. & Frost, L. (1994). The picture exchange communication system. *Focus on Autistic Behavior, 9*, 1-19.

5   For a complete and up-to-date source of research and related publications about PECS visit www.pecs.com.

5) other environments, and so on.

The third phase of training focuses attention on selecting specific pictures associated with particular wants and needs. While some learners readily acquire discrimination between pictures, others need to be taught this skill. Training protocols involve a variety of strategies developed within the field of ABA and include specific strategies associated with error correction.

The fourth phase involves teaching users to build a simple sentence using the icon "I want." From here, the PECS protocol diverges into two paths. One path leads to expanding vocabulary by teaching users to include various attributes in their simple sentence constructions (e.g., "I want *big* cookie"; "I want *red* crayon"). Lessons involving such attributes are far more motivating than learning these same concepts within a receptive mode (e.g., "Touch the *big* circle"; "Point to the *red* circle"). The other path leads to the fifth phase of training in which users are taught to respond to the direct question, "What do you want?" At this point, it is important to ascertain that the user can both respond to this question and request spontaneously when warranted.

The final phase of training involves teaching users to comment, first in response to direct questions (e.g., "What do you see?"; "What do you hear?"; "What is it?") and then spontaneously, including incorporating all the attributes acquired within the request function.

The initial publication written by Bondy and Frost about PECS was in 1994. Since that time, there have been over 86 publications, in more than 15 countries, about PECS. These include case studies, group comparisons, and discussions regarding theoretical issues. One recent review of the literature (Tincani & Davis, 2010) concludes that "...results support PECS as an evidence-based communication intervention." While the original work involved very young children with autism, publications now support the effectiveness of PECS with other children and with adults, and across a wide array of different abilities. Improvements also have been noted in terms of increased social approach, reductions in behavior management targets, increased peer interactions, improvisational use of pictures, and improvements in the acquisition and use of speech (see Bondy & Frost, 2009, and Sulzer-Azaroff, Hoffman, Horton, Bondy, & Frost, 2009, for comprehensive reviews of the literature regarding PECS). More research is needed to better understand the aspects of the PECS protocol that will help produce the greatest impact upon speech emergence. However, it should be noted that the primary intent of PECS is to promote the rapid development of functional communication skills, and the current research strongly supports this main effect. Other targets of research have included demonstrations that parents can readily and accurately learn to promote PECS use at home, staff can reliably implement the system in group home situations for older individuals, and that improved joint attention can be achieved without requiring eye-contact as a precursor to beginning PECS training. For a comprehensive list of PECS related publications, visit www. pecs.com.

Select Critical Communication Skills.

Alberto approaches his teacher and frantically tugs her arm. When she doesn't move because she doesn't understand what he wants, he begins to bite his arm and slap his face. Minerva's teacher tells her to do a job. Minerva drops to the floor and begins hitting her head on the tiles. Dominick is putting on his coat to go outside to play when his teacher approaches him saying, "It's raining outside. We can't go out until it stops raining." Dominick stares at her for a moment and then punches his head.
All these children obviously are upset with their situations. Alberto wants to get something, Minerva wants *not to* do something, and Dominick appears not to understand that if he waits for a while he will get what he wants. It is essential for these children to learn to calmly communicate their wants and needs by becoming competent in using particular basic critical functional communication skills. What are those critical skills?

Critical Productive Skills.

One set of critical skills deals with productive, or expressive, communication. That is, skills the individual uses (as the *speaker* or *communicator*) to communicate effectively with others. These include such important functions as:

1. Asking for powerful reinforcers (including materials, activities and events).

2. Asking for help.

3. Asking for a break, or to end an activity.

4. Answering "yes" or "no" to "Do you want X?"

Why are these skills so crucial? Because, if the person cannot calmly and effectively communicate to get what he wants or needs, then he most likely will try other ways to obtain those outcomes. When Alberto wanted something important like a cookie, he became upset after his approach to the teacher failed. If he is six feet tall, weighing 250 pounds, the person between Alberto and the cookie he wants surely hopes he can communicate rather than use other means to get that cookie.

Asking for help

Asking for help is universally important. Every one of us has experienced situations in which we needed to depend on someone other than ourselves to solve a problem, like repairing our automobiles, piloting our plane home, performing a surgical procedure essential for our survival, or simply reaching something more readily accessible by someone nearby. A child may not be able to reach a toy displayed on a high shelf, open her favorite cereal box, push her straw into the juice box, nor open a heavy door. Unless the child can request a helping hand a tantrum could result. At that point, an observer might realize the nature of the problem and be tempted to approach the frenzied youngster reminding her, "You need to *ask* for help!" Even if the child did stop and ask for help following the prompt, what would we predict would happen the next time the child needs assistance? There is a good chance she again will start to cry; leading someone to prompt her, and the entire cycle repeats itself, as in Figure 5-3. The solution is to teach the child to ask for help before a tantrum begins.

Figure 5-3

A Vicious Cycle for Getting Help

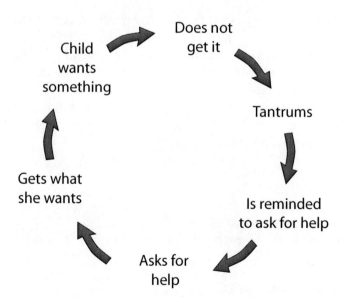

Child wants something

Does not get it

Tantrums

Is reminded to ask for help

Asks for help

Gets what she wants

Asking for a break

Asking for a break as a form of relief also is critically important. We all have experienced situations in which the demand is so great, long, or difficult that it's fatigued us. In these cases, we may request time to recuperate recognizing that, after our break, we will return to work. Certainly we adults negotiate our vacation days when contracting to do a new job, knowing that we periodically need to get away from tedious routines. Similarly, learners also need to have a calm way to ask for a break and we must teach them how. As with learning to ask for help, the key will be for the learner to ask for a break prior to escalating into an emotional outburst. Asking to terminate something (e.g., "All done") also has great importance. Not all communication to avoid or escape needs to have a return to the activity.

Accepting or rejecting

Accepting or rejecting offers from other people also is an essential skill for surviving. Billy hates pickles - their very smell makes him gag. Walter walks over to Billy and offers him a pickle. How will Billy react? In large part, it depends upon Billy's communication skills. He may say, "No thanks!" However, if he can't communicate, he still will convey his disgust - maybe dramatically in some unpleasant or even painful way. If, on the other hand, Walter shows Billy something the boy likes, if Billy cannot calmly communicate "yes" he might just grab the item, an outcome reasonably safe for both of them.

Notice that answering "yes" or "no" to an offer is functionally different from responding "yes" or "no" to a question like, "Is this an X?" When we say, "yes" to "Do you want a cookie?" we get a cookie. The utility of this kind of affirmation is similar to that of a request; it is a critical functional skill. When a youngster answers, "yes" to "Is this a cookie?" he does not get the cookie. Instead, the teacher says, "You're right! It is a cookie!" Here the function is similar to that of a comment. Thus, two different lessons are needed - the first of which is especially critical.

Critical Receptive Skills.

A second set of critical communication skills is concerned with understanding important messages from other people, independent of how that message is delivered. These receptive ("listener" or "communicative partner") skills include:

1. Functional instruction/direction following (to auditory and visual cues/prompts).

2. Transitioning from one activity to another.

3. Waiting patiently when asked to 'wait,' and coping calmly with being told 'no.'

4. Schedule following.

These particular skills are viewed as essential because failure to understand the message could be dangerous or distressing. Contrast a teacher shouting, "Move! There's a car coming!" with "What is this called?" while holding up an apple, or with someone saying, "Hello!" In the first instance, failure to respond correctly could be life threatening, whereas nothing critical would result from not following the others.

Following Directions

A learner's general well-being demands he or she learns to follow directions; otherwise others will need to continue to do everything for the learner. The most reasonable way to accomplish this goal is to teach direction following that leads to functional outcomes. The teacher should design lessons in which naturally reinforcing consequences follow the directions. "Go to the door" should lead to going out the door; "Go to the refrigerator," to opening it and getting something good to eat or drink. Teaching someone to obey, "Go to the wall," which only leads to, "Good job! Now come sit back down," may improve compliance (if that is a current problem), but is not the most effective way to build understanding of instructional words and content. Attributes like colors can be made functional by using the name within an instruction important to the learner, as in "Your favorite toy is in the red box."

Sometimes we give directions because they help us in some way. Dad may be thirsty and would like to ask his daughter to please bring him a soda. He realizes he only can get his drink if his daughter understands what he said. So he considers teaching her that skill. But how would his daughter gain from the interaction? Presumably, her father would thank her or maybe give her a smile or a hug. However, we should recall that not all learners with disabilities find smiles or hugs very motivating. When they don't, it's better to begin to teach the learner to follow directions that will produce some direct reinforcement rather than those primarily benefiting the instructor.

Just as people use various modalities to convey their messages, they need to receive and understand communication others send in different ways. Beyond the essential ability to understand when we talk to them, to be a productive member of our society, everyone must learn to respond appropriately to messages conveyed in other forms. For example, drivers must adjust their reactions to different traffic signs, lights, and lines painted on the road, independent of any spoken cues. We assemble toys or furniture by relying solely on diagrams to guide our actions, especially when the suppliers serve an international clientele. Although we can competently use speech, as well as read and write, frequently we find ourselves in situations where we must rely upon information conveyed in visual form. Regardless of whether they speak, sign or use pictures to express themselves, we must plan also to teach learners to respond appropriately to a range of pictorial, written or other types of visually-based signals, as well as spoken instructions.

Transitioning from One Activity to Another

A child has a major temper tantrum upon arriving at school. You firmly take him to class. After 20 minutes or so, he calms down and plays with a toy. Then you approach him and say, "It's time for gym!" He immediately starts to cry and scream. Firmly, you take him to gym where he continues to cry for another 15 minutes before settling down to play with a ball. Then you walk over and say, "It's time to go back to class!" His tantrum picks up where it left off earlier. Following each transition throughout the day, this cycle replays itself.

What is happening here and why do we list transitions under receptive skills? Probably the child did not recognize that another reinforcing activity will begin shortly. Instances of this nature are not as rare as we might think. Transition times tend to be problematic because they not only signal what's next, they signal the termination of an ongoing, presumably reinforcing activity, as well as a delay until the next one begins. These are the times when learners are most likely to get into trouble - inflicting damage, or attacking others, or even themselves. Part of this reaction has to do with the delay issues we just discussed. However, a significant part of the learner's maladaptive response to transitions is *elicited* by the loss of the current reinforcer[6]. What can we do about it?

The kinds of visual scheduling cues we described earlier may help, but often are insufficient. While the symbols aim to inform learners about the upcoming activity, they may not provide enough information about the next reinforcer. While we, as adults, tend to think about moving from activity to activity, it may be helpful to consider that the learners are moving from reinforcer to reinforcer. Thus, we need to shift our focus from the activity itself to its related reinforcer. This element is crucial as the transition signals the loss of the current reinforcer. Rather than describing the

---

6   See Chapter 6 regarding Contextually Inappropriate Behaviors for a complete description of this behavioral function.

next activity, the teacher can signal the next reinforcer. One tactic is to use props as transitional objects. While the learner is playing with blocks in the classroom, the teacher can approach with a ball used only in the gym. When the learner is playing with a ball in gym and the teacher wants him to return to the classroom for snack time, she could highlight the reinforcer first by saying or showing something familiar about the snack before informing the learner about the necessary transition. In each situation, to obtain the next reinforcer, the learner must change activities. This strategy shifts the emphasis from what the learner must *give up* to what the learner *will get*. So, when dealing with transitions, focus on communicating about the learner's primary concern - reinforcers!

Waiting Patiently

Dominick, you recall, punched himself in the head when he misunderstood the instruction, "Wait." Waiting is unpleasant for everyone because it means the anticipated reinforcing event is being delayed. Even we adults probably could do a little better in the patience department - as our mothers constantly reminded us! What are we trying to communicate to someone when we say, "wait?" A complex message: "I know what you want and you are going to get it but not for a while." What factors do we need to consider in teaching this difficult but crucial message?

The first step in teaching patience is to determine what the learner wants. Then we must consider whether we can control the delivery of that reinforcer. We would not choose to teach patience in a setting like a fast food restaurant at lunchtime, because we could not be certain about exactly how long we would need to wait before getting our food. A better choice would be to begin the lesson when we have prepared the lunch ourselves and it's ready to be served. In this type of situation, allowing access to the reinforcing items is completely under our control.

The next important factor in this lesson is controlling how long the learner has to wait. The general strategy is to begin with an interval so brief that the learner cannot fail to be successful. Then, we gradually stretch the waiting period. As we expand the length of the intervals, if the learner fails to wait calmly, then we might slightly shorten the waiting interval for the next few teaching opportunities. If a learner does not wait patiently, we should not blame the learner or think he failed. In fact, we are the ones who set the interval, so the responsibility remains with us. Next, just as the yellow traffic light signals that we should get ready to stop at the upcoming red light, we should consider adding a visual cue to help the learner succeed with this task. A bright pictorial or written "wait" signal, along with a visual representation of the item the learner is waiting for, may help him better tolerate the delay. We can add stars to the wait-card that can serve as a clock helping the user to better understand how long (i.e., how many stars) before the reinforcer is delivered.

Finally, as we extend the period of time to wait, we should prepare alternative reinforcing activities for the learner to do during the waiting period. What did *you* do the last time you sat in the waiting room before you were called in to be examined by the doctor? Because they know all of us hate to do nothing while we wait, doctors supply their patients with magazines, books or toys. Clever parents, teachers, and camp counselors teach their learners to sing songs, skim books, or play games during the interval to keep them out of trouble. Therefore, as the intervals for waiting are stretched by the teacher, learners should be taught how to stay out of trouble by occupying their time. It is helpful to consider the types of magazines left in the doctor's waiting room. They are not so reinforcing that you would ever go back just to read them. They are low-level reinforcers that give you something simple to do. So it should be with the wait-interval activities - mildly reinforcing items and activities, not the big reinforcers that the learner is waiting for. See Figure 5-4 for an example of a visual cue for waiting.

Figure 5-4

A Visual Cue to Wait for Lunch

In the situation where a learner is waiting, he is experiencing a delay in getting access to reinforcement. In other instances, we are not asking our learner to tolerate a delay in reinforcement, but may be asking him to tolerate a denial of reinforcement. That is, everyone needs to react appropriately to the reponse, "No." Some parents say, "You never can tell my child "no" because he will have a tantrum." If this is the case, the request from the parent is to always make to be sure the learner gets what he wants. How great it would be if we could arrange for this to occur all the time! Sadly, this is not realistic and the world is not so generous (nor is it always a safe practice). As children get older, especially when they begin to crawl and walk, they get a lot of exposure to hearing "no." Just observe a 1½ year-old walking around his house shaking his finger and saying, "no, no, no." He has probably been told "no" several hundred times per week! Over time, and with this practice/exposure, children get better at responding to this condition. The same would be true for our learners. We need to arrange for situations where they are told they cannot have something, and then are praised for their acceptance of this condition. We can start by offering less preferred items to a learner and then, as she requests the item, tell her, "no" and do not allow her access to the item. As the learner calmly accepts not getting the item, she can be provided with a reinforcer unrelated to the one she was denied. In this case the girl is building a history of calmly responding to denial of reinforcement. More reinforceing items can later be introduced and interspersed with other reinforcers to allow the learner greater exposure to this condition.

Following a Schedule

How do you keep track of all the important things you need to do today, this week, or this month? Perhaps you use some type of date book to help you organize your activities, instead of depending on memorizing when you're supposed to be doing what. Learners also like to know what is expected of them and when those activities should occur. Therefore, we should teach them to refer to visual reminder systems (similar to the one in Figure 5-5 that we use at Pyramid) to inform them about their future schedule of activities[7]. Those with good reading comprehension can depend on written words just as we do. If a learner has difficulty with pictures, objects representing activities and places can be used instead. Learners who do not understand text can learn to refer to schedules depicted by images and objects, especially when those sym-

Figure 5-5
A Pictorial Schedule

---

7   Instructions for designing schedules are included in Frost, L. & Bondy, A., (2002) *The Picture Exchange Communication System, 2nd Edition*, Newark, DE: Pyramid Educational Consultants.

bols have been previously included successfully within their instruction following routines. We believe it is best to consider this a two-step process: 1) What do the pictures mean? (i.e., what to do when I see a particular picture), and 2) How do I use the schedule? A golden rule in teaching is "one lesson at a time." Thus, be sure the learner responds appropriately to the individual pictures before constructing a schedule consisting of a series of pictures.

Communicating About Emotions

Many parents and teachers think that it is very important to teach individuals with special needs to express their own feelings and emotions. To better understand how we can teach our learners to communicate about their emotions, consider how typically developing children appear to learn this skill. Amanda is seated on the park bench watching her two-year-old son, Billy, trying to climb onto the slide. The toddler falls and scrapes his knee on the sidewalk. Billy's knee is bleeding and he is crying. His mother runs and comforts him, "Wow, you poor boy - I bet that hurts!" In this scenario, Amanda used information about 1) the *context* (i.e., she saw him fall and she saw blood), and 2) his *affective display* (i.e., she saw him crying) to label how Billy is feeling. On other occasions, when Amanda saw Billy laughing and giggling while devouring an ice cream cone, or when his uncle swung him high into the air, she commented to Billy about how happy he was feeling. In short, others were teaching Billy to communicate about how he was feeling by using situational and affective cues to tell him what he was feeling. Later if Billy fell on his elbow, he might say, "My elbow hurts!" meaning that his elbow now feels like his knee felt when mom said his knee hurt. Similarly, when he tastes a delicious candy, or laughs when his mom tickles him, he tells her he's happy! Describing one's feelings in words may be preferable to acting them out, especially when the emotions are negative. Saying, "It makes me feel bad when you say that" is far better than a child shouting, screaming, and flailing out when her parents say something that distresses her[8].

Billy's statement about his feelings is a form of comment. That is, he is describing something happening inside himself. Children typically learn to comment about external things before they can describe events inside themselves. When we want to teach learners to comment about their feelings, we will need first to determine that they already can comment about common things in their environments, or we may find ourselves spinning our wheels. It is safe to assume that when he talks about the way his knee feels, Billy has already learned to comment about things surrounding him,

---

8   This analysis is based upon Skinner's (1957) discussion about *tacting* private events.

such as about toys, furniture, and his family.

Teaching learners with autism how to label their emotions can present a special challenge, especially if they do not cry, laugh, or otherwise express affect as their contemporaries typically do. Joey burns his hand on the stovetop. Although he pulls his hand away immediately and strenuously avoids touching the stovetop again, he doesn't cry. Catherine eats ice cream as vigorously as other children, but neither smiles nor laughs. Fewer cues are available to their teachers and parents to guide them to label the learner's feelings. Lacking those affective cues, they are less likely to label feelings for the learners. Do these individuals have feelings? Absolutely! Joey avoids the stovetop henceforth, and Catherine will reach for more ice cream when given the opportunity. Communicating effectively about emotions is not the same as having the emotion.

How can we arrange to teach learners like Joey and Catherine to tell us about their feelings? The teacher must be fairly certain of their current status before naming the feeling for the learner. Doing this is a lot easier for positive affect because teachers need only to pile on those reinforcers known to be effective with that learner after withholding them for a while. Labels of negative feelings, like sad, angry, and hurt, are harder to teach because intentionally arranging for unpleasant situations is problematic. Teachers generally would not want to provoke unpleasant feelings and indeed are responsible for doing everything possible to prevent learners from getting hurt. Therefore, they need to be prepared to seize the opportunities when they present themselves naturally.

Under circumstances when a typically developing child would be expected to display a negative reaction, the teacher should interrupt whenever possible whatever else is happening, label the appropriate emotion, and encourage the learner to do the same. Gradually the teacher should diminish the prompts guiding the learner's labeling. (See Chapter 8 for additional details about fading prompts.) One major dilemma presents itself if the opportunity to teach a learner to label his discomfort does not occur often enough. Are there, then, ever situations in which it might be defensible to intentionally arrange conditions assuring that the learner will experience negative feelings, such as taking things away from him abruptly, or permitting him to suffer a minor discomfort rather than preventing it? That solution raises obvious ethical concerns, best discussed openly between teachers, parents, and community representatives.

Communicating Skillfully in Social Circumstances

Several communicative skills appear to be crucial for initiating and sustaining productive social relations with other people. Among these are making eye-contact, greetings, and maintaining and terminating interactions.

Eye Contact

Individuals with autism often are at a disadvantage in cultures where making and maintaining eye contact is considered essential to polite communication, because many do not display this skill. In fact, teachers frequently find themselves cueing the learner to look at them, whether it actually is specified in the learner's educational plan or not. But they may overlook the *reciprocal function* of eye contact: A young girl's mother answers the telephone. In need of help while her mother is conversing, she calls out, "Mom!" But her mother ignores her. The girl then begins to tug at her mother's apron, then on her sleeves and shoulders and, finally, she grasps her mother's face, turns it toward herself, and shouts, "Mother!" In this situation, the girl understood that unless her mother was looking at her there was no point in trying to communicate her needs. Thus, at an early age, typically developing children learn the importance of both looking at others and having others look at them. Consequently, when we want to teach learners who do not make routine eye contact, we need to be certain to address both *initiating* eye contact and *eliciting* eye contact from others. Furthermore, we should recognize that eye-to-eye contact is not the only skill that indicates, or corresponds to, 'paying attention.'

Greetings

Greeting one another appropriately also is important in society. If the learner fails to return our "Hi" or wave, some may conclude she's rude. However, learning this skill is deceptively complex. It is one thing to learn to imitate someone else's greeting. Learning to initiate a greeting is much more difficult, especially because there are subtleties to when, where, and how to greet under particular circumstances. Furthermore, individuals need to initiate a greeting when they enter a room occupied by one or more people, as well as when someone else enters their room. Finally, people must learn to greet only once within an interaction because repeatedly saying, "Hi" within a short time frame is considered impolite.

Communicating within Social Interactions

Conversational or play interactions include four distinct components.

How we respond when someone approaches us is one set of skills. For example, approaching Justine, Phillip may say, "Let's play ball," or he might ask, "Did you watch the Power Rangers last night?" An appropriate response in the first situation would be for Justine to join Phillip in a ball game; in the second, to begin talking about Power Rangers. A different set of skills, though, is involved in teaching a learner to *approach others*. That is, we also have to teach Justine how to approach Phillip. Some learners may approach by formally communicating in speech, sign, with pictures, or by offering a simple object (i.e., Justine brings Phillip a ball). Often individuals with communication difficulties seem to find it easier to learn to respond to social approaches than to initiate them.

Once a learner has either initiated or responded to an initiation, other skills are needed to *maintain the interaction by taking turns*. When Phillip throws the ball to Justine, she should catch it and throw it back. Each needs to learn to take turns. When Phillip tells Justine about the Power Ranger show from the night before, she should continue discussing that topic.

The final interactive component - one often neglected - involves the skills essential for *politely ending an interaction*. Phillip may tire quickly of playing ball, but his peers might be unwilling to play with him again if he abruptly walks away in the midst of the activity. Social graces include comments such as, "Hey, thanks for playing. I'm going to get a drink now!" or "Wow, my arms are tired. Let's take a break!" Justine may not enjoy watching or talking about Power Rangers. Still, rather than simply turning her back on Phillip, she could say, "Well, I didn't watch that show but I did watch *The Simpsons*. Did you see that one?"

Assessing Your Learner's Most Critical Communication Needs

As you can see, speaking words is but one facet of communication. Other elements, such as how someone says a word, how other aspects of their behavior influence the meaning of their words, or the way someone reacts to what others say, request, or do can be equally, if not even more, important. Obviously, it would be impractical and inefficient to work on every communication objective at the same time. As so often happens, we are most likely to achieve our best results when we know how things stand currently, where we are headed, and in what order we should address the challenge. A formal critical functional communication checklist is just the kind of instrument that teachers and parents should find especially helpful in sorting out what skills to teach, how to teach them, and when to teach them.

Table 5-1 displays a *Critical Functional Communication Skills Checklist* containing many important skills. First, the instrument helps you to determine the characteristics of an individual's current modes of behaving, in terms of each important communicative function. For example, when Tony wants something to eat, does he grab for things, point to items, take your hand to the item, or ask for it? Next, it asks you to judge if the form of communication is appropriate for someone in that setting. After reviewing all the items on the checklist you can arrange the skills in order of priority by asking which ones will be most important for the learner to acquire first or modify, then next, and so on[9].

Table 5-1

Critical Functional Communication Skills Checklist

Name:	Tony	Date:	05/03/2011
DOB:	05/03/2001	Age:	4

Skill	Example	Appropriate?
1. Request reinforcers		
edibles	Stands in front of cupboard and screams	No
toys	Climbs shelves to get toys on his own	No
activities	Brings Mom to door to go outside	No
2. Request help/assistance	Tantrums when toys don't work	No
3. Request break/all done	Tries to walk away from activity or tantrums	No
4. Reject	Tantrums	No
5. Accept	Takes offered items	Yes
6. Respond to "wait"/"no"	Screams	No
7. Respond to directions		
Visual Directions		
Orients to name being sig-nalled	Does not orient	No

---

9   As individuals begin to progress, the functions of their communication can become increasingly complex. Eventually they may use their skills to solve problems, to create, or in other advanced ways. See *References and Suggested Readings* at the end of the chapter for more advanced sources.

"Come here"	Complies if speaker shows reinforcer while gesturing	Yes
"Stop"	Complies if speaker blocks movement	Yes
"Sit down"	Complies if speaker shows reinforcer and chair	Yes
"Give it to me"	Tantrums if he's holding a preferred item	No
Go get..." (familiar item)	Does not respond	No
"Go get..." (familiar location	Does not respond	No
"Put it back/down"	Does not respond	No
"Let's go/Come with me."	Complies if Mom shoes keys to go in car	Yes
Oral Directions		
Orients to name being sig-nalled	Does not respond	No
"Come here"	Does not respond	No
"Stop"	Does not respond	No
"Sit down"	Does not respond	No
"Give it to me"		No
Go get..." (familiar item)	Does not respond	No
"Go get..." (familiar location	Does not respond	No
"Put it back/down"	Does not respond	No
"Let's go/Come with me."		No
8. Transition between activities	Tantrums unless he knows what next reinforcer is	No
9. Follow visual schedule	Never attempted	

Play

Play situations provide individuals with valuable opportunities to communicate. Although not the equivalent of communicating, the ability to play interactively certainly is essential if language is to develop at a reasonable pace. The mechanical requirements of play, such as how to manipulate toys and play materials, though, are distinct from the social components of play. While the manipulative skills may be taught independently of playful interactions, we need to be skillful in planning ways to enable the application of those skills within a social context.

Mechanical Requirements of Play. In planning ways to foster interactive play, the teacher needs to decide the best route to follow. Is it better to aim at skills essential for playing in a particular way, or should teaching take place in groups from the start? If manipulating toys and play materials is the ultimate objective, we might teach those skills separately from playful peer interactions. Assuming the ultimate purpose, though, is to promote social play by teaching the use of toys, like Lego®, modeling clay, or toy cars for props, we might begin our instruction in a setting that includes at least one other player. Then there are some play materials that require interaction from the beginning. Another person, for instance, has to be there to throw a ball if catching is to be learned.

A reasonable way to choose toys is to include those that tap into currently powerful reinforcers. For example, if we have noticed that a child likes to watch objects spinning round and round, like wheels on a toy car or a top in motion, selecting toys with similar qualities should help motivate the child to learn to play with that toy. Children who do not often spontaneously look at pictures in books or magazines may not find putting a puzzle together highly motivating, because they may fail to 'see' the picture revealed by the completed puzzle.

Learning how to play with toys and other play materials, though, does not assure that interactive social play skills will generalize automatically to social play. Instead, parents and teachers need specifically to plan ways to promote social play.

Social Play: Parallel, Interactive, and Imaginative. As they develop, children tend to move through various stages of play. Initially, very young children play alone, even when they use the same materials in the same place as their peers. Watch infants in a sandbox or at the beach - all use shovels to move sand around, but each remains an 'isolated island unto herself.' The children are said to be engaging in parallel play at this point.

As they begin to mature, you will notice the same youngsters building upon each other's piles, asking for different tools, or making or following a suggested design. Now the children truly are interacting while playing. Interactive play also may advance to using props or costumes like hats, shoes, or fancy dress to enable children to act out various pretend roles, such as police, doctors, cowboys or cowgirls. Shovels and sand become props for make-believe baking, serving, and eating cookies. Costumes transform them into super heroes, moms and dads, teachers, cops and robbers, the fireman, or the policeman.

You can teach children who do not show more advanced play skills by systematically shaping each of the essential elements (see Chapter 4). We should not assume, though, that if we teach play in one certain way, that skill will suddenly appear while around peers; nor should we assume that we effectively promote the rate of social play solely by providing reinforcers by ourselves. In fact, be careful to create a reinforcing social situation for such play skills by assuring that peers can provide meaningful rewards to those with whom they are to interact. For instance, typically developing classmates of preschoolers with autism have been systematically trained to teach and reinforce their delayed peers for taking turns and engaging in pretend play[10].

Empathy and Sympathy - Reading the Emotions of Others. It's Friday night and 17-year-old Alex, who has just received his driver's license, wants to borrow the family car. Going over the checkbook, his mother mutters angrily to herself. His father is calmly reading a magazine. Alex probably will choose to ask his father for the keys. As we grow up, we learn that people's feelings may impact upon our chances of getting what we want or need. Of course, such material concerns are not the only reason we learn to read other people's emotions. If a girl sees her parents or teachers enthusiastically laughing and clapping their hands, she may join in and enjoy sharing their responses. If a boy sees his brother looking at a broken toy with a sad expression on his face, and he puts an arm around his brother's shoulders or offers some sympathetic words, his brother may thank him sincerely and his parents praise him for his compassion.

How do we teach our learners to become sensitive to other people's emotions? We could develop a lesson in the form of a simple receptive drill: "Point to the picture of the girl smiling." We even could teach a learner to imitate someone else's emotional display: a smile, a frown, or an angry scowl. However, do these skills truly demonstrate the learner's ability to understand what a smiling person is feeling? Do they go far enough, or do we need to ask how we can make knowing about someone else's feeling important to our learners?

Labeling and imitating other people's emotions are only parts of displaying empathy. Such a sophisticated skill involves many different ways of reacting to emotional signs - offering help to someone who looks frightened, smiling and laughing along with someone's joyful expressions, or providing assistance or sympathy to a person who looks unhappy. As with other lessons involving communication and social skills, the use of visual cues, either expressively or receptively, may aide in teaching these skills. Pictures or words may help learners 'remember' to express their feelings

---

10   See, for instance, Lifter, K., Sulzer-Azaroff, B., Anderson, S. R. & Cowdery, G. E. (1993). Teaching play activities to preschool children with disabilities: The importance of developmental considerations. *Journal of Early Intervention, 17,* (2), 139-159.

through communication, as opposed to more dramatic forms. Social Stories™ is a strategy that helps learners review and rehearse potentially difficult interactions in a safe format before encountering the real situation[11]. With this strategy, learners and teachers identify difficult social situations - responding to teasing, responding to or telling jokes, how to tell someone to leave you alone, etc. - and then review potential alternative solutions. Pictures then are designed to help the learner identify the scenario and review alternative choices. These options are initially practiced within controlled role-playing situations, and then gradually introduced into real circumstances. This orientation permits the teacher to review common and unique complex social encounters for each learner.

Summary

In and of itself, talking is not the essence of communication. Rather, communication involves directing behavior toward others, who characteristically respond in a reinforcing way - by providing something material, paying attention, saying something in return, or in other forms. Without the use of language to make their wants and needs known, people are at a distinct disadvantage because they will use whatever works to obtain these outcomes, including harmful or distressing conduct.

Teachers and parents need to choose very carefully which communicative skills to teach by asking what functions these skill will meet, whether appropriately initiating or responding to someone else is involved, plus where and when these skills should be demonstrated. The modality to be used and understood also needs to be carefully considered.

At the beginning phases of learning how to communicate, teachers need to consider several *productive* skills, like asking for powerful reinforcers, help, or a break, or answering "yes" versus "no." Also crucial are certain *receptive* skills, like following directions and schedules, waiting patiently, and transitioning from one activity to another.

To live effectually in our society it is important for individuals to communicate in socially acceptable ways about their emotions, to make eye contact, greet appropriately, and participate in groups by suitably initiating and maintaining interactions, and appropriately departing from these groups. To interact with, and gain from, relationships with peers, children also need the essential mechanical and social skills demanded of play, including responding appropriately to others' emotions. We need to teach each of these skills systematically, using a mix of strategies and modalities that work currently, while keeping an eye on future demands.

---

11   See Carol Gray (1995). Teaching children with autism to "read" social situations. In K. Quill (Ed.), *Teaching children with autism*. New York, NY: Delmar Publishing

Chapter 5 Resources

Communication and Social Skills.

To	Read
Become familiar with verbal behavior from a behavior analytic perspective.	Hayes, L.J. & Chase, P.N. (Eds.) (1991). *Dialogues on verbal behavior.* Reno, NV: Context Press. A series of individually authored conceptual papers on language. *Journal of Applied Behavior Analysis,* 1968 to present. Presents behavior analytic research on many aspects of communicative behavior. Skinner, B.F. (1957). *Verbal behavior.* Englewood Cliffs NJ: Prentice Hall, Inc. Skinner's conceptual account of how verbal learning takes place, on a simple and complex level. Sulzer-Azaroff, B. & Mayer, G.R. (1991). *Behavior analysis for lasting change.* Wadsworth Publishing. Chapter on Communicative Behavior. Contains varied methods for teaching various classes of verbal or communicative behavior.
Become familiar with the behavior analytic research in communication in developmental disabilities.	*Behavior Analysis in Developmental Disabilities.* A reprint volume of research in developmental disabilities from the *Journal of Applied Behavior Analysis,* including language and numerous other topics.
Learn how to teach individuals lacking communication skills to use the Picture Exchange Communication System.	Frost, L. & Bondy, A. (2002). *The picture exchange communication system, 2ⁿᵈ edition.* Newark, DE: Pyramid Educational Consultants, Inc.

Learn how to teach children with developmental delays using sign.	Sundberg, M.L. & Partington, J.W. (1998). *Teaching language to children with autism or other developmental disabilities.* Danville, CA: Behavior Analysts, Inc.
Learn how to teach social behavior and communication to children.	Koegel, L. (1995). Communication and Language Interventions. In R.L. Koegel & L.K. Koegel (Eds.). *Teaching children with autism* (pp. 17-32). Baltimore, MD: Brooks. Hawkins, D. (1995). Spontaneous language use. In R.L. Koegel & L.K. Koegel (Eds.). *Teaching children with autism* (pp. 43-52). Baltimore, MD: Brooks. Frea, W.D. (1995). Social-communicative skills in higher functioning children with autism. In R.L. Koegel & L.K. Koegel (Eds.). *Teaching children with autism* (pp. 53-66). Baltimore, MD: Brooks. Lovaas, O.I. (2002). *Teaching Individuals with Developmental Disabilities: Basic Intervention Techniques* (pp. 291-303). Austin, TX: Pro-Ed. Maurice, C., Green, G. & Luce, S., (Eds.) **(1996).** *Behavioral Intervention for Young Children with Autism.* Austin, TX: Pro-Ed. Chapters 13 & 14. Quill, K.A. (2000). *Do-Watch-Listen-Say.* Baltimore, MD: Brooks.
Learn how to teach functional spoken language to those children with autism who can produce spoken words and phrases.	Lovaas, O.I. (1981). *Teaching developmentally disabled children: The me book.* Austin, TX: Pro-Ed.

Teach independent behavior by means of activity schedules.	McClannahan, L.E. & Krantz, P.J. (1999). *Activity schedules for children with autism.* Bethesda, MD: Woodbine House.

To	Do
Learn how to teach individuals lacking communication skills to use the Picture Exchange Communication System.	Attend a PECS workshop - www.pecs.com

To	View
Learn how to teach activity schedules at school and home, choice making, prompt fading and more.	Princeton Child Development Tapes Princeton Child Development Institute 300 Cold Soil Road Princeton, NJ 08540 E-mail: njpcdi@earthlink.net
Gain an overview of the potential advantages of the Picture Exchange Communication System.	An Introduction to PECS DVD, Pyramid Educational Consultants, Inc. www.pecs.com

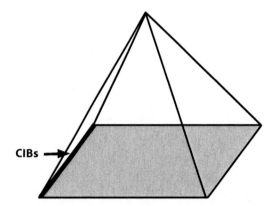

CIBs

6

Preventing and Reducing
Contextually Inappropriate Behaviors

"Kill them," screams a youth. He shakes his fist, jumps up on a chair, grabs the person beside him, and pulls at his clothing. A woman sits quietly, hands folded, head lowered, mumbling inaudibly. A child moves her fingers rapidly up, down and across one another, non-stop, for twenty minutes, completely ignoring everything else.

Are these inappropriate behaviors? Well, that depends. In the first instance, if the youth did that in a restaurant or classroom, we might say, "Yes." But suppose it happened during a football or soccer game. The behavior is perfectly acceptable; everyone else is doing something similar. Lacking any additional information, your initial reaction to the description of the mumbling woman might be that she is suffering from some sort of mental illness. A few more clues about the context, though, could cause you to change your mind: a black book in her hand, an organ playing, everyone else doing the same thing; a person clad in black standing on a raised platform. Of course, she's praying. This form of behavior is totally acceptable in the context of a house of worship. By now you're suspicious. Does the finger-flicking female have autism? Perhaps yes, if the behavior continues for hours on end, with no functional outcome. Probably not, if the fingers are contacting ivory keys and producing scales or a beautiful melody.

As you realize by now, it is not behavior *per se* that is inappropriate. It is the context in which it occurs that matters. Almost any act you can think of could be inappropriate if it happened in the wrong place, at the wrong time, persisted too long, or was too weak or forceful. Recognizing this fact enables us to revise not only our assessment about what is acceptable or unacceptable conduct, but also alters the way we go about addressing it. No longer is the challenge of what to do insurmountable because, instead of needing to eliminate a behavior, the task becomes one of changing when, where, and how often the behavior takes place. That is what this chapter is about - examining the kinds of *contextually inappropriate behaviors* we need to deal with, why they probably are happening, and what to do about them.

General Precautions

Acts of violence, property destruction, and terrorism are unfortunately far more prevalent in our society than any of us wish. Reducing and preventing them requires that we take every reasonable precaution to avoid their happening in our homes or organizations. Among these preventative actions are:

- Developing and consistently applying policies relating to personnel practices, learner and staff protection, health promotion, visitors, weapons, and so forth.

- Promoting health by providing good nutrition, medical services, and opportunities for regular exercise.

- Instituting stress-reducing methods for learners and staff including, among others, physical activities, a comfortable physical environment, and relaxation exercises.

- Minimizing a punitive, and maximizing a positively reinforcing, social ambience and instructional curriculum.

- Organizing small group or team activities in which cooperating on a task results in reinforcement for every member.

Promoting the Well-being of Learners with Special Needs

Parents, teachers, and other providers of services to learners with special challenges are all similar in being concerned with maintaining the wellness of those in their charge, and of themselves. Regardless of the composition of the learner body, the purpose of any school is to enable all learners to learn and grow. The same broad goals reflect the long term aims of adult facilities as well. Yet, unfortunately, people occasionally do things that interfere not only with their own learning and health, but with that of others.

We are talking about harmful and socially obnoxious behaviors, like hurting oneself or others, destroying property, or disrupting others' ongoing activities with loud noises. Then there are attention grabbing and socially unacceptable actions, such as disrobing in public, or interminably repeating strings of words, gestures, or songs. Although any of us might, under certain circumstances, spin a top, pull a string off a package, sing along with a favorite TV commercial, curse, snap our fingers, and so on, when a person spends hours on end repeating those, or other disturbing mannerisms, it becomes an issue to be addressed. Not only are the individuals themselves so engrossed in those activities that little else penetrates their awareness, but also they are interfering with the progress of others. When a team (i.e., the Individual Educational Planning or Overall Plan for Service team) deems it justifiable to intervene directly to reduce or eliminate a behavior pattern, we call the objective a *contextually inappropriate behavior (CIB) target*[1]. No matter how intrusive, aversive, or benign a strategy may be, as long as the purpose of the intervention is to reduce or eliminate a behavior, the focus behavior retains its label as a CIB. In contrast are strategies aimed at increasing or expanding behaviors. We broadly refer to these as *education*.

The kinds of behaviors we have been describing are problems because they happen too frequently or too forcefully, or often at the wrong time or place. Just knowing that reminds us that the person has been learning a good deal, but of the wrong thing. The preferred solution is to promote more socially acceptable substitute behaviors by *systematically* applying behavioral principles as effectively as possible. These *intervention procedures* can vary considerably, though, depending upon a number of factors. These include the functions of the CIBs, their resistance to change, the availability of more acceptable substitute behaviors, and the ability of the environment to support those alternatives.

---

1   The terminology and orientation to intervention described in this section follows the state guidelines for the establishment of Peer Review and Human Rights Committees for the Delaware Autism Program. These behavior intervention targets include actions that are harmful to the learner (e.g., self-injury), to other people (e.g., aggression), or to the environment (e.g., tantrums, property destruction); that interfere with traditional educational approaches (e.g., self-stimulation, disruptive noise), either for the learner, or for other learners, or that may bring social sanctions against the learner or caretakers (e.g., disrobing in public, speaking in a weird or bizarre manner, certain lengthy rituals).

Assessing the Function of the CIB

Behavior analysts accept the notion that conduct of any kind develops for a reason, not just by happenstance. We assume the functional nature of all kinds of actions, including those that are adaptive, like caring for oneself, mastering learning tools, getting along with others, succeeding on the job, and so on, as well as those we are concerned with here, the contextually inappropriate ones. Each of these actions either: 1) has a history of being reinforced by resulting in getting something or escaping/avoiding something, or 2) was elicited by the circumstances.

"I can see how a tantrum might produce reinforcement," you might protest, "but how could spinning an object, twirling a string, singing commercials, twiddling one's fingers endlessly, lashing out at people, or destroying things have done that?" The answer most likely lies in some sort of pairing of the response with possibly unintended, or even accidental, reinforcement. Do you know people who carry around a lucky charm or recite a phrase in the hope that it will ward off evil or enable them to win? We call these *superstitious behaviors* when we're convinced that one thing has nothing to do with the other. How did they evolve? In all likelihood, through experience. Two events happened to coincide in time: the *superstitious* behavior and a powerful real, or vicarious, reinforcing consequence for the person. Because that kind of learning happens so swiftly, often it is difficult to determine what happened earlier to bring it about.

Inquiring of parents, teachers, and other caregivers might or might not provide some clues. Yet all is not lost if those original reinforcing conditions elude us. Recovering sufficient information from a person's past is not absolutely essential. What is crucial is finding out *what events are maintaining the behaviors* so that you can design methods for permitting the person to secure those same reinforcers in a more acceptable way. The objective is to determine what in the environment is *functionally* related to the unwanted behavior, and to teach preferable alternative ways to respond which duplicate that function. We refer to this strategy as the *functionally equivalent alternative behavior* strategy, abbreviated as *FEAB*.

One way to search for the antecedents provoking, or consequences maintaining, the behavior pattern is to ask yourself, or watch, what tends to typically happen just prior to and following the behavior. Does the antecedent hint that it might gain the individual what he appears to want or need? Is extra attention sometimes a consequence? Does the CIB result in access to preferred objects or events? Allow her to seal herself off from the rest of the demanding or distressing world? Keep unwanted contact at bay? If the consequences are apparent, you can use them to shape alternative responses. For example, withhold those consequences until you note the beginnings of a more acceptable alternative action, and then deliver them on the spot.

A more thorough, and for especially troubling CIBs a more ethically defensible way, to discover maintaining conditions is to conduct a formal functional analysis (which may include a comprehensive Functional Assessment)[2]. Briefly, this method systematically supplies the individual with different classes of antecedents and reinforcers to discover which are lawfully related to increases in the rate or intensity (i.e., forcefulness) of the behavior of concern. In a typical functional assessment, distinctive sessions are planned in which the client is:

1. Provided with some type of positive reinforcer (e.g., social attention, interactive engagement, material items, and internally modulated events).

2. Allowed the opportunity to escape or avoid some type of consequence (e.g., of a social, material, or activity variety) as a function of engaging in the CIB.

3. Observed to see if the response is being elicited by specific or global antecedent events (e.g., pain, reinforcer removal or loss, dramatic reduction in the schedule of reinforcement).

Rates or intensity are measured for that session in an attempt to detect patterns revealing which of those functional relationships produces the largest increase in the rate of the CIB. Often this assessment allows you to discover at least one aspect of the environment, including the social environment, you now can apply or terminate to promote alternative acceptable behaviors. Of course, in the real world, CIBs are unlikely to be a function of only one set of factors, so it pays to continue to search for other supportive conditions in effect.

Identifying Functionally Equivalent Alternative Behaviors (FEABs)

Functional assessments are based on the assumption that behaviors do not take place within a vacuum, but are related to factors in the learner's external or internal environment. Nor, when we intervene, will those behaviors simply be eradicated and be replaced by behavioral voids. Instead, we must:

---

2   For a detailed description of this method, see the following articles in the *Journal of Applied Behavior Analysis*: Carr & Durand, (1985), *18*, 111-126; Iwata et al., (1994), *27*, 197-209; Iwata et al., *27*, 215-240.

- Anticipate that when a behavior intervention target is successfully minimized, or entirely eliminated, other behaviors will take its place.

- Plan the specific reactions and consequences that are to follow the occurrence of the CIB.

- Identify (and teach, if necessary) more acceptable *functionally equivalent alternative behaviors* (FEABs).

- Set up an optimal reinforcement system for building those alternative behaviors. That is, try to ensure that the FEAB is associated with higher rates of reinforcement than the CIB.

- Try to use, or develop, FEABs that involve less effort than the CIB.

Comprehensive plans for behavior intervention must identify the FEAB before complex interventions are designed and implemented for the target behavior. Fundamental to the FEAB strategy is the assumption that events in the environment (i.e., antecedents and consequences, broadly defined) shape and control each person's behaviors. If these environmental factors are not altered, even a strong attempt to suppress a CIB will fail over the long term. Why? Because the person's original wants and needs remain or return, and the target behavior has been the only way he has fulfilled them in the past. Thus, long-term improvement is unlikely.

Take care to distinguish between functionally equivalent and teacher-selected alternative responses. The FEAB is determined from the individual's, rather than the teacher's, perspective. For example, if a learner is screaming, the FEAB is not simply replacing it with silence, although that may be precisely what the teacher wants. The FEAB is dependent upon why the learner was screaming in the first place. Learners who scream to get attention must be taught more appropriate (and hopefully more effective) means of gaining attention. Although attempting to eliminate a *behavior* from a learner's repertoire is reasonable, eliminating important *reinforcers* from the learner's life is not. Nor, as just suggested, is that likely to work. Instead, staff (or parents) and the learner can 'negotiate' when, where, and even how often, to attain the reinforcer. Remember to use the "Let's make a deal" strategies described in Chapter 4, *Powerful Reinforcement Systems.*

Many problematic behaviors gain the person access to some sort of reward, like a specific item or activity, or someone's attention. In those situations, a reasonable plan is to teach requesting the desired item calmly, using any effective modality - from speech to using pictures, signs, written words, or even just pushing a button. Perhaps the types of attention they are seeking vary according to a particular situation, as in the case of wanting recognition for their efforts versus needing assistance. In those cases, we would have to plan two distinct lessons, one to teach "How am I doing?" another for "I need help."[3]

Attention is not the only reinforcer supporting problematic behaviors. A young girl likes to run around the classroom, not for attention, but because it simply makes her 'feel good.' Were the teacher to use some arbitrary reward for calm sitting, or even punish running, it probably wouldn't work because running remains a reinforcer (or it results in an automatic reinforcer), and a readily accessible one at that. A better intervention would be to choose a FEAB that permits the girl to run, but only on request and under conditions, and at times, that would not seriously interfere with ongoing classroom routines. Alternatively, the teacher could determine when and how often the girl runs around the room and build running into the schedule accordingly. Again, the learner still gets to run around the room but the teacher gains some control over when and how much running (or perhaps a form of a high energy-expenditure activity that has a similar effect) will take place.

If escape or avoidance is the reinforcer maintaining a target response, teach a socially acceptable alternative, such as requesting a break, or signaling a desire to leave the situation or to end a conversation. Each of these would be FEABs to the original escape or avoidance target behavior. To teach this type of response, the teacher sets up a controlled situation that includes a relatively mild "dose" of what is currently avoided. For example, if when presented with difficult work a teenager hits his peer, we could prepare a card that says, "break" on it and place it nearby. Staff then would assign him a mildly difficult task, but not so complex as to generate an immediate tantrum. A second trainer would assist the learner to deliver the break card. Upon receiving the card, the teacher would guide the youth away from the work for a brief break. Over time, the backup staff's assistance could be faded, while the primary teacher would begin to increase the difficulty associated with the demand.

Sometimes the same target behavior is being supported by an array of different consequences, such as relieving discomfort, and gaining attention and/or food. Under those circumstances, promoting a single functionally equivalent response is more difficult. We need to:

1) Search harder for antecedent conditions, like insufficient rest, sleep or food, internal or external irritants, a recent loss of reinforcers, or

---

3   Carr, E.G. & Durand, V.M. (1985). Reducing behavior problems through functional communication training. *Journal of Applied Behavior Analysis, 18*, 111-126.

others that are establishing those varied consequences as reinforcers at the moment.

2) Relieve those conditions and…

3) Teach distinctively different functionally equivalent alternative behaviors to replace the problematic ones.

When Allison is suffering from an ear infection, has not had enough to eat, or is trying to learn a list of new, difficult words, she cries and whines. Unfortunately, it is difficult to detect which one factor or combination is responsible for the crying. We need to systematically vary the suspected conditions, say by having her examined by her pediatrician and providing her with pain-reducing medication and watching what happens to the rate of crying and whining. If it drops, we then can suspect it was the pain of the ear infection. The FEAB for this circumstance might be to teach her to communicate, "My ear hurts." Similarly, if the crying diminishes when she is fed, we would teach her a distinctive way to request something to eat. To test if the academic demands are too stringent, we could try to give her easier work and see if the crying stops. Then we know to teach her to ask for easier work or for help, or at least to intersperse or precede the more difficult with less difficult assignments.

Sometimes alleviating the stressful situation is beyond us; it just remains. It's hot in the house and Cele wants to cool off. There is no air conditioner or fan, nor any way to take her to the pool or let her run under the sprinkler. In fact, mom is totally occupied bathing the baby and cannot help her older daughter. A FEAB for such circumstances is to provide Cele with an alternative way to express her frustration, perhaps by teaching her to describe her feelings. We may teach Cele to express, "I'm hot," "I'm angry," "I'm sad," "I'm scared," "I'm lonely," and so on. Although caregivers may not eliminate the eliciting factor, they may more quickly offer supportive comments and actions, such as listening, sharing their own feelings, offering some alternative activity (e.g., "I'm angry, too. Let's take a walk and talk about it."), or promising to deal with the issue as soon as the baby is down for her nap, and following through accordingly.

In many cases, someone wants something that cannot be delivered at the moment. The child misinterprets, "You need to wait," as "No! Not now! Not ever!" and reacts by exploding in frustration. None of us lives in a world where all our desires can be instantly gratified. It is extremely important for everyone to learn how to wait patiently. Everybody needs to have this skill reinforced repeatedly - toddler, child, adolescent, and adult - because there is always room for improvement in this department. Given sufficient control over the reinforcer, the key elements of the lesson involve

1) cueing the availability of a reinforcer, and 2) gradually increasing the size of the delay between the learner's response and the delivery of the reinforcer. Some of these strategies were reviewed in Chapter 5, *Functional Communication*.

Just as one set of events can induce a troublesome habit pattern, and other conditions can maintain it, the same may be true of a single instance of a problematic behavior, like one tantrum. We need to keep this in mind when designing a CIB intervention plan because if we overlook both of these factors we could inadvertently make matters worse. For example, an adult at a work site may begin to tantrum in response to a boss' even mildly stated demand to perform a "difficult" task - one associated with a low probability of reinforcement. Once the tantrum has begun, reactions to the tantrum may serve to positively reinforce its continuation. If we were to focus only on the role the attention plays in sustaining the tantrum we might overlook what instigated the tantrum in the beginning - the difficulty of the work. By removing all attention, we inadvertently would be reinforcing beginning to tantrum, because demands now would be removed. While we may choose to ignore the tantrum, we would also continue with some demands, preferably interspersed with some easier requests.

Manipulating Antecedents

If you are fortunate enough to identify whatever antecedents reliably set the scene for a CIB, and if you can bring those antecedents under your control, you should succeed in heading off the CIB readily by preventing or alternating its occurrence using that trigger. Parents are universally familiar with the way young children often react when told it is bedtime. Elsewhere we have discussed how to rearrange antecedents to signal not the end of a reinforcing event, but the beginning of a new one. One is to say, "As soon as you're in bed, I'll read you a story" and, of course, keep the promise. Another is to offer a choice such as, "Do you want to go to bed with a glass of water or juice?"

One of us was acquainted with a boy we shall call Peter, whose temper tantrum was reliably set off by someone asking him to "say" something, like "Peter, say 'car.'" We did notice that he would imitate our play activities, though, especially when we reinforced his imitation with affection and praise. So we decided to build up and broaden his set of imitative skills to include sound effects. We would join him in manipulating cars and trucks, adding the roar of a truck or the siren of a fire engine, and he would imitate. Soon we snuck into our dramatic play words like "come on" and "water." Inadvertently, Peter echoed what we modeled and before long he was speaking aloud, without any need to direct him to speak, along with the inevitable tantrums.

You also can arrange antecedent events like written or spoken phrases, pictures, or other visual signals to promote behaviors incompatible with the inappropriate ones. It is important to make these antecedents clear, while consistently pairing them with reinforcing consequences. In other words, *keep your promises*. "Let's work on your arithmetic workbook until the timer buzzes. Then we can stop and take a play or snack break." By carefully scheduling a timer to sound in a shorter time than you know his attention typically lasts, you can establish the signal as a reliable indicator that reinforcement is on its way. Later, over time, you can begin to stretch the time interval, seeing to it that the youngster works longer without resorting to a CIB as an escape tactic.

Differentially Reinforcing Acceptable Behaviors

The strategies we have just described require that we reinforce just the acceptable behaviors but not the others. When we concentrate on increasing some, but not other, behaviors, we are using a method called *differential reinforcement*. The more systematically we differentially reinforce, the more rapidly change will take place. This strategy requires dispensing considerable reinforcement - much more than any the problem manages to garner - for the behavior we are attempting to promote. The right way is to *"catch 'em being good."* Yet, this obvious solution is easier said than done. Parents and classroom teachers are beset by a multitude of responsibilities, requiring their intense concentration. Larger group situations compound the difficulty even further, especially when a class includes several learners, each of whom displays varying problems. Maintaining the level of reinforcement that effectively promotes ongoing improvement in behavior requires a well-crafted system.

There are several differential reinforcement techniques from which to choose (see Table 5-1). Some are based on a period of time passing during which the CIB has been absent. In that case, we are using *differential reinforcement of other behavior (DRO)*. In this case we can choose to reinforce any behavior, as long as it is not the target one. For example, ten minutes have gone by without Phyllis having a tantrum. She may happen to be working at a task or staring out the window, tying her shoe, rocking, or singing. Anything goes, as long as she is not engaged in a tantrum. By contrast, we can select one particular alternative behavior to reinforce. In that case, we are using *differential reinforcement of alternative behavior (DRA)*. For example, Lou can be called on only when he raises his hand but never when he shouts out. Or we could wait until we see a behavior that is physically incompatible with the behavior we are attempting to discourage. This is *differential reinforcement of incompatible behavior (DRI)*. For example, Toni slaps herself in the face whenever she walks down a hallway. We could reward her for carrying an object with two hands, or for keeping her hands in her pockets or at her sides. As long as she has both hands on the object, in her pockets, or at her sides, they are not available to slap her face. The crucial element is to assure that reinforcing consequences do not follow the CIB (see Iwata, 1993). That is, the CIB must undergo extinction to whatever extent is feasible, while the rate of reinforcement for other behaviors continues to increase.

Sometimes the problem behavior persists to such an extent that the acceptable alternative only happens every once in a long while. In that case we can use a progressive *differential reinforcement technique (DROP)*. We administer a small reward when the problematic target has been absent for a very brief period of time, and correspondingly larger reinforcers as that time period lengthens. For example, one piece of candy after a minute, but a full bar after ten. Use this progressive DRO technique, too, when you decide that a target behavior occurs so frequently that attempting to eradicate it completely would be unrealistic, or when you conclude that completely eliminating a CIB may not be a fair long-term goal. Either of these would be acceptable provided it occurred just once in a while; a two-year-old child's temper tantrum is an example.

Should it be too much of a challenge to demand the complete absence of the target during a given a time interval, you can instead concentrate on gradually lowering its rate. In this case, reinforcement is triggered when the number of times the CIB occurs falls below a given level within a time block. Ulrica slaps herself 10 times a minute. Should the number of slaps drop to, say, eight times per minute, she would receive a reward. Be sure, though, to wait for a few moments during which the CIB is *not* ongoing to deliver the reinforcer, otherwise the *CIB-Reinforcement* connection may be reestablished. As the rate of the unacceptable behavior begins to fall, you can then tighten the rate requirement to, say, no more than six per minute, and so on. Here you gradually are rewarding progress toward diminishing (not necessarily eliminating) the frequency of the CIB. The term that applies to this method of scheduling reinforcement for only responding at some pre-selected low rate, is called *differential reinforcement of low rates*, or DRL (where "L" stands for low-rate). The procedure focuses on gradual improvement, not immediate perfection.

Here is an illustration of a creative way a teacher applied a DRL method: To communicate to a learner just how much screaming would be tolerated, the teacher provided the boy with a card containing ten stickers. Every time the boy screamed, the teacher would calmly remove one sticker. If at least one sticker remained at the end of one hour, the boy could trade it in for some preferred item. Over time, as the boy consistently earned his rewards, the teacher began to reduce the number of stickers on the card. The card now only contained nine, then, assuming success, eventually dropped to eight, then seven, and so on. This procedure can help to gradually reduce the rate of the CIB without requiring its complete elimination right away.

Another variation is to remove more highly preferred reinforcers contingent on the CIB, while less preferred reinforcers remain available. For example, one teacher placed three of the learner's most preferred toys on a shelf where he could see, but not reach, them. One was his most favored, the second a little less, and the third the least preferred of the three. When the learner engaged in the CIB, the teacher would remove the most preferred toy from the shelf, leaving the other two. If he engaged in the CIB again within the target period, she would remove the second favorite toy. In this manner, the learner could see that, while he may have lost the opportunity for the preferred toy, others remained available for him to access when he made appropriate improvements.

Combining strategies can be tempting, such as using the same token system to reward good academic performance and to remove tokens for CIBs. More effective, though, is to have one system for *good work* (whether academic or involving any other performance criteria) and another for *good behavior* (such as a DRL for yelling).

Table 6-1

Differential Reinforcement Procedures

Procedure	Behavior(s) (Bs) Reinforced (R+_	Change over time
DRO	Any other behavior	Gradually increase interval over sets
DROP	Any other behavior	Gradually increase interval within a set
DRA	A specific alternative	Increase interval or increase B to R+ ration
DRI	An incompatible alternative	Increase interval or increase B to R+ ration
DRL		Increase time or reduce number within time

Advantages and Disadvantages of Differential Reinforcement

Each of these differential reinforcement (DR_) systems has its advantages and disadvantages. However, staff needs to incorporate some kind of differential reinforcement procedure within the daily program whenever a severely inappropriate behavior is regularly displayed. While differential reinforcement schedules would be expected to be most effective when CIBs are maintained by gaining some type of reward, the procedures also serve to provide everyone, including those whose problematic behaviors are controlled by escape/avoidance contingencies, with a context rich with reinforcement.

Practical Hints for Using Differential Reinforcement

Remember to *monitor the absence* of the CIB. Do you recall being plagued by flies or mosquitoes at a recent picnic or outing? Noticing their presence required little effort. "If those creatures would only go away, I'd be so grateful!" is what you probably were thinking. But right now, unless you've just been out of doors, you probably haven't given any thought to how wonderful the absence of those pests is. Just as we fail to notice the absence of irritants, like the fact that it is neither too hot nor cold in the room, that we aren't sick, or that no flies or mosquitoes are tormenting us at the moment, we are unlikely to notice the *absence* of a nuisance behavior. That is unfortunate, because attempting to reduce a behavior by means of a *differential reinforcement schedule* requires that we take action when the target behavior is *not* taking place. Given the myriad of other demands on their time and attention, parents, educators, or caregivers may find it difficult to remember to differentially reinforcer the absence of the behavior. Fortunately, a number of timing and signaling devices are available to remind everyone to adhere to the differential reinforcement plan.

Setting a kitchen timer or stopwatch to sound a tone every fixed or variable amount of time is one simple method. To encourage steadier good behavior, obscure the exact time when reinforcers will be delivered by using a variable-interval, rather than the fixed-interval, schedule. Here, you set the timer around a given average, like approximately every five minutes.

As we noted in Chapter 4, we also can prepare a CD with tones or beeps recorded at time intervals averaging around some set interval, such as 1, 2, 3, 5, 7, or 10 minutes. When a tone sounds, staff momentarily stop and reward those displaying behavior that favorably conforms to the differential reinforcement contingency. CDs can be programmed to combine two or more sets of tones associated with two or more variable intervals - a chime for Henrietta and a piano chord for Archie. With replay on the CD player, one can operate the CD continuously throughout the day.

You can use a series of recorded signals like these also when systematically increasing the length of the interval over the course of the school year. You might begin with a CD containing signals for a DRO 2-minute interval. When the learner's responding reaches a pre-determined level (e.g., 80% of the intervals are target free), following a rule to increase the intervals by no more than 50%, you might switch to a DRO 3-minute interval. Now the learner gradually receives fewer rewards for increasingly longer stretches of time containing only appropriate behaviors. We have used this system with some adolescents with autism. At first, they were allowed a sip of soda within the classroom approximately every two minutes, provided the problematic behavior had not occurred in the interim. Two years later, at the work site, the intervals were up to two hours and the reward consisted of allowing the youths to buy and drink a can of soda.

Reacting to Contextually Inappropriate Behavior

Although we heavily favor promoting functional alternatives to contextually inappropriate behaviors as the primary approach, some CIBs are deemed by responsible parties to be so dangerous (e.g., producing tissue damage, injuring others), destructive (e.g., breaking equipment, costly materials or furniture), disruptive (e.g., commanding attention with exceedingly loud noises, seriously interfering with other's ongoing activities), or obnoxious (e.g., smearing feces, masturbating in public), that they must also be responded to directly. As with DRO and other reward-based systems, teachers, parents, and other caregivers all must be consistent in the way they react. For someone with a long history of spitting at other people, even the best preventative systems cannot assure that you won't be spat upon again. What will you do? The key is neither to be surprised nor to get creative. There must be a team plan guiding your actions following such behaviors.

An array of behavioral procedures is available, including presenting something the person clearly does not want at the time (i.e., punishment), such as an arduous work requirement or a reprimand, or withdrawing or terminating reinforcement for a time period (i.e., response cost or timeout from positive reinforcement). Such procedures also need to be applied with exquisite care, because subtle differences in the way the procedures are applied, like how often, intensely, rapidly, with what cues, and so on, can speed up or delay short- and long-term success. The use of these strategies requires optimal personnel training and management. Comprehensive descriptions of these interventions, along with guidelines for their appropriate application, can be found in Sulzer-Azaroff & Mayer (1991).

Additionally, considerable controversy has been, and continues to be, associated with these direct reductive strategies. In the first place, people's opinions differ about what constitutes acceptable and unacceptable behavior. Secondly, although some consider given interventions relatively benign, others see them as overly harsh, immoral, or otherwise inappropriate. Discussing at length the primary issues associated with the use of aversive, or seemingly aversive, procedures is beyond the scope of this chapter. Suffice it to say that the individual teacher should avoid unilaterally deciding how to proceed in attempting to eradicate a given behavior. This is a job properly delegated to a Peer Review and/or Human Rights Committee, composed of wise, respected and informed professionals, parents, and other community representatives.

Furthermore, systematic review of direct reductive procedures should not be limited to those deemed "aversive." Interventions that appear "non-aversive" nevertheless may be detrimental or harmful, producing unwarranted negative side effects (cf., Balsam & Bondy, 1983), or be virtually ineffective. For example, although rocking a 15-year-old boy with autism while feeding him with a bottle may not sound aversive, or may conform to someone's theory about what the youth needs, many would object strongly to such an intervention on ethical and/or humanitarian grounds.

Many local, state, and national educational and rehabilitation agencies have adopted ethical or peer review systems. In Delaware's public school program for learners with autism, for instance, a system of review exists for all interventions designed to reduce the rate, duration, or severity of a CIB among learners with autism. All such interventions are defined as *behavior intervention procedures*, regardless of whether they contain intrusive or aversive components. A Peer Review Committee and a Human Rights Committee (PRC and HRC), composed entirely of individuals not associated with the public school program, annually review all potential CIB intervention procedures. These committees classify proposed procedures within one of three categories: 1) proceed with this intervention, 2) proceed with the intervention but report monthly data on learner behavioral outcomes to the PRC, or 3) use this procedure only after case-by-case review and approval by both committees. Often the very same procedure can vary from one to the next application only in terms of the size of the time interval, the number of reinforcers or repetitions of a work requirement, or some other parameter. With such variations, the rate of reinforcers, and/or the level or intensity of the penalties, influences which of the categories applies. A very brief timeout - planned ignoring for five seconds - is quite different from isolating someone for fifteen or twenty minutes. Therefore the former might be assigned to the first category, the latter to the third.

The particular interventions used within a program should be based upon effective interventions described in the applied literature. Ones in Delaware include minimally intrusive procedures, such as redirection, planned ignoring, mild verbal reprimand, or briefly stopping an ongoing activity, as well as more intrusive procedures, such as isolated time-out, or contingent exercise. Although no intervention is forbidden *a priori*, few highly controversial procedures have been used since these policies have been adopted.

Each intervention plan contains a generic description, a listing of behaviors commonly addressed by the intervention, and the parametric details needed to implement the procedure. For example, if a plan calls for picking up blocks or toothpicks from the floor and putting them into a box, then staff must detail how many blocks will be used, the degree of staff assistance, how long the intervention should last, how many staff may be necessary to complete the intervention, and other details.

Summary

In and of itself, any given behavior is neutral. Its context is what may make it inappropriate. Preventing or reducing the rates of contextually inappropriate behaviors requires a multifaceted approach, including the organization taking general precautions, and applying several specific methods for promoting wellbeing. Conducting a formal assessment to determine the function of the CIB is especially important because it often allows us to identify and apply a strategy to promote a more acceptable functionally equivalent alternative response. These alternative responses need to be viewed from the individual's, not the teacher's or parent's, perspective, and designed to serve the same function as the CIB. Access to desired items, activities, attention, or assistance, or escape from, or avoidance of, unwanted circumstances are typical examples. Just as they do to support any reinforcement program, antecedents - such as words, pictures, gestures, or signs - can foster the change process.

Most essential, though, is the reinforcement program itself. In the case of CIB reduction, this involves two operations: 1) assuring that the acceptable behavior is powerfully reinforced, while 2) the unacceptable behavior is not. This *differential reinforcement* process may be conducted according to various schedules, depending upon *what specific behavior* is the focus of change and *when* and *how often* reinforcement is to be accessed. Given the natural tendency of teachers, staff, parents, and the rest of us to overlook gradual improvements, we have offered a number of tips for reminding ourselves to adhere to the selected reinforcement schedules.

There are times when CIBs are so dangerous, destructive, or socially inappropriate that they cannot be ignored and must be responded to directly. Punishment, response cost, timeout, and other directly reductive methods need, along with the more benign ones, to be applied according to very clear standards, including oversight by a peer review or human rights committee. Along with ethical and humanitarian considerations, the approach must be decided on the basis of scientifically documented evidence of effectiveness with similar individuals.

Chapter 6 Resources

Preventing and Reducing Contextually Inappropriate Behaviors

To	Read
Learn about the role of punishment and coercion in society and our daily lives, the impact it has on those who apply it and those who receive it, and how to change ourselves to make the world a better place.	Sidman, M. (1989). *Coercion and its fallout.* Boston, MA: Authors Cooperative, Inc. Publishers.
Learn how to conduct a functional analysis.	The following articles in the *Journal of Applied Behavior Analysis*: Carr & Durand, (1985), *18*, 111-126; Iwata et al., (1994) *27*, 197-209; Iwata et al., (1994) *27*, 215-240.
Gain an overview of scientifically documented programs to "promote effective change and reduce or prevent severe problems from occurring in the natural environment... p. 4".	Koegel, L.K., Koegel, R.L., Kellegrew, D. & Mullen, K. (1996). Parent education for prevention and reduction of severe problem behaviors. In L.K. Koegel, R.L. Koegel & G. Dunlap (Eds.) *Positive behavioral support: Including people with difficult behavior in the community* (pp. 3-30). Baltimore, MD: Paul Brooks Publishing Co.
Mount an argument to support early intervention with problem behavior and design a comprehensive treatment for children with serious behavior problems.	Dunlap, G. & Fox, L. (1996). Early intervention and serious problem behaviors. In L.K. Koegel, R.L. Koegel & G. Dunlap (Eds.) *Positive behavioral support: Including people with difficult behavior in the community* (pp. 31-50). Baltimore, MD: Paul Brooks Publishing Co.

Attain an overview of current behavior analytic research in autism in the areas of disruptive and destructive and self-stimulatory behavior, language development and social skills.	Frea, W.D. & Vittemberg, G.L (2000). Behavioral interventions for children with autism. In J. Austin & J.E. Carr (Eds.). *Handbook of applied behavior analysis* (pp. 247-273). Reno, NV: Context Press.

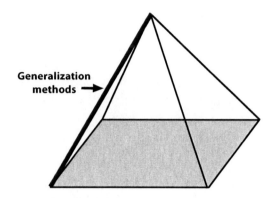

Generalization
methods →

7

Generalization

"No, Marie," shouts her mother, as the child lunges for a slice of bread and stuffs it into her mouth. Marie begins to howl and hit herself in the face while her mother sighs with frustration. "Marie, stop it. You're twelve years old. Too big to act like that."

Marie's mom, Wendy, begins to replay in her head the conversation she has had with herself so many times before. Her daughter is beginning to mature. What will happen when Marie is a full-grown adult? Wendy wonders if she still will be able to handle her. How about when she herself ages and dies? What then? How about getting a life of her own?

Then she thinks about the parent's meeting she attended last week. Among the points the speaker made is that hoping children with significant special needs eventually will become more self-sufficient is reasonable. Today many do live away from their parents, even caring for themselves in community living quarters with minimal guidance and support from social service agencies. But those young adults who have acquired some crucial communicative and activities-of-daily-living skills, and can manage their emotions, will lead far richer lives.

Another of the speaker's points that struck her was that persistent behaviors - good, bad, and indifferent - tend to have a function. The things people repeat, including hurting themselves, most often happen because they have produced something for the individual. Why would Marie be hitting herself in the face? Maybe she became agitated because in the past this usually led to getting some snacks.

A few days later Wendy meets with Marie's teacher to talk about how she might help Marie to ask for food instead of grabbing it or hurting herself. They discuss various alternative objectives. Shall they teach her better ways to ask for food, ways to get it for herself, or both? They decide on the latter because that will serve all the purposes Wendy had identified: enabling Marie to ask for her food, while becoming more self-sufficient at the same time.

There are many different kinds of lessons that Wendy could conduct to enable her daughter to achieve those objectives, but they decide to look toward the future. A good first step will be to teach Marie to prepare her own sandwiches - not just one kind, but several. There will be different kinds of bread: white, rye, whole-wheat; rolls, pita bread. Fillings too will vary: peanut butter and jelly; cheese and ham; maybe later even tuna salad.

At first the task seems overwhelming. So much is involved, including gathering the necessary utensils and ingredients, using them safely and correctly, and assembling the whole thing. Yet the teacher was wise in guiding Wendy to take this real-life approach, for a number of reasons. She knew that Marie liked to eat those particular sandwiches.

1. The activity would therefore contain its own natural reinforcement. Learning to make sandwiches would help Marie to become more self-sufficient.

2. Teaching Marie to obtain her food in a less damaging and more socially acceptable way would be advantageous for all.

3. By setting the lessons in the natural environment, Wendy could make good use of *incidental teaching*. This is a big advantage because it has an excellent chance for promoting increasingly complex, relevant, and general learning.

4. By using varied ingredients, Marie would have to learn a variety of skills - not just one. These could come in handy for other purposes later on.

A few weeks later, one hour ahead of their usual weekend lunchtime, Wendy is supervising Marie in the sandwich-making operation. Velcro®-backed pictures of ham, and cheese, plus labels from the mayonnaise, peanut butter, and from two kinds of jelly jars are displayed on the cover of her PECS communication book. Similarly, pictures of dark and light bread are affixed to the breadbox. On the table is a breadboard and knife. Wendy waits. Marie stands, flicking her fingers. Wendy touches her gently and says, "Let's make sandwiches," pointing to the breadbox. Marie gets a picture of white bread and hands it to her mother. Her mom exclaims, "White bread!" and gives her daughter two slices. They continue with the process, until Marie has put together a reasonable peanut butter and jelly sandwich for herself. Eating it is the best part.

In the above episode, we can see the cleverness with which the lesson was designed. Not only did it permit Marie to learn to make choices, communicate, and perform a skill, but it also set up a situation favoring *generalization* and *maintenance*. Marie would learn to make different kinds of sandwiches and because she eats lunch daily, the skill would have a good chance of maintaining.

Why Discuss Generalization So Early?

Maybe you're wondering why we have placed a chapter on the way behavior spreads from one stimulus situation, or from one response, to another (i.e., generalization) ahead of material devoted to teaching *per se*. Shouldn't we teach a skill until it is mastered and then begin planning for generalization? Well, behavior is always sensitive to changes in the environment, as well as changes in the manner in which an action is formed. These changes begin immediately and do not wait for us to complete some initial 'phase' of learning. Just as we stress that planning for reinforcement must precede the start of a lesson, where the lesson is going in the long run needs to be planned before we start the lesson. For instance, maybe without further consideration, we proceed to drill a skill in a quiet, separate area day after day until our learner 'masters it.' Then, we will plan for this skill to 'show up' in the real world. However, all of the time we spent in this unusual situation will actually interfere with our hopes to see it occur in other situations and in other circumstances.

We have noticed that in their eagerness to *do* something, teachers often wait far too long to begin planning for generalization. They may neglect to anticipate when, where, and with whom the learner ultimately will need to make use of the skill, thereby failing to prepare necessary supportive strategies. For example, in conducting Phase I of the Picture Exchange Communication System™ (PECS), Donna has just successfully taught Denise to exchange a single picture for a piece of candy. The only person Donna teaches Denise to give the picture to is Donna herself, and no one else. They practice this exchange over a period of several weeks, while remaining within arms-reach of one another. What would happen at this point if Donna suddenly moved across the room from Denise? Or Donna suddenly appeared with one of Denise's favorite toys instead of the candy? Or, if they were out together in the community? Or, if someone else were holding the candy? Probably in each of these new conditions Denise would fail to communicate appropriately. Many would describe the situation as, "Denise's failure to generalize."

From our perspective, Denise did not fail at anything. It is not the learner's responsibility to generalize - it is the responsibility of the teacher. More often than not, generalization failures are due to the way teaching is structured, not to some deficiency in the learner. The way to avoid this kind of trap is to plan for generalization well before we begin a lesson. That is, before starting, we should know in the broadest sense, exactly what is to be accomplished. In this chapter, with this long-term goal in mind, we address generalization before sharing our perspective on how to design effective lessons.

Types of Generalization

There are two different kinds of generalization. One is called *stimulus generalization*. Stimulus generalization describes a situation in which a response learned under one set of circumstances occurs under a range of similar conditions, like with other people or materials, or at varied places or times. If after Wendy taught Marie to make her sandwich at home with white bread, the youngster made different kinds of sandwiches in different locations, we would say that Marie's sandwich-making skills had generalized across those different stimulus situations.

The other category of generalization is *response generalization*[1]. With response generalization, it is not the situation or the circumstances that change, but the behavior itself that varies. In Marie's case, if after she learned to spread hard butter she also could spread soft mayonnaise, we might say her skills related to the pressure she exerts on the knife have generalized to suit the new demands.

In and of themselves, stimulus generalization or response generalization are neither good nor bad. It depends on the circumstances. Often we hope a skill we teach will generalize to a new situation. We may teach children in a classroom to calculate the amount of change they should receive when making a purchase, with the intention that the learner will transfer or generalize the skill in the real world. Sometimes stimulus generalization is inappropriate. Treating pennies the same as dimes is a big mistake - often referred to as *overgeneralization*. So is wearing a nightgown out of doors. Shunning someone who is harmless, but who resembles in one irrelevant way a person who has harmed us in the past is over-generalizing, a form of prejudice.

---

1   Some use the term "response induction" to describe this phenomenon.

The same is true of response generalization. Varying the way Marie applied spreads to the bread was quite adaptive. But if she used a variation - such as using a sharp knife and pulling it toward herself - that could be dangerous. If you drive a stick shift but rent a car with automatic transmission, you will need to adjust the sequence of your driving responses to operate the car smoothly; but if you vary the form of your driving responses too much, as in the case of over-steering, you may end up in a ditch.

The important point here is that, before you plan a lesson, you need to refine the objectives to include how much of what kind of generalization you are hoping to achieve. You also want to be very clear about the opposite: what limitations to generalization you want to happen. If you were about to have open-heart surgery, you can bet you would want your surgeon to adjust her skills (i.e., response generalization) to working with your own distinctive cardiovascular system (i.e., stimulus generalization). But you sure wouldn't want so much variation that she cut too deeply or treated you as if you were a much smaller or larger person.

We also should point out that teaching in several situations, or teaching variations of a skill, are not direct indicators of generalization. That is, if we teach Scott to say hello to three people, and he does as he's been taught, he has merely acquired the specific target skill. Only if he were to say hello to someone not included in the set, or say hello in some manner not yet taught, would we say that generalization has occurred. The key is to test for generalization in novel circumstances or behavioral forms.

Promoting Stimulus Generalization

As already mentioned, teachers and parents often assume that generalization will happen "automatically." If learners learn in the classroom to exchange a picture of a ball for a real ball, or to follow the rules for organizing a paragraph, to spell a word, to assemble a widget, or to participate in a PECS training session, they should apply the skill

Stimulus Factors
People
Environmental variations
Materials
Time

properly in real life situations. Stokes and Baer (1977) have labeled this the *Train and Hope* approach to generalization. Unfortunately, training and hoping for spontaneous generalization frequently fails. This chapter focuses on ways to promote wanted generalization[2]. Conveniently, behavior

2   By contrast, if the issue is avoiding over-generalization, you should refer to the material on errorless learning and error correction.

analysts have learned many ways to promote appropriate generalizations across people, places, materials, and responses, as well as how to maintain such changes across time. We summarize and illustrate those here:

1.   Assess the environment

The first thing to do is to determine stimulus factors such as with whom, where, with what, and when the given response and related responses should or shouldn't occur. We do this assessment to ensure that we haven't overlooked some important detail. For example, you are teaching your learner, who is applying for a job, to follow the proper steps with each potential employer, not only in simulated conditions but in actuality, by mail, over the telephone, and in person, during normal working hours. By comparison, acting correctly in the classroom is of relatively little value if behavior is not properly controlled outside.

2.   Teach to natural reinforcers

Look at each of the settings and see who and what stands ready to reinforce, as naturally as possible, the action you are teaching. Train to those conditions. If you want to teach a youth how to shop, bring him to a store where a shopkeeper naturally would deliver an item on request. Be sure you don't need to go shopping at the time so that you can completely focus on teaching and reinforcing the new skill. Find out who can be counted upon to comply or make a big fuss about any new accomplishment. Maybe Grandma and Grandpa's house is the best place to teach requesting a video or how to set up the wading pool.

3.   Teach across trainers and other people

Next, in addition to any discrete-trial training, arrange to have as many of the people who will be present in the learner's various natural settings teach the skill in those different places: the parents in the home, in the park, at the beach; teachers in the classroom, hallways, cafeteria, gymnasium; caregivers out in the community; supervisors on the job. The more of these people who learn the *Pyramid Approach*, the more rapidly and effectively change will occur.

4.   Use many examples of the same or very similar materials

If you are teaching a learner how to use a pen, have several pens available from the beginning - the same would be true for using spoons, forks, and other utensils. When attempting to expand language skills, rather than use only one object to be associated with 'red,' to promote rapid generalization you would want to have many different red objects. Stokes and Baer (1977) discussed using sufficient exemplars, and others have described this as using multiple exemplars. To further promote generalization, you also would want to assure that any objects used to teach colors also are used to teach other attributes, such as size or number. In this way, no object is uniquely associated with one attribute and no attribute is uniquely associated with one object.

5. Teach loosely

Closely related to this approach is what Stokes and Baer (1977) referred to as *training loosely*. Many times, we become so focused on getting the correct response to be correctly repeated that we begin to 'groove' the response. That is, we repeat under such narrow circumstances that the response becomes 'stuck' - unable to get out of the groove we created and into other situations. That means if you are trying to teach someone to ask for a ball, vary the kinds of balls available: softballs, large rubber balls of different colors, footballs, small rubber balls, and so on. This prevents the learner's response from attaching an irrelevant feature, like color or size, to the concept of ball. What you want is for him to use appropriate descriptive adjectives later on for the general class "balls," and to avoid requesting and receiving the exact same object every single time and showing frustration when that doesn't happen. This rationale also is the reason we suggest that in teaching PECS that you vary the teachers, their roles, the materials, and so on early in training.

6. Minimize prompting

We will discuss the use of prompts more clearly in Chapter 9, but suffice it to say here that prompts are things teachers do to help a learner perform a task. Over time, we must get rid of our prompts. However, the more heavy handed we are from the start with our prompts - we repeat them over and over, we use many different types of prompts at the same time, etc. - the harder it will be to eliminate the prompt and promote generalized independence. Prompt as little as necessary to evoke the response. Pause for a reasonable time after you prompt. If what you try isn't working to help the learner perform the target skill, try something else. Give learners a chance to respond correctly without further help.

7. Spot check for "mastered" skills

Mastering a response is not the same as retaining the response. A youngster may seem to precisely follow her schedule for a day or two but then appear to have lost this ability. We need to probe by taking data periodically to see if the newly acquired behavior is persisting intact or deteriorating, and re-teach accordingly. There is a natural degree of response variation for all behaviors. No one performs at 'their best' every moment.

Therefore, spot checking skills that appear to be intact will help you decide whether the learner is merely 'having a bad day' or truly needs some refined teaching.

8. Fade prompt levels and thin reinforcement schedules gradually

None of us is rewarded for every single effort we make. Our learners need to be prepared for irregular payoffs, and diminishing guidance. The best way to promote persistence over time is to lessen the prompts and reinforcers so gradually and systematically that the learner fails to notice the change[3]. One strategy is to have your learners take turns with one another in groups of increasing sizes. Performing in small groups is a natural and effective way for learners to learn to tolerate delay and react under less intense guidance. Also, the prompts can shift from the carefully arranged teacher-directed tell, show, and guide methods to those inherent in social situations as the other learners model the correct response.

Promoting Response Generalization

As in teaching for stimulus generalization, you should identify in advance permissible response variations for each of the skills you are teaching. Then you will teach those selected variations. The art teacher might encourage and reinforce the learners' use of different kinds of brush strokes to obtain different effects. Children just learning to communicate could be given what they indicate they want, whether they make the request in the form of a picture, a sign, or a spoken or written word.

Response Factors
Number
Rate
Duration
Complexity
Acccuracy
Durability

By varying the materials used within a lesson you also assure variations in the responses under those different circumstances. If you were coaching an ice hockey team, you would be sure the players experience all the kinds of ice conditions they might be faced with: smooth, rough, wavy, and so on. These modifications of the ice would allow you to teach them how to adapt their movements and rates

---

3   Psychophysics used the term *just noticeable differences* (JNDs) to describe the degree of change in a procedure below which the individual cannot sense any differences. Essentially, this is what we suggest you do when you diminish how heavily you prompt, and how regularly and frequently you reinforce a response.

of speed to those changing situations. Marie's mother would show her daughter how to press down on the butter harder than on the mayonnaise (but not too hard because the bread might tear apart, an error that then would need to be corrected). In these cases, you will note a combination of methods: a) teaching the learner to differentiate one condition or material from another, then b) adapting the form of the response accordingly.

1. *Fully describe the various response qualities*

Determine in advance the kind of response variation you wish to see transfer and maintain. Then you will know when to provide reinforcement and when to withhold it.

A.   Number of responses

How many times should the response be repeated?

Examples:

- I will do 10 push-ups.
- My teenage daughter will learn 12 new Spanish words.
- Each sales representative will make 30 calls.
- The trainee should fill 200 envelopes.

B. Rate

How frequently should the response occur per unit of time?

Examples:

- The trainee should fold 10 inserts a minute.
- I will work out three times a week.
- My four-year-old son will brush his teeth twice a day.
- Each sales representative will make 30 calls a day.

C. Duration of responses

How long should a given behavior persist?

Examples:

- My work-out will be twenty minutes long.
- Heather will participate in organized games on the playground for at least five minutes.
- The learner should remain seated at the work bench for 15 min-

utes.

- The boss will spend ten minutes a week out on the shop floor.

D. Complexity

How varied are the components of the response?

Examples:

- Does the learner spend all his time folding enclosures, or does he prepare envelopes for mailing: folding the enclosure, slipping it into the envelope, sealing and stamping the envelope?

- The work-out routine consists of stretching, aerobics, and upper and lower body toning.

- There are 29 different steps included in the "Job-Club" method for finding a job[4].

- The child will increase her MLU (mean-length-of-utterance) from 1.5 to 2.5 words.

E. Accuracy

How closely does the response conform to the definitions of a correct response?

Examples:

- Do all four corners overlap exactly? Does the learner place the stamp in the upper right-hand quadrant?

- Each of the 29 steps of the "Job Club" method match the description in the book, according to our checklists.

- Our sales staff follows the script 99% for making an effective sales call.

F. Durability

How long should the skill be maintained?

Examples:

- Does the response, as described above, persist for at least three months?

- If we were to return a year later, would we see the boss spend at least ten minutes a day on the shop floor?

---

4   Azrin, N.H. & Besalel, V.B. (1982). *Finding a job.* Berkeley, CA: Ten Speed Press

Assessing the environment also allows us to predict how likely it is that the behavior of concern will be reinforced and not punished. You may teach a learner to fold inserts very meticulously, but this takes more time than the hiring organization is willing to invest. Now you have a dilemma: teaching the person to operate more rapidly, and perhaps less precisely, or negotiating a different set of standards to be applied with your learner. All of this could have been avoided had details of the work environment been investigated in advance.

2. *Strategies to promote changes in response rate*

Teachers frequently design lessons directed toward helping learners learn *a particular skill in the presence of particular environmental cues*. To eliminate any ultimate dependence on prompts, teachers gradually shift from the prompt to the natural cues. When attempting to shift controlling stimuli, we suggest that teachers avoid presenting the same verbal (or other) prompts repeatedly and instead substitute a different prompt strategy of the type discussed in Chapter 9. Thus, when teaching a child to imitate saying a word, the teacher presents the stimulus once and waits a set period of time before adding another visual, physical, or gestural prompt. The teacher controls the pace of the lesson by beginning each trial with a distinct cue or prompt.

When our focus is on response generalization, though, our goal sometimes is related more to rate than to stimulus control per se. For example, suppose our intent is for a child to run faster, not merely to have the child run when we say, "run." The way we prompt learners to run faster would be quite different from teaching when to run. To illustrate, one adaptive physical education teacher's concern was to improve children's cardiovascular performance - to raise their heart rates and breathing levels - by teaching them to run longer and faster. He used many different verbal and physical prompts and aids. Whether learners were running independently or in response to verbal prompts, or having their hands held throughout the run, was not important. What did count was that they ran at a particular speed for a given length of time. The teacher's goal was not to achieve some type of stimulus control as in the objective, "Given the instruction, '*run*,' the child will run," but rather to have learners reach some specific rate and duration.

Watch a coach working with her players in the weight room. She shouts encouragement to get players to try harder, go faster, and persist. The potential harmful effects of repeated verbal prompts are of little concern because achieving stimulus control over the responses is not the main objective.

Does coaching sometimes occur in the natural course of events, and can such cases help suggest different teaching strategies? We all have watched parents interact with their very young children beginning to babble. Parents tend to group their 'prompts' into bursts and then pause. They do not just say, "Say 'ba'" once, and then pause for 5 seconds before repeating the single presentation. Instead, they repeat the stimulus: "ba, ba, ba, ba, BA!" often with a rising inflection before pausing. Parents also use differential reinforcement in a way that guarantees the child's success! No matter what the child does, the parent pleasantly continues to model various sounds. Whenever the child responds in kind the parent provides more social reinforcement by way of changes in inflection, broader smiles, louder praise, claps, tickles, and so on. Should the parental modeling be construed as prompting, contrary to our suggestion that we avoid repeating verbal prompts? Or should the modeling be viewed as coaching (i.e., interspersing feedback and reinforcement among the prompts)? Our take on the matter is that because the parents are not trying to achieve stimulus control over specific responses, these repetitions are much more focused on encouraging a broad response class - any kind of vocal responding. Neither are the parents expecting their child to say a single "ba," nor the child to repeat the same number of "bas" as they modeled.

Good teachers act like coaches when their concern is promoting response generalization[5]. Watch effective coaches and you will notice them using a procedure called *differential reinforcement of high rates* (abbreviated DRH). They organize reinforcement to be set for delivery when the response is repeated a particular number of times within a given time limit. The youth stuffing fliers into envelopes earns his soda if he has finished at least 100 in an hour or less. The teacher praises his pupil's oral reading when the passage is read correctly in less than thirty seconds. The way to use this method is to build up the response-per-time ratio requirement gradually, in small increments - 30 per hour, then 40, 50, 60, and so on. If the learner falters several times in a row, drop back a bit and later proceed more cautiously.

Another related strategy involves allowing the learner to control the pace of a lesson. During a sight-word drill, the teacher controlled the pace of the lesson by handing the learner the words one-by-one, asking the learner to place a printed word on its corresponding object. Under those circumstances, he successfully placed 26 words in 45 minutes. We then

---

5   For detailed descriptions of strategies that promote response fluency, see Johnson, K. R. & Lyang, T.V.J. (1992). Breaking the structuralist barrier: Literacy and numeracy with fluency. *American Psychologist, 47*, 1475-1490 and Lindsley, O.R. (1992) Precision teaching: Discoveries and effects. *Journal of Applied Behavior Analysis, 25*, 51-57. For the influence of behavioral momentum see Mace, F.C. et al., (1988) Behavioral momentum in the treatment of noncompliance. *Journal of Applied Behavior Analysis, 21*, 123-141.

rearranged the lesson by placing 10 objects on the table and handing the learner all 10 printed words. He correctly placed the words on all 10 items in 40 seconds. Of course, had he made discrimination errors, the teacher would have had to respond appropriately; but by focusing on improving his rate, his performance was significantly smoother.

Summary

Just as learning about scuba-diving only in a classroom would inadequately prepare us to try diving in the sea on our own, teaching our learners in a classroom and then hoping they will practice their newly learned skills whenever and wherever needed often turns out to have been overly optimistic. Instead, for any new skill we plan to teach we need to have considered many factors. Are we seeking stimulus or response generalization or both? After answering that question we then need to describe in detail the nature of the generalization we would like to see happen. We need to assess the stimulus factors present in the environment to see whether we have described our instructional objectives in sufficient detail. Included in the list are people, environmental variations, materials, time, and so on. Ideally we need to determine what reinforcers are in place currently, so we can teach to these natural reinforcers. Then we can teach sequentially across these different environments, adjusting to the circumstances that vary from one to the next. Included in the list of response generalization elements are number, rate, duration, complexity, accuracy, durability of the response, and perhaps others. The learner's response pattern is more likely to be flexible and less rigid when we provide many different examples for a generic response. Similarly, loose training prevents learners from attaching an irrelevant feature to the concept they are learning. Generalization over time (i.e., maintenance) is supported when we minimize prompting, intentionally promote high, steady rates of the response of interest, spot check for the mastered skills, repairing if necessary with "booster shots" of training, fade any remaining prompts, and thin the schedules of reinforcement.

Response generalization also may not occur "spontaneously." When response variation is called for, we need to plan and conduct our teaching to take advantage of those differences meeting the demands of the situation. Here we teach the learner to distinguish between particular circumstances, and adapt the form of the response to each one accordingly. Most important is that we do our best to plan in advance what these variations are, and how to adjust to the diverse requirements necessary for appropriate behavioral generalization.

Chapter 7 Resources

Generalization

To	Read
Understand the need for, and choose and use, methods for promoting generalization.	Cooper, J.O., Heron, T. E., & Heward, W.L. (1987). Part 10. *Applied behavior analysis:* Englewood Cliffs, NJ: Prentice-Hall. Sulzer-Azaroff, B. & Mayer, G.R. (1991). Chapter 29. *Behavior analysis for lasting change.* Atlanta, GA: Wadsworth Group: Thompson
Discover the various ways a response can generalize, and how to promote or hinder this effect.	Baer, D.M. & Stokes, T.F. (1977). Discriminating a generalization technology. In P. Mittler (Ed.) *Research to Practice in Mental Retardation. Volume II. Education and Training,* pp 331-336. Baltimore, MD: University Park Press. Charlop-Christy, M.H. & Kelso, S.E. (1997). *How to treat the child with autism.* (Chapter 16) Claremont, CA: McKenna College. Kirby, K.C. & Bickel, W.K. (1988). Toward an explicit analysis of generalization. *The Behavior Analyst, 11,* 115-129. Stokes, T.F. & Baer, D.M. (1977) An implicit technology of generalization. *Journal of Applied Behavior Analysis, 10,* 349-368. Stoke, T.F. & Osnes, P.G. (1989). An operant pursuit of generalization. *Behavior Therapy, 20,* 337-355.
Analyze the sources of the problems that stand in the way of learners transferring newly acquired skills to novel situations.	Cuvo. A. J. & Davis, P.K. (1998). Establishing and transferring stimulus control. In J.K. Luiselli & M.J. Cameron (Eds.) *Antecedent control: Innovative approaches to behavioral support.* (pp. 347-369): Baltimore, MD. Paul Brooks Publishing Company.

Experience vicariously ways that one family promoted their autistic child's generalization of new knowledge and skills.	Chapter 21 in Maurice, K. (1993). *Let Me Hear Your Voice: A Family's Triumph Over Autism*. New York, NY: Fawcett Columbine.
Arrange a classroom environment to support children's communication.	Kaiser, A.P. & Hester, O.P. (1996). How everyday environments support children's communication. In L.K. Koegel, R.L. Koegel & G. Dunlap (Eds.*) Positive behavioral support: Including people with difficult behavior in the community.* (pp. 145-162). Baltimore, MD: Paul Brooks Publishing Co. (pp. 145-162).
See how some have organized the environment and taught learners skills to manage their own behavior	Janzen, J.E. (1996). *Understanding the nature of autism.* San Antonio, TX: Therapy Skill Builders, (especially the chapters on Expanding Communication and Social Competence – Chapter 22 & Teaching Self-control and Self-management strategies – Chapter 23.) Koegel, R.L., Koegel, L.K. & Parks, D.R. (1995). "Teach the individual" model of generalization. In R.L. Koegel, & L.K. Koegel (Eds.) *Teaching children with autism.* (pp. 67-77). Baltimore, MD: Paul Brooks Publishing Co.
Become familiar with a wide range of ways to support community integration.	Koegel, R.L. Koegel & G. Dunlap (Eds.*) Positive behavioral support: Including people with difficult behavior in the community.* Baltimore, MD: Paul Brooks Publishing Co.
Locate sources describing methods to support socialization, including script following, peer mediation, incidental teaching and others.	Refer to reference list in Krantz, P.J. (2000). Commentary: Interventions to facilitate socialization. *Journal of Autism & Developmental Disorders*, 30, 411-413.

Discover how teaching pivotal skills can contribute to children's development of social skills.	Koegel, R.L. & Frea, W.D. (1993). Treatment of social behavior in autism through modification of pivotal skills. *Journal of Applied Behavior Analysis, 26*, 369-378.
Learn how to design and use activity schedules, a tactic for promoting independence, choice, and social interaction among people with autism.	McClannahan, L. E. & Krantz, P.J. (2010). *Activity schedules for children with autism: 2nd Edition, Teaching independent behavior.* Bethesda, MD: Woodbine House
Become familiar with strategies that promote response fluency.	Johnson, K. R. & Lyang, T.V.J. (1992). Breaking the structuralist barrier: Literacy and numeracy with fluency. *American Psychologist, 47,* 1475-1490 Lindsley, O.R. (1992) Precision teaching: Discoveries and effects. *Journal of Applied Behavior Analysis, 25,* 51-57.
Appreciate the influence of behavioral momentum in promoting response maintenance.	Mace, F.C. et al., (1988) Behavioral momentum in the treatment of noncompliance. *Journal of Applied Behavior Analysis, 21,* 123-141
To	View
Learn more about teaching independence and choice.	*Teaching Independence and Choice.* Princeton Child Development Institute, 300 Cold soil Road, Princeton, NJ 08540
Watch teaching learners how to relax and use imagery.	Groden, J., Cautela, J.R., LeVasseur, P., Groden, G. & Bausman, M. (1991) *Breaking the Barriers I: Relaxation Techniques* and *Breaking the Barriers II: Imagery Procedure.* Champaign, IL: Research Press.
To	**Do**
Practice programming for generalization and maintenance.	Exercises in Sulzer-Azaroff, B. & Reese, E.P. (1982). *Applying behavior analysis.* (Chapter 7) New York, NY: Holt, Rinehart & Winston

| Teach a child or yourself to relax in new or difficult situations. | Read and follow the instructions in Cautela, J.R. & Groden, J. (1978) *Relaxation: A Comprehensive Manual for Adults, Children and Children with Special Needs.* Champaign, IL: Research Press. |

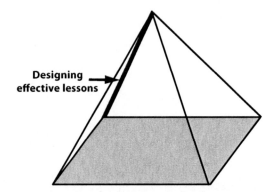

Designing
effective lessons

8

Designing Effective Lessons

Although she cheerfully sorts her blocks in neat precise rows, five-year-old Alicia still doesn't talk. Instead, when she wants something beyond reach, she screams and tears at her clothing. Nor does she play with her brothers and sister, or seem to notice who is in the room. Despite trying many different methods, her parents and teachers have seen Alicia make little progress in language or social development. Recently, while attending the child's Individual Educational Plan (IEP) meeting, they learned from her new teacher about the *Pyramid Approach to Education*. They can see how those methods may help Alicia to: begin to communicate more successfully; get along better with adults and children in school and at home; and begin to learn important academic skills like reading, writing and arithmetic.

The teacher recognizes the importance of being systematic, though, and explains to Alicia's parents the value of well-designed lesson plans that describe the times, places, materials needed, teaching steps to take, and information to observe and record. Here we present the general game plan teachers, staff, and parents should follow.

Preparatory Steps

Suppose you and your family are invited for the first time to a colleague's house for a Sunday barbecue. Finding your way there will be much easier if you know the town, street and house number, and have access to a road map. The same is true when you decide to develop a teaching strategy for each learner you teach. Only if you are clear about both where you are now, and where you are headed, will you arrive safely at your destination. So, before actually designing any lesson, begin by reviewing the objectives included in the learners' Individual Educational Plans (IEPs). Then, decide in what order to address those objectives, preparing instructional methods by adjusting the format and content of the lessons to each particular learner.

Review Objectives

It might be tempting to begin teaching a particular lesson because it is timely, others in the group will be working on it, it is something you or someone else seems to want the learner to learn at the time, or for some other reason. If, before beginning, you refer back to the objectives in the learner's individual educational plan, you might save valuable time and effort. See if the lesson matches the individual learner's current needs. If it does, great. Otherwise, review the learner's objectives to see how they can be woven most seamlessly into your teaching day.

Remember, too, that learners differ in terms of how they can deal with various levels of complexity. Some need to proceed in very small, simple steps; others are capable of moving in larger, far more complicated ones. Even if you decide to teach three learners in your group about Halloween pumpkins, one may be ready only to point to a pumpkin, so you target teaching him to indicate a pumpkin when other vegetables are present. Another can say "pumpkin." You may want to teach that learner to say "Jack-O Lantern." The third is capable of describing it as the vegetable we use for making Jack-O-Lanterns. You use the situation as an opportunity to teach her how to describe the process of creating the Jack-O-Lantern. In general, the goal is to expand upon the learner's current skill level. If, as suggested in Chapter 3, you have specified the dimensions of the instructional objectives, you and others also will easily tell when they have been reached. Together, you should then celebrate the accomplishment.

Match Lessons to the Objective

Beyond allowing for individual differences, we also need to look at the objective itself to see what kind of lesson would work best in any particular case. Sometimes an objective, such as teaching to ask for food, naturally lends itself to an event within the daily routine, perhaps snack time. Other lessons require careful arrangement or should be contrived, such as teaching writing your name.

There are two distinct types of lesson strategies associated with teaching specific skills, whether involving basic actions or communication (expressive and receptive). There also are two broad directions for each type - in terms of who typically initiates the lesson. For the present, we will just list them and will provide further details later:

1. *Discrete trial* formats for lessons involving relatively direct and straight-forward instructions or cues, and relatively simple responses.

2. *Sequential* lessons for skills that require a series of distinct small responses put together in a particular order (often referred to as *behavior chains*).

Point of Origin for Lesson Strategies

1. *Teacher initiated* lessons involve activities wherein the teacher begins the interaction with an instruction - either for a discrete trial (e.g., "How much is two plus two?") or sequential (e.g., "Let's set the table for four.").

2. *Learner initiated* lessons (sometimes referred to as *incidental lessons*), suited to encouraging the initiation of the action in response to naturally occurring cues from the physical (i.e., things) or social (i.e., people) environment.

Plan Ways to Incorporate and Apply Laws of Learning and Behavior Change

The *Pyramid Approach's* foundation in science distinguishes it from many other instructional approaches. The more we know about, and use, scientific principles of behavior, the better our lessons will work. Let us take a look at how this operates.

Learning involves systematic changes in behavior. These changes can involve 1) the acquisition of a new form of behavior, 2) behaviors occurring under new conditions, 3) new sequences of behaviors, and 4) new qualities associated with behaviors, such as how rapidly they are repeated, or how long they continue. *Teaching* is doing things to support learning. In this case, typically two or more people are involved: the learner, whose behavior is to change, and the teacher, who acts to support the change in the learner's behavior. Teaching happens before (i.e., *antecedent* to) and after (i.e., as a *consequence* of) the learner's behavior. We also adhere to this simple adage - *If the learner didn't learn, the teacher didn't teach.*

Antecedents and Consequences

What are antecedents? Antecedents are things (i.e., stimuli) that come before a behavior that may influence aspects and features of that behavior. We can view antecedents as if they were the props, sets, background music, and lighting for a play. Dim lights, a dark street, a bat flying overhead and somber, discordant music prepares the audience for a mystery or dark drama; bright lights, cheerful colors, and sprightly music hints of a romance or comedy. In a similar way, antecedents signal something about what behavior 'should' or 'should not' follow. In the former, reinforcement is likely to follow as a consequence. In the latter, reinforcement is not likely to follow as a consequence. In behavioral jargon, antecedents set the occasion for a particular response. For example, being presented with fleshy, seedy, farm produce, especially if it is sweet, should be an antecedent to the label "fruit." Instructions are supposed to be antecedents to learning certain behaviors. Much of the work done by teachers, staff, parents, and curriculum designers involves developing and arranging antecedents such as text, pictures, audio-visuals, rules, instructions, and so on.

Different Kinds of Antecedents

Technically an antecedent is a *stimulus*. The term 'stimulus' has a long history in psychology and education. Most often it is associated with the phrase 'stimulus-response,' as when referring to certain reflexes. For example, often when we smell fresh baked bread our mouths begin to water. If a pin sticks a baby, she immediately cries. These types of stimuli seem automatically to lead to particular reactions. If the name Pavlov is familiar, it's probably because you remember that he studied how dogs would come to salivate at the sound of a bell. As we noted in Chapter 2, Pavlov noticed that if the sound of a bell reliably preceded placing food into a dog's mouth, the dog would begin to salivate at the sound of the bell, even when no food was immediately provided. This type of learning has been called *classical conditioning* and, in that case, the antecedent stimulus is termed a *conditioned stimulus*. While such conditioning does play a large role in our emotional reactions, it seems to be less important to the acquisition and development of more complex skills, especially those related to social, communicative, and academic skills.

Consequences

Thorndike first studied another type of learning early in the twentieth century. He examined the impact of certain consequences upon given behaviors. As noted in Chapter 2, B.F. Skinner then refined those discoveries by observing that certain consequences - *reinforcers* - would increase the future probability of the response those consequences had followed. However, Skinner did not limit his analyses to just the impact of consequences upon behavior. He also studied the influence of reinforcing consequences upon the combination of particular events (or stimuli) that consistently preceded those reinforced actions (i.e., its antecedents) and the response. He and his colleagues discovered that when a particular stimulus reliably was paired with a particular behavior, and that sequence was followed by a reinforcing outcome, then that behavior occurred more often in the presence of that stimulus. Such a stimulus is called a *discriminative stimulus* or S^D (pronounced "ess-dee") for short. It is important to understand that any object or event in the environment may become an S^D. When an S^D has been created, we also say that the S^D has gained *stimulus control* over the behavior with which it is associated.

Control by Discriminative Stimuli

What is the nature of the control that S^Ds exert over behavior? It is important to understand that S^Ds do not physically force a particular action to occur. Rather, think of them as signals that the particular action will lead to a particular outcome. Loosely, we might say that an S^D suggests a particular behavior will lead to reinforcement. For example, consider the line painted down the center of a two-lane road. In the United States we have learned that keeping the car to the right of the line generally leads to reinforcement - that is, getting to our destination safely. The painted line does not physically force us to drive on its right side. We can drive on the left of the road. In that case, however, we would be far less likely to arrive safely. Driving to the left of the line is *not* associated with reinforcement. Perhaps we learned this lesson when we were first taught to drive and our instructor scolded us for driving slightly to the left of, or even on, the line. Notice that in Britain they use the same type of paint on their roads and yet, over there, driving to the left of the painted line is associated with reinforcement. It is the history of reinforcement that gives the paint specific 'meaning.'

Antecedent Stimuli and Lesson Planning

Let us consider how understanding stimulus control will influence the way we teach our lessons. Assume we want to teach Sarah to choose a spoon when we say, "Please get your spoon." We may start the lesson when Sarah has a bowl of cereal in front of her but no spoon. We then say, "Please get a spoon," and guide Sarah to get a spoon from a silverware tray containing only spoons. Quickly, she begins to retrieve a spoon each time we give her the instruction at breakfast time. Does Sarah really know what a spoon is? Can she discriminate it from a fork or a knife? In other words, has the word "spoon" gained stimulus control over Sarah's choosing spoons? One way to check would be to add forks to the silverware tray without any cues, like a bowl of cereal, before her. If we then ask Sarah on a number of different occasions to get a spoon, and she comes back with the right utensil, we could move on to a more advanced lesson. By contrast, should she often select the wrong utensil, we would suspect that our verbal instructions lacked stimulus control over her choices. More likely, she had been responding to various accessory or contextual cues, such as the contents of the bowl or plate. Then we would need to design a lesson to teach her to respond correctly to our instruction. So, one of our rules of teaching will be always to *test whether our intended S^D truly is working by trying out other, non-related stimuli to see if a learner responds differently to them than to the cue we hope has taken control.*

> **Test the control exerted by an intended discriminative stimulus by displaying other similar stimuli and evaluating whether the response occurs only when it is supposed to, but not otherwise.**

Teaching Scientifically

Our survival, growth, and adaptation to society depend upon stimulus control. What that means is that certain stimuli commonly cue our behavior. The flashing pedestrian signal tells us when it is safe to cross the street; the date stamped on a perishable product lets us know whether to buy and eat it; words on a page guide the way we assemble our lawn mower; our bosses expression indicates whether this is a good time to hit her up for a raise; one set of positions of the hands on the clock cue us about when to go to bed, and another when to catch our ride. Identifying these natural cues prior to teaching is essential if our instruction is to succeed efficiently. We include them as conditions in our objectives, and teach toward that cue-response combination.

Enabling a learner to behave reliably according to a given natural cue, like telling the time by the position of the clock's hands, though, is more easily said than done. To succeed with learners who face special challenges, we need to use the best available instructional technology. In this case, a technology based on the science of human behavior. The guidelines we present below derive from that science.

Teach by Trial and Success

Baby Billy pulls himself up to a standing position, moves his wobbly leg forward, totters a bit, and flops back on to the floor. Maybe he'll cry;

maybe try again. Eventually he succeeds and, before long, he's walking. Probably Billy learns to crawl, walk, feed himself, and many other skills, through trial and error. But suppose he never succeeded after weeks or months of effort. Eventually, unless he received some assistance or formal training, he might give up trying. Because success is so essential to progress, the *Pyramid Approach* stresses the importance of *designing instruction to maximize learner success and minimize learner errors*.

Why do we intentionally try to bypass the 'error' part? Because committing an error does not result in reinforcement and may even be punished. When that happens repeatedly, learners not only fail to learn but, just as we are tempted to do when the vending machine swallows our dollar without delivering our selection, they can become aggressive or try to flee the situation. When reinforcement rates substantially drop, problem behaviors are likely not far behind.

Minimizing learner errors, though, is not always easy. It can take a cleverly planned sequence of steps, often combined with a mix of natural cues and artificial prompts, to get the responses we are seeking. We may have to progress in very small steps, physically guide, or otherwise prompt, the behavior by showing or telling the person what to do, or exaggerating differences between the right and wrong antecedents. A complete description of how to deal with errors can be found in Chapter 10, *Error Correction*.

Shape for Success

Later, Billy toddles over to the swing and stands there babbling. His mom responds by saying, "Oh Billy, you want to have a swing!" as she lifts the child into the seat and pushes him. Mom pushes Billy each time he makes a sound more and more closely approximating the word "up." Eventually he says "up" nearly every time. Mom then can use the same method of reinforcing successive approximations to encourage Billy to build his vocabulary. "Up, swing", "Go up swing", "Please swing", "Please up swing".

This method, noted in Chapter 4 as *shaping*, takes lots of patience, but the price is worth it. You can get the behavior you are hoping for without needing to resort to discipline. The trick is to make the required changes so small that only rarely does the learner have to wait to obtain the reinforcer.

Beware of the teacher's trap, though. Our temptation is to tell, tell, and re-tell the learner what to do instead of waiting patiently until that exact moment when the slight progress occurs. This tendency might be related to the false allure of response production - "I'll do anything to get him to respond!" We need to remind ourselves that if, like the mother bird in the cartoon (Figure 8-1), orally instructing the learner didn't work the first few times, it probably won't work any better the next several dozen times.[1] What *does* work is reinforcing progress, and withholding reinforcement when there is none.

Figure 8-1

If need be, though, teachers can speed up the shaping process by adding assistance (see below) that is known to work effectively with that learner under those circumstances. Having observed Billy's penchant for imitating his playmate Rory's behavior, Billy's mom could pick up and swing Rory when Rory says "up." Billy immediately imitates and mom now can reinforce his progress. The following sections concentrate on establishing, using, and fading out, various kinds of prompts.

Prompt for Success

When a child cannot perform a task, we - as teachers or parents - would provide some type of help to assure a successful outcome. Four-year-old

---

1   Interestingly, this trap is by no means limited to teaching young children or learners with special challenges. Even in business and industry, when workers fail to follow given procedures, such as adhering to specific safety precautions, the natural tendency is to bring them back for retraining, instead of the much more powerful technique of shaping their progress toward optimal performance.

Danny cannot wash his hands so we will help him wash. There are many things that we could do to help - spoken instructions, gestures, modeled demonstrations, or even physical assistance. In the case of teaching discrimination between visual stimuli, like the hands on a clock, numbers, letters, words, or pictures, we might enhance, highlight or exaggerate an aspect of the stimulus by making it bolder, brighter, larger, or more. Any modification we put into the lesson to help the learner perform the task is called a *prompt*.

Consider, however, when we will know that the lesson has been learned. What would we observe? In the case of hand washing, we would observe the learner completing the task independently. That is, without any help; without any prompts. So, the key to any lesson that involves the use of prompts is to not only figure out which one works, but to be sure to eliminate that prompt.

Cues versus Prompts

As we've seen, one of our main responsibilities is teaching learners to respond correctly to important physical and social stimuli native to their environments. For example, to watch TV, I need to learn which buttons to press; to make toast, where to put the bread, and what switches to push; to choose the right public bathroom, symbols related to male vs. female; and, as noted earlier, to drive a car, I need to understand where to position the car relative to the lines on the road.

Often, what other people do is part of the natural learning process. For example, putting toys and other things away when the teacher says, "Time to clean up," to turn to the right page when told, "Everyone turn to page 10," and line up when the teacher says, "It stopped raining! Let's go outside and play!" In each example, the instructional stimuli are natural to the setting and will not necessarily need to be eliminated in the future. Just think how hazardous driving would be if all painted lines disappeared! We will refer to discriminative stimuli that remain, or are inherent in the environment, as *cues*. As you might anticipate, if they are to function independently in that particular environment, learners' behavior ultimately needs to be controlled by natural cues.

Unlike Billy, Rory is very good at imitating what he hears his parents say to him and is responsive to their gestures. If he whines for his dessert, his mom or dad will advise him to say, "Please," and he does. If he wants to play his favorite DVD, they point to the receptacle and tell him to push it in. Eventually, though, Rory's parents hope he will function independently of their help. If they fail to remove those prompts effectively, he may continue to rely upon the prompt. In such cases, we say that the learner's responding has become *prompt dependent*.

In fact, prompt dependency is seen so often, particularly among learners with autism, that many have come to view this as a feature of the disability. Some people talk about prompt dependency as if it were a failure on the learner's part - "He failed to generalize because he is so prompt dependent!" We are convinced that prompt dependency develops not through any deficiency in the learner, but as a result of the teacher's failure to plan and conduct lessons that successfully eliminate the prompt. It was not the learner who put the prompt into the lesson, nor is it the learner's responsibility to eliminate such prompts. It is not educationally sound to move learners on to more advanced levels if they require a prompt before performing a given response.

Formal Lesson Design

We noted earlier the aspects of lessons that distinguish between discrete versus sequential, and teacher- versus learner-initiated lessons. Let us look at each in more depth. Regardless of which lesson format anyone uses, it will only be said to have done its job when the learner reliably responds to cues.

Discrete Trial Lessons

We plan discrete trial lessons to be short and simple. If lessons are too complicated, we break them down into their simple components and generally build repetition into the training. Soon you will see how this is accomplished.

What is a Discrete Trial?

A discrete trial, according to Anderson, Taras and Cannon[2] consists of four parts: 1) the presentation by the trainer, 2) the learner's response, 3) the consequence, and 4) a short pause between that consequence and the next trial. Typically, the point of each discrete trial lesson is to teach appropriate responding to a simple instruction (often, but not necessarily, spoken). Such instructions are the S^Ds for the target skill. Remember, though, that not all S^Ds are spoken. That is, if someone were to ask, "What is the S^D for this lesson?" it would not be correct to assume that the S^D would have to be a spoken word or phrase. Many lessons are designed to teach appropriate responses to non-verbal social or physical-environmental cues, such as a signal like the fire bell or a V-sign to quiet down.

2   Anderson, S.R., Taras, M., & Cannon, B.O. (1996). Teaching new skills to children with autism. In C. Maurice, G. Green & S.C. Luce (Eds.) *Behavioral interventions for young children with autism* (pp. 181-194). Austin, TX, Pro-Ed, pp. 181-194.

Objectives Suited to Discrete-Trial Lessons

We can teach either verbal or non-verbal responses within a discrete trial format. For example, verbal responses are required by instructions such as, "What's your name?", "What color is the ball?", "What is it?", "What number comes after two?", and "Say, 'ball'." On the other hand, we would anticipate non-verbal responses to instructions such as, "Touch your nose," "Put with the same," "Give me the car," and "Go to the door." As we discussed in greater detail in Chapter 5, *Functional Communication*, it is important to understand that even if a learner can respond appropriately to the instruction "Give me the car," we should not necessarily expect that learner to ask for the car, or even imitate the word "car."

Assuring Learner Attending

When beginning a lesson, we want to be sure the learner is paying attention. In the beginning, we may need to use a general cue to attend, such as "Look at me," or "Get ready." Notice that these instructions specify something about being attentive. In *form*, they are not the same as when we say a learner's name prior to asking him to do something (e.g., "Andy, please give me the spoon."). However, the function is the same. That is, each is a cue that essentially says, "Get ready to listen because the next thing I say will be important." If the learner does not respond to the cue to pay attention, the teacher shapes that response by pausing until the learner appears to be attentive (e.g., is making eye-contact) or, if necessary at first, by gently physically guiding the learner to "pay attention."[3] However, eye-contact is not the only way we can judge that someone is paying attention, nor is a verbal instruction the only way to capture attention. Orienting to a powerful reinforcer that you are holding also indicates that the learner is attending, as when we begin Phase I of PECS[4]. Within this lesson, we would not say, "Look at me" prior to beginning the lesson - rather, once the learner reaches for the reinforcer we are ready to begin.

---

3   The fact that a learner is looking at you is no guarantee that he actually is paying attention; looking at someone just tends to correlate with increased attention. The only way to really find out is to see what happens next. That is, whether or not the learner responds appropriately to the stimuli you are presenting.

4   A recent study concluded that "...the PECS curriculum can successfully teach a generalized means of showing coordinated attention to object and person without requiring eye contact to children with ASD." Yoder, P. & Lieberman, R.G. (2009). Brief report: Randomized test of efficacy of Picture Exchange Communication System on highly generalized picture exchanges in children with ASD. *Journal of Autism and Developmental Disabilities, 11*, online version.

Presenting Instructions

How the teacher states the instruction is an important issue. We could say, "Beth, would you please reach over here and pick up the red ball and place it into my hand?" Many learners will miss the essential information buried within this long statement. When introducing new terms, it is more effective to use simple statements such as, "Give me the ball." As the learner learns to respond to the instruction, the teacher may adjust its form gradually to what would be expected to occur in the natural (non-teaching) environment (e.g., "Give it here," "Toss it to me."). How narrowly or specially defined is our instruction will influence the learner's generalization to other instructions and situations (See *training loosely* in Chapter 7 on *Generalization* for more details). For example, if we only use the phrase, "What's your address?" in this form for 12 months of training, the learner may not answer a parallel question like, "Where do you live?" or "What is the number of your house and the name of the street you live on?" We also should take care not to provide too short of an instruction, such as, "Touch nose" or "Match." First, we know of no evidence that such hyper-truncated instructions are more effective than the simple ones noted. Furthermore, simple words, such as "the" function as important discriminative stimuli to listeners that the *next* word is likely to be important. (e.g., "Touch *the* blue ball").

Presenting Consequences

After giving the instruction, wait patiently for the answer *for at least 4 to 5 seconds* and, if the learner responds correctly, deliver praise. It is a good idea to have everyone on your team practice how long 5 seconds truly is. You'll be surprised at the initial wide variation within the group! Sometimes when there is reason to believe that praise or other social rewards presently are not effective reinforcers, pair praise with additional rewards, such as snacks or treats.

Using Prompts if Necessary

If the learner fails to react within the allotted time limit, or responds incorrectly, the teacher typically, though not necessarily, says "no" or "try again" in a neutral, not harsh nor punitive, tone. The reaction is meant to be informative and educational (The specific way the teacher should react to the learner's error will be discussed in more detail in the chapter on *Error Correction.*). In this case, the teacher next repeats the instruction and simultaneously adds a prompt likely to assure a successful response. The type of prompt chosen varies according to the kind that regularly works with the learner within that type of lesson.

How many prompts should be used?

Just as reinforcers are defined by their impact upon behavior, and not our intent, so too are prompts defined by their impact upon behavior. Recall that prompts are helpful. If what you do, perhaps a gesture toward an item, is *not* helpful (i.e., it does not result in the proper behavior), then your gesture was not a prompt. No matter how we try, some of our attempts to prompt will fail. In these situations, it will be very tempting to try many prompts at the same time. Point to the item, while showing a picture of the item, while naming the item, while simultaneously providing physical assistance - surely this will work! However, you've now used *four* prompts at the same time and the lesson will not be completed until all four have been removed. That is why we urge you to try one prompt. It is hard enough to eliminate that one prompt, and removing one prompt will be easier than trying to remove four prompts. We will discuss more details about the use and elimination of prompts in our next chapter.

Providing Opportunities for Repetition of the Correct Response

So far, we have described the sequence within a single trial: Present the instruction; wait for the learner to respond; and provide an appropriate consequence. However, a successful single correct response is no guarantee the learner has mastered the objective of the lesson. Therefore, the trial is repeated. But in what manner? There are several factors we must consider at this point.

Repeating Trials. A single success hardly guarantees learning. The trials need to be repeated, but not just haphazardly. We need to consider such factors as how long to wait between trials, how many trials to conduct, whether they should be repeated one right after the next, or trials of a different kind interspersed, plus other details.

Frequently Posed Questions about Discrete Trial Teaching

1. *How much time should pass between trials?*

    The time between trials[5] generally is fairly short - a few seconds. The reason for using short intervals is to avoid the learner becoming distracted by other stimuli in the immediate environment. However, over time, it will be important to stretch the length of the interval because simple instructions or other cues rarely are repeated in the real world.

---

5   Those who appreciate the precision of technical jargon will refer to this as the inter-trial interval.

2. *How many trials should be carried out within a teaching session?*

Some lessons readily lend themselves to repeated trials. For example, putting spoons in the dishwasher often involves many spoons (and ultimately other utensils). Putting toys away, all socks of one color in one pile and all of another color in a different one, the tall books on one shelf, the small books on another, all illustrate situations naturally calling for repeated trials. When repetitions are not necessarily inherent in the situation, choose a criterion for

> **Naturally Repeated Discrete Trials?**
>
> A parent related how, at Halloween, she designed a picture for her son, who used it to symbolize "Trick or Treat!" The boy toured the neighborhood with his friends, presenting the card to each neighbor answering the door. The rewards - candy and other treats - also fit the context naturally! Obviously, he went to many homes that night, repeating his simple request over and over and ...

determining the number of trials to repeat before changing the lesson focus, say, *when the learner responds correctly for four trials in a row*, or some similar criterion.

3. *Should trials be repeated directly one after another (massed), or should they be interspersed within (distributed) other activities?*

There is no simple formula for balancing massed vs. distributed practice. In general, trials tend to be massed in the beginning, and then become more distributed. However, over-emphasizing massed practice significantly postpones the distributed work. This strategy, in turn, can delay introducing the skill within the more natural context, and seriously interfere with generalization. Begin to apply the discrete trial in its natural context as soon as possible - that very day if possible! Instead of sorting socks at the table, move to the wash basket next to the clothes dryer.

Finally, some discrete trial lessons do not lend themselves to massed or rapidly repeated trials. For example, when teaching a girl to say "Hi," it would not be effective to prompt her to say "Hi" for 10 or 20 massed trials. In fact, if this approach is used, when she leaves the teaching table and chair, she may not say "Hi" to anyone. Indeed, her responding may well have become dependent on the discriminative stimuli specific to the lesson, like sitting in a chair, repeating the instruction, and so on.

4.   May we address more than one lesson within a session?

Traditionally, discrete trials were rapidly repeated to help keep learners engaged, while minimizing any tendency for them to become distracted or to turn to self-stimulating. Today, we question this assumption, opting instead to intersperse other instructional trials periodically within the session, while sustaining a high pace for responding. Additionally[6], research has shown that interspersing activities tends to improve the learner's ongoing attention to the task.

Figure 8-2
Tips for Successful Discrete Trial Instruction

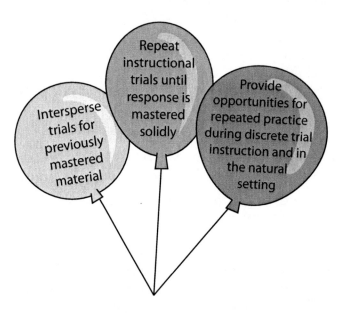

In our section on reinforcement, we noted that surprise and novelty are usually reinforcing in and of themselves. Thus, adding trials for skills that learners *already have learned* to a block of trials designed for a new lesson can be very effective. This mixture will help keep learners attentive to your cues and prompts. Requesting previously mastered responses also will give you additional opportunities to reward them for successes, especially

---

6   Neef, N.A., Iwata, B.A. & Page, T.J. (1980). The effects of interspersal training versus high density reinforcement on spelling acquisition and retention. *Journal of Applied Behavior Analysis, 13*, 153-158.

important at a time when they
may be unsure of the correct new
responses. Take care to avoid
presenting two *new* lessons at
the same time. This will virtually guarantee high rates of errors,
low rates of reinforcement, and,
consequently, increases in rates
of disruptive behaviors[7]

> **A Golden Rule for Lessons**
>
> One *new* lesson at a time!

Sequential Lessons

Much of what we do in everyday life consists of routines composed of
a complex of many simpler steps, as when we prepare meals, get dressed,
clean the house, operate our DVD players and computers, groom ourselves,
and play. As suggested earlier, skills of the sort we might instruct within
a discrete trial format often need to be combined with others, typically in
a particular order. If we change that order, we change the outcome - often
not for the better! For example, socks over our shoes may look cool, but
wouldn't be very practical. Consequently, when teaching such sequential
skills, first consider what steps compose the sequence. This process results
in the development of a *task analysis*.

Designing Effective Task Analyses

When teaching sets of sequential skills, the first requirement is to identify each of the steps. Here is a sequence of steps, itself a task analysis,
which you might follow when analyzing a task:

1. Envision how you and others do that activity - an *armchair analysis*.
   Of course, if several people are working on the design, you may find
   that different people suggest slightly different ways of accomplishing
   things. For example, is it critical that the plates be put down before
   the glasses? One big advantage is that teachers usually know the skills
   themselves! The tricky part is accepting the idea that how we do a
   task may not be exactly the same as the way someone else does it, even
   though we both end up with good outcomes. We may consider these
   differences in style, not function. Bob might put on his left shoe first,
   fold one loop of the lace and wrap the other behind the loop, and pull
   the first one through. Henry may put on his right shoe first, double
   loop the lace, and twist and tie them into a simple knot. Yet both walk

---

7   Adapted from Pryor, K. (1999). *Don't shoot the dog! The new art of teaching and
training.* New York, NY: Bantam Books

out of their bedrooms without tripping. Must the salad fork be on the left of the dinner fork? Probably you will realize there are various acceptable ways to sequence a task analysis for most complex behaviors.

2.   Watch a few experts performing the skill. Note each element. When you see differences in the content or order of components, discuss it with the others to decide which elements you absolutely have to retain and which can be optional.

3.   Sometimes published task analyses can be found in professional journals and books. A good place to begin is by checking for "task analyses" in the indexes of journals like the *Journal of Applied Behavior Analysis.*

4.   Consider the characteristics and abilities of the learner. You might need separate task analyses for two different learners due to differences in their skills or other distinguishing features. For example, a task analysis designed to teach a seven-year-old to shop in a supermarket would be different than one for a 15-year-old. The sequence for someone who reads may be different than for someone who depends upon picture cues.

5.   Putting the task analysis to the test is essential. The only way to know whether what you've written is clear and effective is to use it and see how well it works[8]. Be prepared to make adjustments accordingly.

Task Analyses and Behavioral Chains

Another term used to describe a complex response consisting of a sequence of steps is a behavioral chain. One property of chains is that each link, or response element, in the chain is connected both to the link before and the link after it, as shown in Figure 8-3. Ultimately, in a smoothly executed chain, the link preceding each element functions as an S^D for it; the link following as its (conditioned) reinforcer. The same applies to each of the components of a task analysis.

---

8   The Murdoch Center Program Library is a collection of almost 1000 task analyses applicable to the habilitation of people with severe special needs. Murdoch Center Foundation, P.O. Box 92, Butner, NC 27509.

Figure 8-3

Washing Hands in Preparation for Lunch

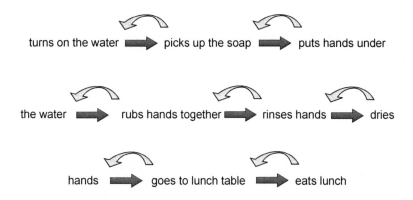

turns on the water ➡ picks up the soap ➡ puts hands under

the water ➡ rubs hands together ➡ rinses hands ➡ dries

hands ➡ goes to lunch table ➡ eats lunch

Now, because each step is supposed to act as the effective discriminative stimulus for the next one, be very cautious about adding unnecessary prompts into the sequence. For example, it would be very tempting to add verbal prompts to each step. While teaching a child to wash hands, we could say, "Turn on the water...pick up the soap...put your hands under the water...rub your hands together... rinse your hands..." etc.. However, as noted in the section on prompting, all prompts must be removed before independence is achieved. Although verbal prompts are easy for teachers to use, in practice, once the learner begins to depend upon them, they can be difficult to remove. Why? There is no evidence that one type of prompt is inherently more difficult to remove than any other type of prompt. Most likely, it is because using verbal prompts is so easy that we often neglect to notice that we've put them into the lesson. Without knowing a prompt is there, it will be hard to create a plan to remove it. Thus, in addition to determining the sequence of steps within the task analysis, it is important to identify which types of cues will be in place when the sequence is completely learned. To wash hands effectively, a child must learn how to manipulate soap, water, the faucet, and so on. Understanding spoken instructions is not a necessary aspect of washing hands. How to use prompts to teach the sequence of steps and permit the natural cues to become effective will be reviewed in our section on *Arranging Effective Lessons*. Figure 8-4 displays another task analysis: one for preparing a peanut butter and jelly sandwich.

Figure 8-4: Preparing a Peanut Butter and Jam Sandwich

1. Place breadboard on table	16. Wipe knife off on other piece of bread
2. Get knife from silverware drawer	17. Close peanut butter jar
3. Get plate from cabinet	18. Open the jam jar
4. Get package of bread from breadbox	19. Use knife to scoop some jelly out of the jar
5. Place next to breadboard	20. Spread jam onto second piece of bread
6. Get peanut butter jar from cabinet	21. Repeat if surface not completely covered
7. Place next to board	22. Close jam jar
8. Get jar of jam from refrigerator	23. Turn over and place the side of the bread with peanut butter on top of the piece with jam
9. Place next to breadboard	
10. Take two slices of bread	
11. Open the jar	24. Cut sandwich in half
12. Place the cover beside the jar	25. Put the sandwich on a plate
13. Use knife to scoop some peanut butter	26. Return peanut butter to cupboard
14. Spread the peanut butter on one slice of bread	27. Return jam to refrigerator
15. Add more peanut butter if parts of the bread are not covered	28. Put knife in the sink

Initiating the Sequence

In designing effective sequential lessons, consider how to begin the sequence. What is the cue for the activity? Sometimes, a verbal cue is appropriate. For example, a teacher announces to the group that playtime is over and that everyone should get ready for lunch (e.g., "It's time to wash hands."). The bus has just driven up and mom says, "Time to dress to go outside." The music teacher says, "Here's my guitar," or "Now we can sing." Although it's tempting to always use these kinds of verbal cues, teachers should try to encourage learners to be more independent and thereby, over time, less reliant upon an adult's directions. Thus, for any particular activity or element of a chain, assess if verbal instructions can be dispensed with in favor of other environmental cues. For example, learners ultimately should respond to fire bells and not someone telling them what to do after the fire bell sounds. Bringing out the guitar could just as well signal sitting on the rug in a circle as telling the group to gather. Seeing the bus drive up could cue getting dressed to go to school and so on.

Reinforcement during Sequential Lessons

The types of reinforcers associated with a task should be considered when designing effective sequential lessons. As noted in Chapter 4, *Powerful Reinforcement Systems*, use reinforcers that fit the situation - those that are contextually relevant. Some of these rewards can be thought of as intrinsic to the activity. Many of us find something about throwing and catching a ball is enjoyable, independent of social reinforcers. It just feels good.

On the other hand, some contextual reinforcers are connected to what happens following completion of an activity, but not necessarily while the activity is in progress. For example, maybe a learner doesn't care about the 'feel' of tying his laces, but loves to have his sneakers on when he runs around outside. Creating a relationship between completing something that *is not* naturally reinforcing, and the resulting access to something that *is* naturally reinforcing, opens up some interesting options. You could be direct and instruct, "Put on your sneakers," running the risk that the only time the learner will put on his sneakers is when he is told to do so. However, at a time when the learner's sneakers are off, you could say, "Hey, let's go outside!" At this point the learner is likely to bolt for the door! Now, you could say, "Uh oh. We wear sneakers to go outside" (or some such similar reminder). What happens when the learner has completed putting on his sneakers? Does he get M&Ms for nice lacing or being compliant with the demand? No, because praise and quick access to the door are all he needs. The type of reinforcer associated with a sequential lesson influences how the lesson is taught. In general, this strategy involves our emphasis on a 'reinforcer first' orientation.

Table 8-1 provides a list of common sequential skills and potential contextual rewards, both intrinsic to the situation and related to natural outcomes. You may find it helpful to complete the table and add examples of skills you plan to teach.

For some activities, the assumed natural reinforcer for completing the task will occur long after its completion. For example, why do we brush our teeth? Presumably, to prevent cavities. Manufacturers of toothpaste, though, certainly know about manipulating immediate or intrinsic rewards. They add pleasant flavors to the toothpaste and reassure us that our breath will be kissing sweet right afterward. Such additions increase the probability that we will brush our teeth (and thus consume more, resulting in our buying more toothpaste). It also is true that sometimes when we finish brushing our teeth, we enjoy the clean feel of our teeth and mouth in general, but that probably is not a sensation we notice every time we brush.

We also are taught that brushing our teeth (sometimes with certain additives) will help prevent future dental problems. However, as all teachers and parents know, getting children (and even adults sometimes) to do something *now*, in anticipation of some far-off reward, is not easy. Therefore, *arrange to deliver arbitrary reinforcers on the completion of activities lacking naturally reinforcing consequences.* In this particular case, you might arrange a simple deal with the child by requiring that he brush his teeth after snack, but before going to the play area.

Finally, not every sequential lesson can be arranged to be intrinsically rewarding or result in naturally or immediately arranged outcomes. For example, what is the natural outcome for completing stuffing a hundred envelopes with a newsletter for the neighborhood association? Perhaps a sense of civic pride would be sufficient for you. Suppose, though, that the task were for you to pack boxes of manufactured goods for a profit making business. What would it probably take to motivate you to do this activity? Right - a reasonable amount of money. The advantage of using money or *tokens* is that we can exchange it for a variety of rewarding items some time later.

If you decide to dispense tokens during a complex task, watch that they don't disrupt the lesson. If the tokens distract the learner, try placing them out of reach, but in such a way that the learner can detect each time he has received one. Pair the delivery with a sound or word (e.g., "Another chip," "That's sixteen; four more to go"). Place it into a glass jar, or use pegs, puzzle pieces, or other objects that provide a visual cue that the token has been delivered. Display a number showing the amount earned or use some another method suited to the learner.

Table 8-1

Common Contextual Skills and Intrinsic Rewards

Sequential Skill	Potential Intrinsic Reward	Potential Completion Reward
Washing hands	Sensory stimulation (feel, sound, sight, smell, etc.) of soap, water, rubbing hands	Access to meals/snacks, access to activity after cleaning dirty hands
Getting dressed	Feel or look of clothes	Access to next activity (e.g., smock leads to art, t-shirt leads to gym, coat leads to bus/outside)
Brushing teeth	Feel/taste of toothpaste/ toothbrush, water play	Access to next activity or meal, clean feel of mouth
Setting the table		

Putting away groceries		
Putting away plates and utensils		
Putting toys away		
Playing a game		
Washing laundry		

Learner Initiated Lessons

Mindy clearly wants to eat some popcorn. She is standing in front of the bowl of popcorn. She even reaches into the bowl but says nothing to her teacher. Anne appears to want to watch her favorite DVD. She has the disc in her hands and is standing in front of the television set and the DVR, but doesn't know how to put the disc in the machine or how to turn on the TV. Tony has just asked his teacher for an apple, but the teacher wants him to indicate whether he wants the red or green apple. In each of these cases, the learner has started a pattern of actions but is not bringing them to completion, or only can do so in a limited fashion. How, then, can we teach successful initiation of an action, or expand upon current skills? Will it be effective to rely upon the same teaching strategies needed to teach discrete trial and sequential lessons?

Discrete trial and sequential lessons are typically begun with an instruction, such as, "What's this?", "Clap your hands," or "Set the table." It is tempting to use a similar strategy to get a learner to initiate. However, imagine what would happen if a teacher said to a learner, "You start the conversation with me...go ahead...start...you first." If the learner starts to speak at that point, has he started the interaction?

As previously stated, we encourage using motivators that fit the context, or are natural to the situation. Can we use this strategy to help learners initiate and expand their behavior patterns? *Incidental teaching* is one well-researched strategy to expand learner's skills by capitalizing on this idea. This strategy was first used with young children with impoverished speaking repertoires[9], but has since been extended to learners with a variety of disabilities[10].

Your efforts to use incidental teaching should be more successful if you try to adhere to the following strategies:

1. *Observe the learner's preferences.* Rather than choosing what a learner can earn within a lesson, observe what currently motivates the learner. For example, a learner is observed to reach for a truck while saying "truck." Another learner picks out all the red candies from a handful offered by the teacher. Incidental lessons start only when the teacher has observed what the learner wants, or is trying to accomplish.

2. *Use natural cues.* The teacher manipulates various objects and events in the natural setting in order to entice the learner to interact with something interesting. For example, the teacher places a group of toys just out of reach of the learner, or shows the learner a preferred snack inside a closed clear container. Thus, rather than always using a direct strategy, like asking the learner what he wants, the teacher modifies the physical environment, using an indirect strategy to attract the learner's attention[11].

3. *Assess the learner's current repertoire and choose an expansion to teach.* The teacher carefully observes how the learner currently attempts to obtain the desired outcome. For example, when shown a truck, Doris merely reaches for the truck without saying anything, while Lily says, "truck", and Yosi says, "I want the truck." The goal with Doris is to communicate (in any effective modality) her desire for the object, while the goal for Lily is to add, "I want" to her single word. Yosi's goal is to add color or size adjectives to his short sentence structure. Notice that the original approach to each learner is the same, but the lesson changes in relation to the how the learner responds.

4. *Take advantage of spontaneous opportunities.* Another term for a teacher is an instructor - one who instructs. Thus, teachers often feel compelled to give instructions as a way to start each lesson. How can we teach

---

9   Hart, B. & Risley, T.R. (1975). Incidental teaching of language in the preschool. *Journal of Applied Behavior Analysis, 8,* 411-420.

10   e.g., Farmer-Dugan, V. (1994). Increasing requests by adults with developmental disabilities using incidental teaching by peers. *Journal of Applied Behavior Analysis, 27,* 533-544; McGee, S. G., Almeida, C., Sulzer-Azaroff, B., & Feldman, R. S. (1992). Promoting reciprocal interactions via peer incidental teaching. *Journal of Applied Behavior Analysis, 25,* 118-126.

11   This strategy also has been described as contriving an establishing operation, a term described by J. Michael, (1982). Distinguishing between discriminative and motivational functions of stimuli. Journal of the Experimental Analysis of Behavior, 37, 149-155.

without beginning with instructions? One way, as we've seen, is to take advantage of teaching opportunities as they arise across a day, including instances when the learner initiates toward something. For example, while a group of learners are playing at the sand table, one learner begins to walk toward the art area. Rather than assuming the learner must play with sand, the teacher sees this as an opportunity to teach the learner to communicate her desire to change activities. Likewise, a mother may be taking a walk with her son when he bends down to examine a squiggling worm. Instead of insisting on continuing with the walk, the mother comments about the worm and encourages her son to express his interest in a more mature fashion. In a group home, after completing setting the dinner table, an adult reaches for the ice tea. Here's a situation to promote the use of PECS to communicate about the tea. In this way, teaching opportunities are not limited to when the teacher is ready to teach. Rather, teaching occurs when the learner is ready to learn. This can happen almost any time! Like a good photographer, teachers are ready to 'capture the moment' and create a mini-lesson on the spot.

5. *Do not predetermine the exact number of trials in a lesson.* Teachers often set the number of trials or teaching opportunities within a particular lesson. For example, a teacher decides she will put out six objects and teach the learner to name each one ten times. The same is often true for sequential lessons. A teacher asks a learner to set the table with plates, forks, spoons, knives, and napkins for eight. Can we predetermine, however, the number of repetitions within incidental lessons or other types of self-initiated lessons? Adam likes to play with a ball. Can his teacher make Adam want to play with the ball exactly twenty times during the next hour? Of course not. Teachers must observe how strongly a learner wants to play with an item and be ready to move on to a different lesson (or the same type of lesson with a different object) when the learner's interests shifts. So, while a teacher will try to create many teaching opportunities within a set period of time there is no way anyone can precisely determine how many times such opportunities will take place.

6. *Manage the learner's access to high-preference objects and activities.* While predetermining the number of incidental-teaching trials to hold is not realistic, you can arrange to increase the number of opportunities by limiting the amount of time the learner maintains access to the item or event. Use a natural strategy, such as taking turns. After learners have obtained the reinforcing item or event, permit them to enjoy it for a period of time, and then remove access, as people do when they "take turns." Shift to another DVD or program, allow another child a

turn with the toy, or use some other reasonable strategy. Then, after a few minutes, display the reinforcer once again, thus setting up another learning opportunity.

7. *Involve peers in the process, when possible.* Provide the peer tutor with a set of toys or other items the learner prefers. Teach the peer tutor to 1) wait for the learner to initiate, 2) prompt the learner to label the item, 3) turn the object over to the learner, 4) praise the requesting, 5) allow the learner to sample the reinforcer, 6) ask for a turn for her/himself, 7) play with the item him/herself for a short period, and 8) repeat the sequence.

Summary

Designing effective lessons depends on a number of important actions. We need to prepare carefully by reviewing the objectives contained in the learner's individual plan. Lessons should be designed to incorporate principles of effective learning and instruction most likely to succeed, rather than on our intuitive feelings about how to proceed. Fortunately, we are not forced to begin from scratch, because many other instructional designers and teachers have paved the way for us. In fact, today there exists a huge library of behavior-analytic based instructional strategies that have been demonstrated to be effective with typically developing learners and those facing particular challenges. Included among these strategies are discrete trial and sequential formats, as well as teacher-led and learner-initiated methods; methods especially well suited to teaching learners with autism and related conditions. In this chapter we have described each of these approaches along with a number of guidelines to help you succeed in preparing your daily lessons.

Discrete trial instruction is a formal approach to teaching specific skills on a trial-by-trial basis. The learner needs to be attentive while instructions are delivered in a simple, straightforward manner. The teacher needs to be patient in awaiting the correct response and, when it is given, must present rewarding consequences right away. When necessary, prompts can assist the learner to provide the appropriate response. When prompts are used, they must be removed as quickly as possible. Additionally, the learner needs numerous opportunities to repeat the correct response. Other considerations in discrete trial instruction include using short intervals to separate trials from one another, setting guidelines for the number of trials within a session that depend on the nature of the response, and deciding whether to mass or distribute practice opportunities. Nevertheless, introducing multiple lessons at once is to be avoided. One new lesson at a time is sufficient.

Sequential lessons lend themselves best to teaching complex skills; those that consist of many steps. We plan for sequential lessons by designing, or choosing already developed, task analyses. With sequential lessons, we decide in advance what event should cue the activity and plan to capitalize on those reinforcers inherent in the situation, or to deliver them at particular points. The type and pattern of reinforcement may depend on the exact nature of the activity and the learner's history of exposure to it.

Learner-initiated lessons capitalize on the natural motivators for the learner. We can discover those by observing carefully to see what is approached or chosen, or we can make new arrangements to entice interest. With learner-initiated lessons, we need to be familiar with the learner's history of responding in relation to the object or event, so we can build upon and expand those skills. Additionally, we should teach ourselves to be very sensitive and responsive to unanticipated learning opportunities. While making hard and fast rules about the number of trials to repeat within a lesson is not advisable, often we provide for repeated practice by managing access to preferred items and activities. An especially powerful way of accomplishing this goal is to involve peers in the learning process.

In the next chapter we continue along the path of helping teachers to develop and deliver behavior-analytic based instruction. You will learn how to use prompts to get a behavior going, and how to fade those prompts to see to it that the learner ultimately can respond to the cues from within the natural environment.

Chapter 8 Resources

Designing Effective Lessons

To	Read
Systematically choose programs for teaching young children with autism, apply the programs, and assess progress along the way.	Taylor, B.S. & McDonough, K.A. Selecting teaching programs. I n Maurice, C., Green, G. & Luce, S., (Eds.) *Behavioral intervention for young children with autism* (pp. 63-180). Austin, TX: Pro-Ed.
See what elements are important for parents to include to successfully teach their children at home.	Anderson, S.R., Taras, M. & Cannon, B.O. (1996). Teaching new skills to young children with autism. In Maurice, C., Green, G. & Luce, S., (Eds.) *Behavioral intervention for young children with autism* (pp. 181-194). Austin, TX: Pro-Ed.
Choose a curriculum and learn how to apply it in a center-based program or at home.	Harris, S.L. & Weiss, M.J. (1998). Chapter 5: What to teach and how to teach it. In *Right from the start: Behavioral intervention for young children with autism*. Bethesda, MD: Woodbine House.
Encounter an engaging series of examples and 'how tos' of teaching dolphins, dogs, and people through differential reinforcement.	Pryor, K. (1999). *Don't shoot the dog! The new art of teaching and training*. New York, NY: Bantam Books, especially Chapter 6: Clicker training: A new technology. (pp. 165-183).
Design a pre-school program that incorporates discrete-trial, sequential and incidental training.	Charlop-Christy, M.H. & Kelso, S.E. (1997). *How to treat the child with autism*. (Chapter 9, 11) Claremont, CA: Claremont McKenna College Handleman, J.S. & Harris, S.L, (Eds.) *Pre-school education programs for children with autism*: Second Edition. Austin, TX: Pro-Ed (pp. 157-190)

Choose when and how to use incidental teaching and teach others to use it.	Fenske, E.C., Krantz, P.J. & McClannahan, L.E. (2001). In C. Maurice, G. Green, & R.M. Foxx (Eds.). *Making a difference: Behavioral intervention for autism* (pp. 75-82). Austin, TX: Pro-Ed. McGee, G.G., Morrier, M.J. & Daly, T. (2001). The Walden early childhood programs. In Handleman, J.S. & Harris, S.L, (Eds.) *Preschool education programs for children with autism*: 2nd *Edition* (pp 157-190). Austin, TX: Pro-Ed
To	Do
Experience using behavioral methods to design and teach a lesson to your peers.	Exercises in Sulzer-Azaroff, B. & Reese, E.P. (1982). *Applying behavior analysis.* (Chapter 8) New York, NY: Holt, Rinehart & Winston

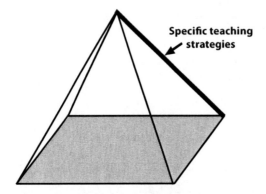

Specific teaching
strategies

9

Specific Teaching Strategies

"She is such a terrific teacher," Carlo's mom comments to her friend during a monthly parents' meeting. "Before he would just yell, scream and kick and we couldn't figure out what he wanted. It was a nightmare. Now he lets us know, with pictures, and sometimes even a spoken word, what his issue is."

"If Kim could only do that we'd feel like we'd won the lottery."

"Maybe she will. Give it a chance. She's only been here for a few weeks. They're teaching you how to follow through at home with her learning objectives, aren't they?"

"We're trying."

"I couldn't believe it the other day. We were in the mall and he handed me his picture of a pretzel - we didn't even see the pretzel-stand!"

"So what happened?"

"Dan rushed him off to get one. That really hit the spot for Carlo!"

None of Carlo's accomplishments happened by chance. They were the result of his teacher carrying out careful discrete trial and generalization lessons. Through a carefully engineered series of steps, she had taught him to use PECS to request his favorite items and activities. She also had him respond to a picture of a toilet whenever there was a scheduled bathroom stop, including while out in the community. Both of these skills helped make going to the mall a fun family event.

Good teachers with all sorts of learners are especially concerned with what people say and do in response to a *particular*, not just any, cue: answering questions, analyzing events, generating solutions, using tools, developing particular motor skills, responding to their own body cues. Good teachers do this efficiently and effectively.

The last chapter described various ways to design effective lessons in general. This one concentrates on ways to eliminate prompts that currently work to get learners to respond to the cues that *should* evoke those responses in the ordinary scheme of things.

Contrast this with the actions of a teacher who has a good deal to learn about effective teaching. As you observe, he says, "Andy, come here ... Andy! Come here ... Come here now! ... Come here ... Come on, you can do it ... Come here, Andy! ... Come here ... Come on, over here ..." Andy doesn't budge or, by the time he does, there is no way of knowing to which signal, if any, he had responded! Unfortunately, that is a trap many of us have fallen into when we first began to teach. When something doesn't work we repeat it, often louder and faster[1].

Is there a better way? Watch skillful instruction and your answer will be, "Absolutely!" Able teachers have learned how to arrange for the response they seek by:

One definition of insanity is doing the same thing over and over and expecting a different outcome! --Attributed to Albert Einstein

• Presenting the natural cue and seeing if that works, like telling Andy to come here once.

• If that cue fails, supplementing it with a prompt, such as a beckoning gesture, a different verbal form (e.g., "Come see what we're going to do next"), lavishly praising another learner who comes when called, or, perhaps as a last resort, going to Andy and gently escorting him over.

• Gradually eliminating those

---

1   The now familiar extinction burst at work.

prompts over time while supporting the continuation of the particular response.

As we emphasized in the previous chapter, one of a teacher's most important responsibilities is to help others learn to respond skillfully, not just when prompted, but when cued by the conditions natural to that situation. These cues may be direct and obvious, such as a stop sign, or more subtle, like a raised eyebrow or the passage of time. When natural cues fail, teachers use prompts that also may vary in terms of how direct or subtle they are. Finding the right prompt to help the learner act in a certain way is not the biggest challenge for teachers, though. Rather, it is how to eliminate that prompt while the learner continues to engage in the appropriate action. In this chapter we will discuss different natural or contrived ways to promote the behaviors we are seeking, along with ways to eventually dispense with any artificial supports. In the next chapter, we concentrate more heavily on instructional techniques for avoiding errors in the first place, or for coping with them when they do crop up.

Prompting

What is a prompt? We must define prompts in a functional manner, just as we have defined 'reinforcer.' That is, we define a prompt by its relationship to certain behaviors. A prompt is something a teacher does to *help* a learner perform a skill. If what we try as a teacher doesn't help in terms of the performance, then we did not provide a prompt. For example, if I point to the correct item for a child to give to me but she still does not give me that item, then my pointing did not function as a prompt. Prompting is one of the most powerful instructional devices we know. As a strategy, it has been examined in great detail by behavior analysts working in the laboratory, as well as in the field. It's tempting to use just any kind of prompting because it's easy and seems to gain the reaction we are looking for in the short term. Yet our concern is to produce learning that takes hold and maintains. Here, the task is far more challenging because there is a lot to learn about effective prompting methods. We need to know what they are, which ones to choose, and where and how to use and remove them. Teachers who take the time to learn these important subtleties will be rewarded, though, by seeing their learners' progress begin to accelerate.

Types of Prompts

There are many types of prompts (see Table 9-1), as well as a variety of strategies to move from one prompt to another, or to change from prompts to natural cues systematically. It is important to understand that these prompts are *not necessarily* **listed in terms of their importance, ease of use, or suggested place in a** sequence. You do not need to start with the prompts at the top of this list and then move down to the bottom, or begin at one prompt and move forward with any lesson. There are guidelines, however, for you to decide whether to use any prompt within a particular lesson and, if so, *which one* to apply. First, though, you need to identify what events ultimately are supposed to lead to a particular behavior.

Table 9-1

Type of Instructional Prompts

1. Verbal (e.g., direct - "Come here"; indirect - "What do we need?")

2. Partial verbal (e.g., "Coo…" while prompting to say 'cookie')

3. Physical (e.g., hand over hand assistance, putting your hand on a learner's back with gentle pressure)

4. Partial physical (e.g., touching a learner's hand or back)

5. Gestural (e.g., pointing to an area or item, tilting your head in a direction, touching an item)

6. Model (e.g., performing the act, saying a word, constructing the item, manipulating the material)

7. Augmented stimuli (e.g., brighter or larger visual, exaggerated tactile, such as sand over a letter, louder or more distinct auditory input, lines on a paper, dotted lines, exaggerated aspects of a cue, overlapping visual cues)

Prompts versus Natural Cues

As discussed in the last chapter, *natural cues* involve those external or internal qualities that are (or should be) dependably associated with a behavior. That is, a yellow triangular sign cues us to slow down, or our bodily sensations suggest to us that it's all right to keep pedaling our bicycles. *Prompts* are those tools that teachers temporarily use to *help* learners begin to progress toward mastering particular skills, like, "Remember, the b looks to the right, where the door is," or when dad runs alongside, steadying the bike while junior is getting the hang of riding. The point of many lessons is to find, and then remove, those artificial supports so the learner eventually responds to the cue, just as everyone else is supposed to. While you may find there are times when it seems difficult to find the right prompt, in general it is more difficult to remove the prompt than to put it into the lesson in the first place. The following sections describe strategies teachers can use to identify the cues that ultimately should take control of a particular response and the kinds of prompts that can aid the process.

How to Identify Natural Cues

A basic *Pyramid Approach* guideline is that teachers should know what the final performance is supposed to look like before starting to teach a skill. Teachers must specify the cue that naturally will be associated with the skill before starting the lesson. For example, once a girl has learned to wash her hands, the cues that control her responses involve her hands, the soap, the water, the sink, and the towel. Notice that when she masters this skill, no verbal cues remain associated with the task. Therefore, before beginning to teach the lesson, carefully decide which types of prompt to use so the learner can ultimately respond to the natural cues in this activity. If verbal prompts are used while teaching this skill, then there must be a plan to remove them, because they are not naturally associated with hand washing. Teachers don't want to create a situation in which the only way the girl washes her hands is when told to do each step. It is easier to avoid the use of verbal prompts in the first place than to remove them. If you don't put it in, you won't have to take it out!

Table 9-2

Cues Inherent in the Situation: Natural Cues

Activity	Natural Environ-mental Cues	Natural Social Cues	Initiating Natural Cue
Washing hands	Hands, soap, sink, faucet, water, towel	"wash hands" "lunch is over" "lunch time" "Gee, your hands are dirty"	Dirty hands Finishing a meal Starting a meal
Tying shoes	Open laces Just put on shoe		

Making a PBJ sandwich	Bread, peanut butter jar, peanut butter, jelly jar, jelly, knife, plate		
Getting dressed	Shirt, pants, under-wear, socks, shoes, buttons, zipper, snaps		
Stacking blocks	Blocks, possible properties of blocks (i.e., color, size, shape, etc.)		
Writing your name	Paper (possible lines on paper), pen/pen-cil, previous written letters		
Using CD player	CD, buttons, place for CD in CD-player		
Greeting people	Someone else enter-ing a room: you enter a room with someone else there; someone says "hi" (or uses some other form of greeting)		

On the other hand, consider a lesson on greeting people, where some verbal cues are integral to the situation. Greeting people politely can happen under one of several circumstances. For example, when Jane walks into a room and sees someone, it is polite for her to greet that person. However, if Jane is in a room and someone enters, then it also is appropriate for her to greet that person. Finally, if someone greets Jane with words or gestures, then she should respond with a greeting of her own. Only in this last instance was a verbal cue a natural precursor to greeting. However, to demonstrate complete mastery of this skill, Jane should greet people under all three conditions. Therefore, we should avoid using verbal prompts for the first two cases, but retain the natural verbal cues when we teach the last skill.

> *Because a prompt is a way to give learners help, the lesson is not complete until they can perform the task independently. That is, without the prompt. Therefore, whenever we use prompts, we must eventually remove them. By recognizing where we are now (i.e., the current prompt) and knowing where we are going (i.e., the natural cue) we can begin constructing the roadway to allow the prompt to gradually diminish in favor of the natural cue. Table 9-2, above, provides some common activities and their associated natural cues. Some areas are left blank for you to decide how you might complete them.*

Prompting Strategies

Researchers conducting basic experimental studies of behavior and learning deserve the credit for investigating methods for teaching their human and animal learners to make very challenging distinctions. Can you tell which of the objects below is different?

Could you see that that the fifth one is more oval? How easy would it be to teach your learners to differentiate that one from the others? Careful programming has enabled children with substantial developmental delays to accurately distinguish among shapes like those. In this, and the next, chapter you will find out about some of the prompting methods that researchers have created and how you can use them for your own instructional purposes.

Selecting Prompts

When selecting a prompt consider the following:

1. Use prompts that work. Does the prompt actually help the learner? Try it a few times. If it doesn't, try something else. To get a learner to pick up an item, you may try pointing to it. If that fails, try tapping on the item. If that fails, try shining a light upon the item. If that fails, picking up the item yourself may work. What you do is only a prompt if it successfully leads to the desired response.

2. Use prompts that are as close to the natural cues as possible. Having

one's attention drawn to what one's peers are doing is much closer to responding independently than is being physically guided. For any given situation, set up a hierarchy of prompts effective with the particular learner, moving from those closest to the cue toward those further and further away. How to move through the hierarchy will be described later in this chapter.

3. Model or demonstrate when feasible, showing the learner exactly what to do, when, and how. Be sure, though, that the learner already has learned to imitate modeled actions. If that is not the case then, naturally, it is very important to teach a learner how to imitate, because this is the essence of "vicarious or observational learning." It is much easier to say, "Watch me (or them). Do it the way I (or they) do it," than to physically prompt someone through an entire activity.

4. Three basic types of modeling prompts are often used in teaching:

    A. Body actions - waving an arm, touching an ear, turning around, holding up one finger, and so on.

    B. Selection of objects - when the teacher picks up a ball, the learner picks up a ball, and when the teacher picks up a spoon, the learner picks up a spoon, and so on.

    C. Actions with objects - pushing a button, scribbling with a crayon, turning a wheel, pulling a string, and so on.

5. When dealing with fine visual, oral, or tactile discriminations consider *embedding* your prompts directly within the stimulus to draw the learner's attention to the finer distinctions. If you want to teach a learner the difference between the spoken words "Stop!" and "Step," you might elongate the short "o" sound and/or make it louder; do something similar with the short "e" sound. To aid reading the word, you could draw a picture of an upheld hand around the o while placing a step beneath the e. Or, instead, you could pair the spoken word "stop" with a hand gesture signaling "stop," and pretend to be climbing up the steps for "step."

5. Use prompts that will be easiest to gradually remove or *fade*. Within any type of prompt, use the least intrusive level. If you were to use physical prompts, assure the performance with the least degree of support from the start. In this way, you are closer to its elimination than if you unnecessarily started with the maximum degree of physical interaction. Suppose every time a bell sounded to signal the end of an activity, you picked Andy up and carried him to the door. It would be

very difficult to get him to line up independently. By contrast, it would be easier to fade physical guidance that involved less physical contact than carrying - perhaps just guiding with a hand on Andy's back. It should be noted that it is virtually impossible to compare 'intrusiveness' between different types of prompts - remember, prompts are defined by their functional effect on behavior, not by some arbitrary scale we create. Our next section tells you how to go about moving from prompts to natural cues.

Eliminating Prompts

Fading Prompts

Billy loves to listen to music on his CD player. You want to teach him to put a disc into the player and then push the "play" button independently. As you analyze the task, you recognize that when Billy has acquired this skill, the CD, the CD player, and the buttons on the CD player should be all he needs to respond to in order to activate it. No one should have to tell him what to do. You also know that Billy does not imitate others readily, so modeling is unlikely to prove effective. Therefore, you decide to assist him physically instead of prompting him verbally, or modeling the skill for him. The teaching question is: "Although we can guarantee a successful action by physically guiding the entire sequence, how do we get Billy to do it independently?" In this case, gradually reducing the amount of physical assistance provided will be the most effective strategy. The gradual reduction in the degree of support provided by a prompt is called *fading*. How a prompt is faded depends upon the type of prompt.

Fading Spoken Prompts

Spoken prompts can be faded along a number of dimensions. For example, you can gradually reduce how loudly a prompt is said, slowly eliminate the number of words used within a sentence (e.g., "go to the door……go to the…..go…."), or even reduce the proportion of a complete word as in, "Say, 'chocolate'…say, 'choco'…say, 'choc'….say, 'ch.'"

Fading Physical Prompts

The degree of physical assistance provided can be reduced over a series of teaching trials. For example, begin with full, hand-over-hand guidance in pushing a button through a shirt-hole. Across trials, gradually decrease the force exerted. Then, use less physical assistance to guide the learner's hand to the button itself. Fading physical prompts may also involve altering where physical contact is made with the learner. For example, start *graduated guidance* with hand-over-hand prompting and then guide the learner's wrist, then his arm, and then merely touch his shoulder. Of course, even the faintest physical prompt (e.g., a finger on a shoulder) provides help that must be eliminated. Therefore, physical prompts are successfully faded only when all contact has been removed.

Fading Gestural Prompts

Gestural prompts may involve pointing to some environmental object or event, including a part of the learner's body. Another example is pantomime or gesture, such as moving your arms and hands in an upward fashion while saying, "Stand up." Increasing the distance between your fingertip and the object is one way to fade a gestural prompt like pointing. Over time, reduce the degree to which your hand, and eventually finger, is extended. Gestural prompts can be faded gradually by reducing exaggerated motions, until they disappear altogether.

Fading Model Prompts

Model prompts can be faded by demonstrating fewer and fewer aspects of the full action - change from clapping many times, to clapping once, to beginning to clap but not connecting hands, and so on.

Modeling the selection of an item is different than modeling an action with an item. Therefore, how modeling prompts are faded depends upon the goal of the lesson. For example, Morris has learned to imitate when his teacher picks up an item from a set of common toys and objects. His teacher now uses modeling to teach Morris how to use each object. However, his teacher only teaches Morris one action with each item - scribble with a crayon, roll a ball, rub a tissue on his lips, and so on. Now, when his teacher picks up an item, Morris immediately picks the same item and performs the learned routine. Is Morris imitating his teacher's action? Most likely, he only is imitating her selection because he now knows what to do with each item. In order to be sure that he is imitating her action, she must teach him at least two actions with each object. Thereafter, he must watch what she selects, *and* what she does with that item, in order to successfully imitate.

Fading Augmented Stimuli

At times, pictorial prompts are temporarily added to a feature in the environment to guide a learner's performance, as when dotted lines are supplied over which learners can trace a letter. In time, the dots are faded by 1) diminishing the number of dots, 2) decreasing the intensity with which the dots are printed, or 3) decreasing the size of the dots. The lesson also could begin with a dashed line and then fade to a dotted line.

In other situations, an aspect of a natural cue is enhanced and then faded[2]. For example, in teaching a learner to distinguish between the letters 'p' and 'q,' accentuate something associated with the letter (e.g., q is for q*ueen; she looks at the door*) or the directions in which the letters face (e.g., p faces the *pig* outside the window), like that shown in Figure 9-1. You could fade by making the lines of the pictorial prompts thinner and thinner, or moving back in steps until the only remaining hint was the nose.

Figure 9-1

Augmenting with Pictorial Prompts[3]

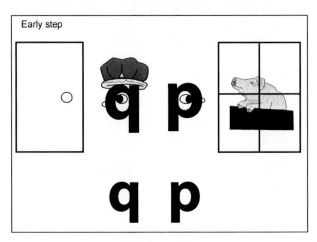

Within the PECS training sequence, a learner may have difficulty placing the "I want" symbol on the left-hand side of the sentence strip. Perhaps because the child is only three-years-old and cannot make such left-right discriminations at this point. One form of enhancement is to add a red line around the edge of the "I want" card, as well as a red lined box on the sentence strip. Over time, we fade the red line, as in Figure 9-2, and the child eventually places the symbol correctly using only natural cues[4].

---

2   Reese, E.P. (1971). Skills training for the special child. Cambridge Center for Behavioral Studies, 336 Baker Ave., Concord, MA 01742.
3   Take care to avoid these kinds of prompts with learners who tend to respond to only a single feature of a stimulus (are highly 'overselective') because shifting back to the natural stimulus may be very difficult
4   Frost, L. & Bondy, A. (2002). *The picture exchange communication system training manual, 2nd edition.* Newark, DE: Pyramid Educational Consultants, Inc

Figure 9-2

Fading Visual Placement Prompts

Another example (Figure 9-3) demonstrates how elements of a picture, such as enhanced circles (resembling an "O") added over the lenses, can be faded until only the printed word remains:

Figure 9-3

Fading Visual Prompts for Reading the Word *"Look"*

Some learners may encounter real difficulty progressing from the real object to its pictorial image. Try superimposing a small picture, or some other two dimensional representation, on the three dimensional symbol, while slowly making the latter less and less visible. Gradually enlarge the overlapping picture until it completely covers the object. Use this combined symbol as before until the learner once again is performing at a satisfactory level[5].

---

5   This strategy was successfully demonstrated by Frost, L. & Scholefield, D. (May, 1996). *Improving picture symbol discrimination skills within PECS through the use of three-dimensional objects and fading: A case study*. Paper presented at the Association for Behavior Analysis convention, San Francisco, CA.

Figure 9-4

Fading from 3-D to 2-D

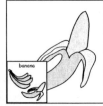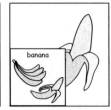

Prompt Hierarchies

When you plan to use prompting strategies such as those just described, you have several choices. You can provide hardly any help at all, adding assistance as needed. Alternatively, you can provide a good deal of support, gradually removing it bit by bit. Each serves separate purposes.

Least-to-Most Prompt Hierarchies

In some cases, a learner may perform some of the actions necessary within a sequential activity. You assess performance by providing as little assistance as possible. Should you need to help, begin in the least intrusive way before gradually escalating support. This strategy forms the basis of the *least-to-most prompt hierarchy*. If you elect to use this strategy, decide in advance:

- The types of prompts you will use.

- In what order you will present the prompts.

- How long you will wait before prompting. The length of the pause may reflect characteristics about the learner (e.g., one learner may benefit from five-second pauses while, with another learner, waiting for more than 3 seconds hardly ever succeeds).

Suppose you want to teach a toddler to stand up when you say "Stand up" so you can help him get dressed. After giving the instruction, pause for five seconds (if that is the interval selected). Then use a hand signal (i.e., gestural prompt) and wait five more seconds. If that doesn't work, model the action, and again wait to see what happens. Finally, physically assist the child to stand. The sequence of prompts is set and so too is the length of the pause used between prompts. Of course, when the child stands, give him praise and possibly other rewards.

One challenge in using this strategy is deciding when the learner simply needs a little more time to do something independently versus when the learner is waiting for you to provide assistance. For example, when teaching a learner to set the table with four sets of plates, forks, spoons, knifes, cups, and napkins, if there are five-second pauses between each of four types of prompts for each item, the table would hardly ever be set! This strategy may lead into a type of stop-and-go pattern throughout a task: the learner independently completes three steps, and then pauses for the next step - waiting for a series of prompts - then completes five steps before pausing again, and so on. This herky-jerky pattern delays the acquisition of a fluid task sequence. Be sensitive to learners who may need extra time to complete a difficult task, while avoiding unnecessarily long waiting periods for those who don't.

Most-to-Least Prompt Hierarchies

Sometimes a learner does not complete any aspect of a sequence. Different varieties of potential prompts are used, to no avail. Obviously, she needs assistance all along the way. In such cases, choose to initially provide as much help as necessary, and over time gradually reduce the number and intrusiveness of the prompts. For example, in teaching a child to load a dishwasher, begin the lesson by using physical guidance as the child puts each item into the dishwasher. Over trials, switch from full physical guidance to merely touching an arm or hand. Later, only point to the items to be loaded. In this case, you would be reducing the successive intrusiveness of the prompts from full physical, to partial physical, and finally, to a gestural prompt. One advantage of this strategy is that it allows little room for mistakes, because the appropriate action is assured by providing the necessary prompt.

When physical prompting of this type is provided within a sequential task, it also is preferable to prompt from behind the learner. For example, two teachers collaborate in Phase I of PECS. One entices the learner by holding a desired item. When the learner reaches for the item, the second teacher, stationed behind the learner, guides the learner's reaching hand to pick up a corresponding picture. Together they give the picture to the communicative partner, who immediately gives the learner the desired item in exchange[6]. At first, the second teacher will need to use full physical prompts to have the learner pick up the picture, reach it toward the teacher, and release it. Over trials, and as quickly as possible, the second teacher

---

6   If the teacher who is enticing the learner also provides physical prompts, she may cause the learner to become overly dependent upon those prompts. Perhaps because prompts from behind the learner are outside of the learner's field of vision, they are easier to eliminate

begins to use less physical guidance, typically by going from full physical to partial physical prompts. In time, all physical prompts are removed and the learner completes the exchange independently. Another example of effectively providing prompts from behind the learner involves the use of visual schedule systems to help learners move through the activities of the day. Such prompting strategies are used for individual pictures as well as sequences of pictures[7].

A potential danger in both types of prompt hierarchies is that by changing from one type of prompt to another, you still must remove that new prompt. Is it easier to remove one type of prompt than another? Most likely not. Therefore, you may want to first try to pick a single prompt and try various strategies (including those we are about to describe) to remove that single prompt before trying to move from prompt to prompt.

In some sense, the most-to-least prompt strategy is similar to fading. That is, assistance is gradually reduced over time. However, in fading we reduce the level of a *single type of prompt*, while with the most-to-least strategy we gradually reduce the assistance using *different types of prompts*. In the next chapter, under the heading of *Errorless Learning*, we offer several additional examples of fading methods.

Delayed Prompting

A learner may respond appropriately to certain types of potential prompts but not others. For example, some learners almost always imitate a word modeled for them. Others reach for whatever picture someone merely points to or touches. Other learners always retrieve the item corresponding to one displayed to them. In each case, the goal of a lesson is to transfer control from these currently effective prompts to natural cues (or other less intrusive types of prompts). *Delayed prompting* can be helpful in these cases. In this strategy, two distinct types of signals are used - the prompt that is already effective, and the natural cue.

Two basic types of delayed prompt strategies are *constant* time delay and *progressive* time delay. As with all delayed prompt strategies, first we identify the prompt and the intended natural cue. For example, without any additional help, Henry does not choose his candy according to the color named by the teacher, as when she says "red" or "blue" when both are presented simultaneously. However, whenever his teacher points to the red one, he picks up the red candy. When his teacher points to the blue

---

7   See McClannahan, L.E. and Krantz, P. (1999). *Activity schedules for children with autism: Teaching independent behavior*, Bethesda, MD: Woodbine House, for a detailed description of this strategy.

candy, he picks up the blue one. In this case, a gesture is the prompt, while spoken words are not.

Delayed prompting involves inserting a time interval between the two signals. In *constant time delay*, a fixed time interval, such as four seconds, is always used. Henry's teacher says, "red" and then waits four seconds before pointing to the red candy. Each time candies are offered his teacher waits the same four seconds between her spoken word and her gesture. Notice that Henry cannot fail at this lesson - either he responds to the spoken word "red" or he responds to the point. In either case, he gets candy! Over time, Henry begins to respond correctly even before his teacher has pointed. In all likelihood, his response shifts from the prompt to the spoken cue because he gets his reinforcer sooner by taking advantage of differential reinforcement.

A variation on this strategy is to use a *progressive time delay*. In this case, rather than using a set duration between the prompt and the cue, you begin with no delay. That is, simultaneously present both signals. Then, over a series of trials, gradually increase the delay between presenting the cue and presenting the prompt. For example, when Mariana is shown a picture of a spoon, she immediately gets a spoon. However, when her teacher says, "spoon" she does not respond correctly. Her teacher begins by saying, "spoon," while simultaneously showing her the picture of a spoon. Next, her teacher introduces a half-second delay between the spoken word and showing the picture. Then her teacher increases the interval to one second, two seconds, three seconds, and so on. As with constant time delay, either Mariana responds to the spoken word or she responds to the picture. In neither situation is she likely to make an error. This progressive time delay strategy is used within Phase V of PECS training. In this case, control is transferred from pointing to an icon - "I want" - to the spoken question, "What do you want?"

With both types of time delay, you can enhance the likelihood of switching from the prompt to the cue by adding reinforcement when responses occur to the cue. Thus, in addition to getting the reinforcer more quickly - he doesn't have to wait for the prompt - you might give him more of the reinforcer, or allow access to it for longer, when you see the response to the cue.

Delayed prompting only works when you know what functions as a prompt. For some very young children, you may find it difficult to find that reliable way to help in the performance of various tasks, thereby limiting the applicability of this strategy for them. However, once any type of aid proves effective, whether physical, gestural, verbal, or modeling, then this strategy becomes very appealing and promising.

Be Careful with Your Prompts!

As we noted in the last chapter, we need to remain aware of the danger of prompt dependency. This dependency occurs when a prompt has been added to a lesson but it has not been effectively removed. As noted, it is the teacher's responsibility to put in prompts and to remove them - you are responsible for that prompt! One tendency many teachers display is using more than one prompt at a time. It seems that if we use a gesture, and a picture, and a little physical help, and a word or two that all will be easier! But if you remember that you must remove each prompt you will see that if you were to use five prompts all at once then you are not done with the lesson until all five have been removed!

> *Removing one prompt can be difficult enough, so here is one simple rule - use one prompt and try to remove it. If you cannot remove it within a reasonable and planned period of time, you have some choices. For one, you could change your prompt strategy - that is, try a different way to remove that prompt. For another, you could replace your current prompt with a different prompt and then try to remove that one. Remember, piling on the prompts may seem to make today easier but will make all your tomorrows more difficult!*

How to Teach Sequential Lessons

A number of strategic questions arise when we teach sequential lessons. Should we teach all steps of the sequence at the same time? Should the first steps or the last steps become the focus? Although there are no universal answers, often some choices need to be made along the way.

Whole or Partial Task

For many activities the entire sequence must be completed each time it's taught. For example, hand-washing requires carrying out the entire sequence, from turning on the water to drying hands, each time. The *whole task* needs to be taught. On the other hand, some activities permit separating segments in the sequence. For example, a learner can practice putting clothes into the washing machine without having to run the machine every time it's loaded. This example uses a *partial task* approach. Concentrate on the more difficult aspects of the sequence when using this method. However, not all steps within the same task are amenable to partial task presentation. For example, while washing clothes, it is not practical to have the learner repeatedly put liquid soap into the machine because if it were then turned on, the results would be disastrous!

Forward or Backward Chaining

As was noted earlier, sequential tasks can best be thought of as a behavior chain, where each element is linked both to its previous step (as a reinforcer) and to the next step (as a discriminative stimulus). Furthermore, completing some tasks can be naturally rewarding for the learner, while extra rewards need to be added for completion of other tasks.

As chains have two ends, teachers have a choice as to which end they want to first teach. In *forward chaining,* the first steps are taught from the beginning of the lesson, with full support provided for the remaining steps. For example, George's teacher wants him to wash his hands. With this strategy, George is first taught through prompting and fading to turn on the faucet and pick up the soap. Then his teacher provides full assistance on most of the remaining steps. So, next, she helps him wet his hands. At this point he independently rubs them together and needs to be guided to move on to the next steps of returning the soap, rinsing his hands, and so on. In general, as George learns the initial steps, the teaching focus changes to the next set of steps.

Other sequences may be taught by focusing on the last steps first, using *backward chaining.* This strategy may be necessary when the first steps are more difficult to teach. For example, to ride a bike, Nancy must get on the bike before peddling to keep her balance. Teaching her to get on the bike first will be difficult because without peddling, she can't stay upright. Instead, her mom helps her onto the bike and then holds her (helping her keep her balance) while she begins to peddle. As she gains control over her balance, her mom lets go and carefully watches to see if she stays upright! Only after she has mastered peddling and balancing is she taught how to hop onto the bike and get going on her own.

Backward chaining also may take advantage of tasks for which there are very powerful natural consequences. For example, putting on sneakers results in an opportunity to run. Thus, the last step - pulling the looped laces tight - is strongly reinforced by the immediate opportunity to use the sneakers. Therefore, Sam's teacher uses full assistance to help him complete all steps in tying laces except for the very last one. Once Sam learns to pull tight the looped laces, his teacher says, "Nice tying your sneakers! Go ahead outside!" During subsequent lessons, his teacher gradually expects him to learn to independently complete the steps just prior to the last one, carefully moving back in the sequence over time. The lesson always ends with Sam running outside.

Figure 9-5

Backward Chaining Sequence to Teach Sentence-Strip use within PECS

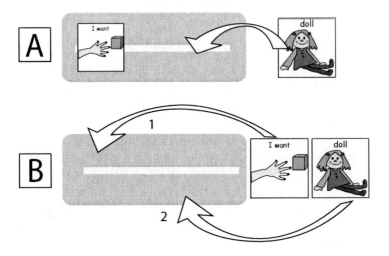

Within the training sequence for PECS, after the user can exchange a single picture, we teach him to place two symbols - "I want" and a picture of the desired item - on a Sentence Strip before exchanging it with his partner. The final performance involves placing both pictures on the strip. Therefore, when we begin this lesson, the "I want" symbol is already on the Sentence Strip (sequence A in Figure 9-5 above). The learner needs initially to learn what to do with the single picture of the desired item. Rather than presenting it immediately, we teach him to place the picture on the Sentence Strip and then to give the strip to the communicative partner. After he learns this, we teach him to affix the "I want" symbol (sequence B above). At that point, the learner can smoothly complete the remainder of the task by placing the picture corresponding to the desired item on the Sentence Strip, as previously learned. One advantage to back-

---

Is Combining Procedures Okay?

Sometimes strategies may be combined to maximize effectiveness. For instance, differential reinforcement may be used with delayed prompting. In such cases, when a learner responds to the currently effective prompt, the reinforcer is provided calmly. However, when the learner 'beats the prompt' (i.e., responds to the natural cue) then enthusiastic praise is provided! Both cases continue to result in rewards; it is only that independence earns more powerful ones than prompted responding.

ward chaining is that while we focus our teaching on one step, the remainder can be swiftly performed without further help.

Summary

Most of our educational objectives consist of learners learning to respond in one way to a particular cue, and differently to other cues: following directions, answering questions, making the right choices, solving problems and many more. When our learners fail to react appropriately, we're tempted to try the same thing over and over again; often faster and louder. An alternative is to interpose a prompt - demonstrating, telling, gesturing, guiding, or whatever else works - to get the learner to respond correctly. Prompting can produce the behavior we are seeking but, ultimately, learning is demonstrated only when the behavior occurs independent of any guidance.

The way to approach the situation is to examine the objective to find out when, where, and under what conditions the behavior is supposed to occur. In other words, we need to be clear about the *cues* that should call forth the response under natural conditions. Then our task is to select a *prompt* - one that is as close to the natural cue as possible. Among the strategies often shown to be effective are demonstrating or modeling a particular bodily action, or our own selection of objects from an array, or our manipulation of a particular object. Imbedding prompts directly within the stimulus can work with those discriminations involving sight, sound, or touch. We must remain mindful of the fact that all prompts will have to be eliminated, though, and consider this aspect when first selecting specific prompts.

We need to examine the nature of each prompt because we realize that our job is not done until all such prompts are eliminated. Then we can act accordingly. Spoken prompts may vary along a few dimensions, like loudness or completeness, so we can diminish the intensity of the sound or reduce the length of the prompt. Physical prompts can be faded by diminishing the forcefulness or changing the location of our guidance. Gestures and modeling prompts can be compressed and augmented; stimuli made smaller and dimmer until they gradually disappear. Interposing a constant or variable delay between the prompt and the cue is an especially effective way to proceed, as learners typically begin to anticipate the cue in time.

The task of removing prompts will be easier if we only supply those that are absolutely necessary in order to achieve the response we are seeking. If we have the patience, we do that by starting with no help and adding it slowly, a bit at a time, until we get what we're looking for. That way we will have identified the minimal prompt intensity necessary. Alternatively, if we want to be absolutely certain to achieve the behavior we are seeking; we can prompt in most-to-least fashion so the learner makes few errors. Then we remove those prompts slowly but surely.

Another valuable instructional tactic to use is chaining, teaching lessons containing sequences of tasks. Depending on what the learner already knows, the reinforcing features inherent in the task, and other aspects, we can either begin by teaching the initial portions or those at the end. While starting at the beginning seems the logical place, going backwards can just about guarantee that the learner will complete the job and come in regular contact with reinforcers every time. We all win!

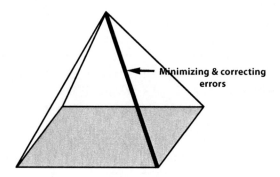

Minimizing & correcting
errors

10
Minimizing and Correcting Errors

"Practice makes perfect." "Learn by trial and error." People familiar with these phrases might be shocked to learn that scientific evidence calls these age-old statements into question. Practice makes perfect only if we practice perfectly, or have improving actions followed by reinforcers. If we repeatedly practice something the wrong way, and get credit or some other form of reinforcement for doing it, we will learn to continue to do it imperfectly. If you are practicing hitting a tennis ball, you could be using poor form, yet get it over the net. That could firmly establish the poor form and get in your way in the future. If you over-broil a hamburger but your guests declare it delicious, you may never learn to make a tender, juicy one.

The same thing goes for *learning by trial and error*. Sometimes errors are reinforced, and when they are, they are apt to re-occur. A better way to learn concepts or skills is by having our more successful efforts reinforced. An effective coach would be sure to reserve positive comment for a perfect (or at least improved) tennis swing, or a reasonably juicy (or improving) quality of hamburger.

> **Reinforcing improving practice makes perfect**

Do we need to discard these sayings altogether? No. Just modify them a bit. Restate *"Practice makes perfect"* as *"Reinforcing improving practice makes perfect."*

Similarly, the phrase *"Learn by trial and success"* is more accurate than *"Learn by trial and error."* In both instances probably you have noticed that shaping can be an important part of the successful instructional process. (For a review of *shaping*, see Chapter 4, *Powerful Reinforcement Systems.*) Shaping is a wonderful teaching tool and we use it whenever appropriate. There are times, though, when a response cannot be shaped because there is no way to improve upon it. Either it's right or it's wrong. A 6 is not a 9. A W is not an M. Hugging family members or friends is fine, but one does not hug strangers in the mall. Sticking wires into electrical outlets, running into a street full of traffic, or eating pills from the medicine cabinet are all unacceptable - your first error may be your last act.

How do we teach rights and wrongs of those kinds? By presenting choices and then 1) reinforcing the correct answers, and 2) withholding reinforcement from, or correcting, the wrong ones. This kind of *differential reinforcement* teaches making proper distinctions or, technically speaking, *discriminations.* Reinforcing repetitions of the correct choice should allow learning of the correct discrimination.

Teaching that way sometimes causes problems, especially when our learners have a difficult time learning to tell slight but important differences between very similar stimuli. First of all, every time they practice the wrong response, there is a risk of reinforcement occurring by chance. The learner, or even the teacher, might fail to note the inverted letter and accept an M where a W belongs. That can happen even to us. You may have used a poor strategy in a card or board game yet won often enough. Now you've learned a better method, but you're playing in a tournament and the pressure is on. You lose the game because you returned to your old faulty ways.

The need to correct errors sometimes can create a second problem, particularly among special populations. One side effect, sometimes called an *extinction burst,* may result when the learner commits an error and, as appropriate, reinforcement has been withheld (technically - *the error has been placed on extinction*) or the learner corrected (technically - *punished*). Extinction bursts can take the form of anger, aggression, escape, and/or total inaction, thereby interfering with the learning process. Trying to teach a new skill to a screaming learner or one who has tuned you out doesn't work very well, and is punishing to you as a teacher too. Is there another way? Yes. Remember, people learn best by trial and success. *Errors are not essential.*

Errorless Learning

Interestingly, if responses were error-free from the very beginning, the results will be even better. There would be no need to shape or correct errors. The advantages here are many:

1) Reinforcement rates can be very rich because the response is right every single time. There is no need to correct or ignore any of its aspects.

2) Extinction bursts are avoided.

3) Development of *bad habits* - accidentally getting stuck at a level of imperfection (e.g., "No matter what I do, my golf ball hooks to the left") - can be averted.

According to researchers and educators, learners whose development is delayed thrive when they learn without making errors. To be right all the time in a learning task is exciting and wonderful; a rare and heady experience. Reading, math concepts, and many other academic responses, can be programmed for errorless learning. So can social and other kinds of skills.

How Do We Design Errorless Lessons?

As described earlier, we conclude that learners have learned a skill or concept when they consistently demonstrate:

• A brand new behavior, like zipping up a jacket.

• A new form of a behavior, like combing one's part on the left instead of the right.

• An older behavior under new conditions (now zipping slacks), or for longer time periods (assembling boxes for an hour instead of a minute), more intensely (brushing teeth until they really shine), at a faster rate (getting dressed in five minutes instead of an hour), or more accurately (filling in every space correctly on a job application).

• A set of behaviors rearranged in a new order (making a shopping list, purchasing the items, bringing them home, putting them away).

Just as there are different types of learning, many of the kinds of teaching methods we read about in the last chapter, and elsewhere in this book, attempt to minimize or totally eliminate errors from the start of the lesson. All of these errorless strategies, of course, work best when we apply the rules for effective reinforcement discussed in the Chapter 4, *Powerful Reinforcement Systems*.

Teaching for "Errorless Learning."

Teachers now have many techniques available to them for helping learners avoid the pain of making errors by hardly ever producing them in the first place. Among these are some already familiar ones and a few new to you:

1. *Blocking errors.* In some situations, parents and teachers prevent an action to avoid severe punishing consequences. We place covers over electrical outlets and never allow our children near streets with busy traffic unless they are holding our hands. In such cases, we would not know if the child has learned until he was no longer prevented from responding. That is, what he would do when electric outlets are not covered, or if no one held his hand at a street corner. Maybe in these cases we don't care just how independently he acts, as long as the youngster can remain protected until he has matured sufficiently to make us feel more comfortable about gradually removing our safeguards.

2. *Shaping.* When trying to teach a new form of an activity, shaping is a highly effective strategy. As noted earlier, the key to successful shaping is to make progressive changes in the response requirement large enough to encourage advancement but small enough to encourage continuing to do the task correctly. In shaping, no response is punished, while just about every response is reinforced.

3. *Physical guidance.* Another way to help create new forms of behavior is to gently physically guide the learner to perform the action perfectly, then gradually to withdraw, or *fade,* the degree of help we provide. Of course, this strategy will not work with everyone - some individuals are described as being 'tactile defensive' and may withdraw when others touch them. In such cases, tolerating touch would have to precede using physical guidance as a prompt.

4. *Graduated guidance.* Sometimes, rather than fading the degree of support *within* one type of prompt for a single action, several prompts across an entire activity are faded. Graduated guidance involves starting with sufficient physical support to assure a successful completion of a sequence, and then subtly reducing the physical assistance across the individual steps. In such cases, the reduction of support is a function of the independence shown and, thus, is not planned for ahead of time. For example, there are several items that are involved with getting dressed, and a learner may be more independent with his shirt than with his pants. In this case, he would need more support for putting on his pants than for his shirt. When all prompts have been eliminated, the sequence is performed in response to the natural cue.

5. *Fading*. Of course, we may support a new form of action completely with prompts other than those involving physical contact - visual prompts, modeling, slow motion demonstrations, and so on. Once it is clear that these fully support the new behavior, we begin to diminish the number of prompts, or the strength of the specific prompt. When using fading, we do not shift from one type of prompt to another. Rather, some aspect of the specific prompt - its force, location, duration, etc. - is systematically reduced, leaving the natural cue in place at the end of the lesson.

6. *Teaching discriminations errorlessly.* As we saw in the last chapter, when teaching learners to choose correctly between things they "perceive" (i.e., see, hear, touch, taste, or smell), we can arrange our instructional stimuli so making the wrong response becomes very improbable. With this strategy, teachers organize the array of materials in such a way that selecting one is highly likely while selecting the other is not. For example, you might place two objects on a tabletop - a ball immediately in front of the learner and a spoon across the table and almost out of reach. Ask for the ball and the learner is very likely to give you the nearest object. Each time the learner responds correctly, you can provide some reinforcement as well as move the spoon closer to the ball (in random locations relative to the ball). Very gradually, as in shaping, begin to move the two objects closer together, while continuing to ask for the ball. This arrangement is only the beginning of a discrimination lesson. In order to assure that the spoken word "ball" reliably results in the response of choosing the ball (in technical language, the choice is "under *stimulus control"),* the learner will need to give you the ball when it is one of several equally available items, and *not* give you the ball when you've asked for something different.

7. *Expanding* some parts of an action. Helping a learner throw a ball farther, walk quietly down a longer hall, go a greater distance across a room to ask the teacher for help, speak more loudly, place a stamp more neatly in the corner of the envelope, and fill the soda machine more quickly all depend upon the learner possessing some current degree of skill. Each of these lessons can be accomplished without the use of prompts by having the teacher shape minute changes in the criterion for reinforcement. Thinning the schedule of reinforcement also involves no apparent prompts. Successfully implementing these strategies requires careful monitoring of information such as the distance involved, the number of required repetitions, the duration of a response, or the frequency of reinforcement.

8. *"Slicing".* When a learner hesitates within, or has difficulty with a portion of, a sequential response, you can take that part and *slice* it

into smaller parts. Then you allow the learner to practice each portion over and over until it looks automatic. Recombining it into the larger part becomes much easier later on. Suppose a youngster were having difficulty tossing a ball into a basket. By examining the performance closely, you note his wrists are placed on the ball at the wrong angle. You show him where they should be and practice just throwing short distances, forgetting about the basket for a while. After he continues to repeat this new position time after time after time (i.e., fluently), you now return to coach throwing toward the basket.

Planning instruction for errorless learning can be challenging and time consuming. Nevertheless, currently available computer graphics capabilities can ease the process substantially. In addition to the kinds of pictorial cues illustrated in the last chapter, we can subtly adjust other properties of the prompts, fading them out slowly, in a series of steps, until none remain other than the critical differences. Notice that the position of the two different letters is switched randomly in order to avoid the learner using position as an erroneous cue.

Fading *color* cues

You may decide that you want to change the color pictures your learner uses to communicate to ones that are black and white (perhaps, in part, to help reduce the cost of the pictures). In this case, you can gradually reduce the color saturation of the pictures in the following manner:

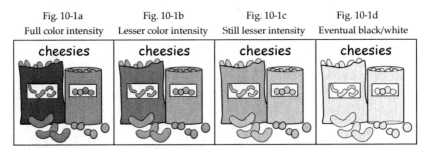

| Fig. 10-1a | Fig. 10-1b | Fig. 10-1c | Fig. 10-1d |
| Full color intensity | Lesser color intensity | Still lesser intensity | Eventual black/white |

Fading *size* cues

While teaching a learner to discriminate pictures within PECS, you decide to take advantage of the learner's tendency to reach for bigger pictures. In this case, when pairing an item that is highly desired (e.g., cheesies) versus minimally reinforcing (e.g., socks), you start by making the "cheesies" picture much larger than the "socks" picture. As soon as the learner reliably uses the larger picture, you gradually change the relative size of the pictures in the following manner.

Figure 10-2a

Large "cheesies" Picture
Small Picture of "socks"

 vs.

Figure 10-2b

Large "cheesies" Picture
Somewhat Larger Picture of "socks"

 vs.

Figure 10-2c

Large "cheesies" Picture
Somewhat Larger Picture of "socks"

 vs.

Figure 10-2d

Pictures of Equal Size

 vs.

Altering *intensity* cues

You may have found that one learner can successfully choose the picture of the "cheesies" only when it is paired with a "blank distracter." That is, a card the same size as the picture of the "cheesies" but with nothing on it but its white background. As quickly as this pairing leads to successful selection of the "cheesies," you gradually introduce a faint picture onto the "blank" card - a picture of "socks." Over a series of trials, the intensity or darkness of the "socks" image is gradually increased until it is just as dark as the picture of "cheesies."

But Suppose Learners Do Make Mistakes? Coping With Errors

A key goal for teachers is to minimize the errors their learners make. However, despite our best intentions, sometimes mistakes do happen. You ask Bill his name, and he answers, "soda." Michelle walks out of the bathroom into your classroom and you hear the water still running. One way to react to these errors is to *fix* them. To Bill, you say his name and he immediately repeats it. He now has said his name. You tell Michelle to go back into the bathroom and turn off the faucet. She does so, and the water stops running. In each case, the problem has been repaired - Bill said his name and the water stopped running. But what did Bill and Michelle learn? Most likely, Bill did not learn anything - he already knew how to imitate his name. And if Michelle acquired any new skill, it probably was that she should turn off the water when her teacher tells her to.

How, then, are teachers supposed to react to such errors? Just as we reviewed different types of lessons in order to design various errorless teaching strategies, so too will we need to link *error correction strategies* to the type of error made within a lesson. As opposed to quick fixes, error correction strategies create small learning opportunities. At the same time, the teacher quickly and frequently assesses what the learner actually learned.

The key to error correction is focusing on the goal of the original lesson. For Bill, the lesson was, "Answer the question, 'What's your name?'" For Michelle, the lesson was to complete a full hand-washing sequence in the bathroom. To select an error correction strategy, first identify the stimuli

("What's your name?" running water) that are *supposed to* control the behavior ("My name is Bill;" turns off the water). Then develop, and follow, a plan to re-establish the appropriate stimulus control. How we respond is dependent upon which of our two prime lesson formats we use - either discrete trial or sequential. Let's see how we can effectively respond to errors in each type of lesson.

Discrete Trials: The 4-step Error Correction Sequence

Step One: *Model/Demonstrate/Show* the Correct Response. The error Bill made took place within a type of discrete trial lesson. A simple stimulus, "What's your name?" should have been followed by a simple answer, "Bill," followed by a reinforcing consequence (e.g., "Yes!" or "Glad to meet you, Bill."). Instead, Bill said, "soda." The teacher naturally would model, or demonstrate, the correct answer. When Bill imitates, should we move on, assuming the problem was licked? No, because Bill's imitation of the word "Bill" is not the same as answering the question, "What's your name?"

Step Two: *Practice* the Correct Response. The teacher now asks his name again. Bill is very likely to respond correctly at this point. Since this is the practice step, we want to assure that no error is repeated. Thus, we might prompt in whatever manner is necessary to assure a correct response. Note that we cannot tell you how to prompt - there are no universal prompts. You must know your learner and the action being taught to best select the prompt. However, should we stop the lesson here? From Bill's perspective, he has just said his name twice in a row - once imitatively, and once in response to the question. When he said his name the second time, though, could we say for sure whether he was listening to us, or was he simply repeating the last thing that worked? Repeating a response that just got reinforced is a very good strategy for any learner; but if that is what Bill did, then his response was not under the stimulus control of the question, but more likely cued by his own previous response. In other words, he is simply *imitating* rather than *answering the question*.

Step Three: *Switch* to a Different Response. How, then, do we check that Bill is truly listening? The teacher now introduces another simple instruction - *switching* to a different question. What we introduce in this step should be something that is in the learner's repertoire. That is, something he is virtually certain to successfully perform. For example, the teacher holds up a known item, such as a cup, and asks, "What's this?" Given that this response is very familiar to Bill, he is likely to successfully respond. The teacher provides him only with a small reinforcer, such as praise, because his answer is not a new one.

Step Four: *Repeat* **the Original Cue (i.e., the set-up for the lesson).** Now the teacher *repeats* the original cue by asking, "What's your name?" If Bill says "Bill," the teacher can feel more confident that the reply was under the stimulus control of the question and not Bill's own prior response. The teacher also provides a big reinforcer at this point. While we will still cover the issue of data collection shortly, it should be pointed out here that a correct response at this step of the error correction does *not* get scored on the data sheet. You've already put a minus (-) at step one!

Other Examples. This strategy also is used within discrete lessons involving discrimination training. For example, within Phase III of PECS, you may offer the learner a choice between a cookie (i.e., a preferred item) and a sock (i.e., a non-preferred item). If the learner gives you the sock picture, you would offer the sock. When the learner rejects taking the sock, the 4-steps would involve:

1. Tap on the picture of the cookie (i.e., *model*).

2. Hold out your hand near the cookie picture (to have the learner *practice* giving you that picture). Praise the learner but do not give the cookie yet.

3. *Switch* to another skill that the learner knows.

4. *Repeat* the initial step by re-enticing with both the cookie and sock. If the learner gives you the cookie picture, immediately give the cookie and praise.

Hints about Switches. The *switch* could involve having the learner do something different, such as pointing to a known body-part. As with a spoken model, the lesson should not stop at that point. Selecting an item or picture someone else just pointed to is not necessarily the same as choosing correctly between an array of items or pictures. The *switch* in this case requires distracting the learner from staring at the item just selected, and assuring ourselves that the target stimulus is truly controlling the response by introducing different items or distracters.

It is helpful to switch to things that the learner already knows. That way, you also have an opportunity to provide the learner with a bit of reinforcement (i.e., praise for a correct response) as an antidote for the consequences of the mistake. Those reinforcers may help establish what is called *behavioral momentum* - making future correct responses more likely. A switch to something the learner knows well also gives you an opportunity to check whether the learner is paying attention at all, or is just not making an effort. Suppose you ask a learner to touch his nose and you are absolutely certain he knows how to do this (because he has done this so many times before), but he touches his ear instead. We should assume that something is wrong with the overall lesson, not just with the target skill within the lesson. A teacher also may consider switching to a completely different type of response - from a lesson target of giving a spoken reply, to an imitative or instructional motor act.

Finally, if some of your learners have not yet learned other reliable responses at this point in their education, pointing to something on the floor, accidently dropping something on to the floor to be retrieved, or even pausing for five or six seconds should provide the necessary distraction prior to the teacher repeating the primary cue.

Although our instructional example involved a spoken response, "Bill," suppose the lesson had involved teaching *receptive language* - wherein the goal is to select a particular picture or item - rather than *expressive language* - where the objective is for the learner to produce a verbal response. In that case, *modeling* could be conducted in the form of a demonstration of, or showing, the correct picture, such as pointing to, or tapping on, the picture.

What Happens if the Learner Continues to Make Errors?

At this point, you may be wondering what happens if the learner makes another mistake at the repeat step. You might duplicate the entire 4-step error correction sequence; but suppose the learner makes yet another mistake. You could keep on looping through the sequence forever! To guard against this, only repeat the 4-step sequence two or three times, at most, before stopping the lesson and moving on to something else. The more errors that build up, the greater the likelihood of a problematic behavioral episode. You either can stop the lesson at the point of the switch (i.e., "You're right! Let's get a drink of water."), or greatly simplify (or even eliminate) the choices provided. In either case, the session ends on a successful note.

Correcting Errors in Sequential Tasks

Backstepping

Michelle was involved in a sequential activity when she made an error - leaving the faucet open. Her teacher noticed the problem when Michelle entered the classroom, but it is clear that the error was made in the bathroom. What should be the appropriate stimulus control for turning off the faucet? In part, that will depend upon the task analysis - the plan for the order of the steps involved in washing hands. For example, the sequence may be:

1. *Turn on faucet*

2. *Pick up soap*

3. *Rub soap on hands under water*

4. *Put down soap*

5. *Rinse hands*

6. *Turn off faucet*

7. *Pick up towel*

8. *Dry hands*

In this sequence, "rinse hands" is the step that precedes "turn off faucet," and thus should come to provide the proper stimulus control over turning off the water. But Michelle is in the classroom with you! Her teacher must now go *back* in the sequence to the *step* before the error if Michelle is to learn the proper sequence. The teacher says, "Wow! Let's try that again!" while walking Michelle back into the bathroom. The teacher re-creates the proper conditions - soapy hands and running water. At that point, the teacher uses a gesture to prompt Michelle to turn off the water once she has rinsed her hands and prompts, as necessary, to ensure that Michelle completes the sequence. Now, Michelle has a good chance of learning when to shut the faucet.

This same Backstep strategy can be used to refine various flawed sequences, even when these are not part of a formal lesson. Suppose that, along with the paper waste, a learner throws her spoon into the garbage. Many teachers would ask her to retrieve the spoon from the garbage can. Although she does need to learn to hold on to the spoon while dumping the garbage, she does not need to learn to retrieve spoons from inside garbage cans. Thus, she needs to take her tray and utensils back to her seat and learn to hold the spoon while dumping the garbage. Suppose a boy bolts out the door and runs down the hallway. Rather than having the learner walk back up the hallway and walk down slowly, the key is recognizing that the learner needs to learn to associate going out the door with walking slowly. Thus, the boy's teacher would lead him back into the room, teaching him to leave the room through the door and walk down the hallway. A learner using PECS places an attribute card in the wrong place on the Sentence Strip (e.g., "I want the ball blue"). Instead of pointing to where the picture should go, have the learner re-create the Sentence Strip, assuring the correct placement of the card at the correct point in the sequence.

Both the 4-Step and Backstep require a fair degree of diligence from the teacher. Given the effort required at the time of the error, you may wonder whether it's worth the bother. A familiar adage may help remind you of your choices: *Pay a little now or a lot later!* Create a learning opportunity through your error correction strategy, or you will see the error appear over and over and over and …

Anticipatory Prompting

While Backstepping is an effective error correction strategy for sequential tasks, you may encounter situations in which it simply is not possible to stop the sequence and go back to an earlier step. Events during instructional activities based in the community may be beyond your immediate control. You take Jake on a public bus. He is supposed to take money out of his wallet and give it to the driver. On this occasion, Jake takes out his money but walks past the driver. An immediate Backstep procedure would require you to ask the driver to stop so Jake could exit and re-board the bus, while you then would prompt Jake to give the driver his money. Imagine the look the driver would give you!

In such a situation, your next opportunity to address the error will occur the next time you take Jake onto the bus - maybe the following week. You know where in the sequence Jake probably will make the error. That is, you can anticipate the error. Therefore, you can use an *anticipatory prompt* to prevent the error from re-occurring. As Jake is taking out his money, you may prompt (i.e., remind) him about the next step - give the money to the driver. How you prompt will depend upon what you already know about Jake. A verbal hint will be effective with some learners - either direct (i.e., "Give the money to the driver") or possibly indirect (i.e., "What will you do with the money?"). Gestures or pictures may work better with others.

As always, you need to eliminate those prompts over time. One way is to use the anticipatory prompt earlier and earlier in the sequence - before boarding the bus you might remind Jake, "Now, remember to give the money to the driver." The intensity of the anticipatory prompt also may be faded over time - a spoken reminder, to pointing to Jake's wallet and then to the driver, and so on.

Some sequential tasks contain recurring sequences of actions. For example, a vocational task may involve collating three pieces of paper, stapling them together, folding them in thirds, putting the set into an envelope, sealing the envelope, placing the envelope in a 'finished' box, and then repeating the entire sequence. Suppose a learner consistently pauses at a particular step in the sequence. For example, Bart pauses after putting the filled envelope in the 'finished' box. His teacher typically waits a few seconds and then tries subtly to prompt him to repeat the cycle. No matter how delicate the prompt - a finger flick, a slight nod of the head - Bart's continued performance remains prompt dependent. Because his teacher knows where in the sequence the error is likely to occur, she can use an anticipatory prompt. At first, while Bart is still sealing the envelope, but before he has put it into the 'finished' box, his teacher touches the pile of papers that start the sequence. While the teacher prompts, Bart looks at the pile of papers but also puts the filled envelope in the right location. He then immediately starts the cycle over. Over time, his teacher moves the anticipatory prompt to a point earlier in the sequence and reduces the intensity of the prompt. In time, she completely removes it and Bart cycles through the sequence until all the materials are used, or the end of the work session is signaled.

Commonalties Among Error-Correction Strategies

Teachers should always seek to minimize errors in their design of lessons. When the goal is to establish stimulus control over a particular action, errors typically involve either responding to the wrong cue, or not responding at all to the correct cue. When the focus is on establishing stimulus control, it is not a good idea to modify the lesson to allow prompts to remain. Choosing between pictures within a discrimination task is not the same as picking a picture tapped by the teacher. Answering a question is not the same as imitating the answer. Hanging up a coat after looking at a picture on a schedule is not the same as hanging up a coat following a verbal or gestural prompt. Teachers need to be prepared to use error correction strategies when the focus of the lesson is correct responding to given instructional or natural cues. Common among all error correction strategies is a sequence within which the intended stimulus (i.e., the instructional, natural, or chained cue) is arranged to connect with the target action. While it is best to apply correction opportunities as quickly as possible, circumstances may prevent repetition of the response sequence until the next opportunity arises naturally, as in the case of the bus rider.

> **Prevent errors whenever possible and plan for appropriate error correction when necessary!!**

Furthermore, by recognizing the nature of the lesson being taught, a teacher should predict the type of error likely to occur. Errors within discrete trial lessons tend to differ from those encountered in sequential lessons. Although teachers do their best to minimize errors, they should not be surprised when some occur. In their lesson preparations, they should include a plan to apply appropriate error correction strategies, if needed.

Summary

Many learn successfully enough by practicing a skill repeatedly and through trial and error. The problem with these approaches is that the repetition of errors can establish the wrong, as well as the right, aspects of the behavior. As we have seen, there are better ways, especially for learners who encounter major difficulties in learning. These *errorless learning* methods have the advantages of avoiding the necessity of correcting errors, extinction bursts, and the development of bad habits. Behavior analysts have designed numerous errorless teaching methods which, when combined with powerful reinforcement strategies, can achieve wonders. Included are blocking errors, shaping, physical and graduated guidance, fading, and teaching discriminations without allowing errors to intrude. The field of behavior analysis frequently develops new error correction strategies, or you may currently use one that you have demonstrated is helpful but, that is the key, whatever you use, it must be effective!

Nevertheless, errors are bound to happen. When they do, it pays in the long run to see to it that they don't become firmly established. Fortunately, another arsenal of strategies is available to us. The 4-Step error correction sequence - *modeling* or demonstrating and then having the learner *practice* the correct response, *switching* to another skill, and then *repeating* the cue followed by a powerful reinforcer - works well with discrete trial instruction. In sequential lessons, Backstepping to an element earlier in, or even to the beginning of, the sequence helps. When necessary, anticipatory prompting can be used to avoid a likely error within a sequence until the learner regularly responds appropriately. Eventually, eliminating these prompts is essential if the learner is to perform the task appropriately and independently.

The important thing to remember when teaching the kinds of advanced skills described here is to remember not to become discouraged. If preventing errors altogether hasn't worked, you now have a number of ways to correct them. Like a good scout, don't let unanticipated errors throw you. *Be prepared* to cope with them by having a correction plan readily at hand.

Chapters 9 and 10 Resources

Specific Teaching Strategies & Minimizing and Correcting Errors

To	Read
Define, describe, and apply methods for chaining and shaping behavior.	Sulzer-Azaroff, B. & Mayer, G.R. (1994). *Achieving educational excellence: Behavior analysis for school personnel* (pp. 110-140). San Marcos, CA: Western Image.
Examine and learn about applying antecedents to motivate and teach learners with autism.	Luiselli, J.K. & Cameron, M.J. (1998*). Antecedent control: Innovative approaches to behavioral support.* (Especially sections IV & V). Baltimore, MD: Paul H. Brooks.
Use prompts to get responses to occur and transfer those prompts to natural antecedents.	Cooper, J.O., Heron, T.E., & Heward, W.L. (2007). *Applied Behavior Analysis, 2nd Edition.* Columbus, OH: Merrill. Cuvo, A.J. & Davis, P.K. (1998). Establishing and transferring stimulus control, In J.K. Luiselli & M.J. Cameron (eds.), *Antecedent control: Innovative approaches to behavioral support.* (pp. 347-369). Baltimore, MD. Paul Brooks. MacDuff, G.S., Krantz, P.J. & McClannahan, L.E. (2001). Prompts and prompt-fading strategies for people with autism. (pp. 37-50). In C. Maurice, G. Green, & R.M. Foxx (Eds.). *Making a difference: Behavioral intervention for autism.* Austin, TX: Pro-ed. Sulzer-Azaroff, B. & Mayer, G.R. (1991). *Behavior analysis for lasting change.* (Section III.) Atlanta, GA: Wadsworth Group - Thompson.

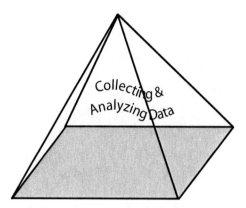

11
Collecting and Analyzing Data:
The Why and How of Data Collection

A teacher you know proudly announces, "Sarah can dress herself!" Another colleague reports, "Marquelle can factor algebraic equations!" When you get home, your spouse mentions that your son, "Worked for two hours all by himself!" On the phone, your mother reports that she completed an art project. And while watching TV, your daughter shares with you that she exercised today. How should you react in each case? Would you react differently if you learned that Sarah put on one sock versus chose her clothes before school, and put them all on neatly within 10 minutes without supervision? Would you react differently if you knew that Marquelle took 3 hours to complete the assignment versus five minutes? What if your mom filled in a color-by-number picture versus painted an original landscape? And what if your daughter did one sit up before eating a pint of ice-cream, versus expended 500 calories during her workout?

What influences your reaction is the quality and detail of the information about the actions - not simply knowing whether or not it occurred. The same will be true while you are teaching children or adults new or refined skills - the information you collect about their performance can help you decide if you've had a significant impact or not. Let's discuss now how to arrange to collect information about your teaching efforts and the behavioral changes you are trying to achieve.

Why Collect Educational Data?

Let's face it - collecting and analyzing data takes time and effort! Most of us have difficulty doing two things well at the same time. So how can I teach effectively and also take relevant data? For one, this issue translates into something like, "Why should I bother to take data?" Other critical questions include, "Who should take the data?" "What type of date should I take?" and "How often should data be collected?" Let's consider the answers to these questions.

It should be recalled that there are no perfect lessons - no one can guarantee that the strategy selected to teach a skill will be effective, because no one can guarantee the future. Some strategies will work and some will not. What happens if we've selected a strategy that doesn't work? Clearly, the learner's skill will not improve. But we should also realize how failed teaching strategies influence our own lives. Teaching is not an easy activity - it is something to which we devote great time and effort. If we continue to use a strategy that is not resulting in learning, then we must admit that we're wasting our own time and effort - not just wasting the time of the learner. Do you have time to waste? We doubt it. Therefore, one critical reason to take good data should be personal (and even selfish!) - take data to assure that you are not wasting your own time and sticking to a strategy that leads nowhere.

Designing and Changing Lesson Strategies

Effective teaching is hard work. While teachers put a great deal of effort into planning and implementing lessons, there is no guarantee that those efforts will be successful. As we noted in Chapter 8, if the learner didn't learn, the teacher didn't teach. If the learner is not learning, something about the lesson needs to change. Therefore, teachers need to collect information to find out whether or not their strategies are working, and if they should continue or change their lesson strategies.

It often is tempting to rely only on informal observations. Yet when the instructional steps are very small, as they tend to be when learners have special needs, minor signs of learner progress might well be overlooked. Some learners progress so slowly that they may appear not to be moving along at all. Collecting data at such times can be extremely important. The information will affect decisions about whether or not to change lesson or behavior intervention plans. Suppose a task analysis for laundering a shirt has 25 steps. In the absence of objective data, the teacher might easily overlook actual progress at the rate of about a step or two a week, and be tempted to change her lesson strategy prematurely. By collecting data, she will uncover how effective her instruction actually has been.

Analyzing the Environment

Data should also serve as the central problem-solving piece when investigating how the elements of a *complex system*, like those in the home, school, community, or workplace setting, affect what learners do. Then, we can analyze the data to help guide decisions about whether, and how, the system should be changed. Consider, for example, pro-social behaviors. Data could be collected on factors known to influence that category of behaviors, including the type of activity, who is present, or the frequency of encouragement or praise from adults that support positive interactions. We then can measure which people, or which actions, do the most to encourage or discourage the learner to practice particular social skills.

In addition, collecting data can serve numerous useful purposes:

- Determining the *current status* of the learner or others. For instance, a standardized language assessment is administered to discover a) whether a learner's placement in an educational program seems reasonable, or b) the average functioning level of the learners in a given program.

- Tracking *progress*, as in a learner advancing through the phases of a language-training program like PECS. Some teaching objectives will be broadly defined, while others will be broken down into very fine steps. Be certain that the type of data you collect reflects the size of the steps you are teaching.

- Supplying evidence of direct *accomplishments*, such as the number of contextually relevant requests a learner makes, or the number of words she reads per minute.

- Monitoring correlated *improvements* (e.g., downward trends in problematic behaviors, such as acts of aggression, self abuse, or withdrawal).

- *Assessing* and *diagnosing* the origin of problems, as in assessing the function of aggressive or self-abusive episodes.

- Yielding information about curriculum, resources, and educational strategies to use as a basis for deciding what to use, and how to use them.

- Serving as a *source of useful feedback* to learners and teachers.

- Providing a basis for setting long range and interim goals.

Who Collects Data?

In a school situation, different members of the IEP team may write particular objectives. It may seem natural that the person who authored an objective should be the one to take the data on that objective. However, it should be remembered that the IEP team, and not any individual, is responsible for implementing, and thus evaluating, the IEP. Regardless of who wrote the program, the whole team, including paraprofessionals, takes responsibility for deciding how data are to be collected and analyzed. For example, both the teacher and the speech pathologist might collect information about PECS or speech performance at various times. However, each of these team members also might collect data on vocational objectives, such as how well a learner requests missing materials for a job. Observers need to be trained to be consistent in the way they score behavior so the information they gather remains objective and reliable.

Resources, of course, dictate who might be in the best position to collect data on a behavior or its results. Progressive organizations will include technical support staff whose job includes collecting, summarizing, graphing, and analyzing data. In the absence of such personnel, you might try to recruit others to do the job. They do need adequate training and supervision, though, until all are confident that their data are reliable and valid. In the absence of that kind of support, professional personnel, the teachers themselves, their peers (other teachers, aides), parents, capable learners, and supervisors need to learn to fulfill this role successfully.

No matter who records, the method of data collection must remain accurate and consistent. Below we describe methods for maintaining this rigor by periodically scheduling simultaneous observations by a second person. Reliability needs to be monitored fairly often, especially in the beginning, so differences in scoring can be used as a basis for refining definitions and training.

Qualities of Useful Data

Formal data collection is reserved for important educational purposes, not just for the fun of it, because the process can be costly. Educators need to balance between the purpose and importance of the data, and methods yielding the most valuable information for the smallest investment. If the goal is simply to get a rough estimate of progress, precision may not be crucial (although realize that the results could be way off base). The following discussion assumes the object is to get as closely as possible to the real truth.

Validity

To be of value, whatever data are collected must be valid. That is, the numbers must mirror exactly, and accurately, what they are supposed to be measuring. The more valid data are those with very carefully defined and tested *objective* definitions of the events being measured. That means avoiding one's subjective feelings or impressions. Instead either a completely objective mechanical instrument, like a tape recorder, or one or more unbiased observers, is necessary. Standardized tests, like individual intelligence tests, or teaching protocols, like the *Picture Exchange Communication System* and *Direct Instruction*, spell out very clearly what constitutes a "correct response," and users are trained to apply those definitions consistently. Under those circumstances, validity is less of an issue.

Sometimes it takes a major investment to design valid measures. Definitions may have to be defined, refined, and redefined repeatedly. Often, though, as we have seen, *function* may be more important than the form or *topography* of the behavior. So what needs to happen is to describe clearly the function of a whole set of related behaviors (i.e., a *functional response class*). Differentiating between a self-hit, bite, and head bang may not be the most important concern. All could be included under the functional heading of "avoidance or escape responses." More important is what any member of that response class appears to accomplish for the learner. Similarly, the data taken could just as well relate to the effect the learner's behavior has on objects (e.g., projects completed, windows broken), or on other people present (e.g., causing them to laugh, cry or surrender a toy).

Reliability

To be considered reliable, a data collection method needs to consistent over time from one observer to the next. In looking at ongoing learner or teacher behavior, arrange for two people independently to collect the same behavior samples at the same time. What do you do if you find that each one scores an event quite differently from the other? Suppose one says a learner is spontaneously initiating a request to play with a given toy, and the other says she is responding to a prompt. Deciding what to do next would be difficult. Should you fade the prompt or concentrate on promoting initiations toward a greater variety of toys? The problem is that the data do not truly represent what is happening; they are unreliable, useless. Problems like this can be fixed by:

1. Revising and clarifying the definitions of correctness, including conditions, timing, rate, and other qualities or *dimensions*. Teaching-teams are ideally suited for this purpose because everyone is familiar with the situation and knows where issues arise.

2. Re-training the observers; having them observe, compare, receive feedback from trainers, and so on, until all agree very closely among themselves not just once, but on a number of occasions.

Example:

Old definition:	Learner initiates a spontaneous choice
New definition:	When presented with two different toys placed equidistant from one another, and with no instructions or gestures from the teacher, the learner reaches in the direction of one of the toys within 10 seconds

As a *quality assurance* strategy, check the data-scoring methods periodically by having two observers collect the same sequence of data (at least ten or so repetitions) at the same time. Of course the observers need to make sure to avoid communicating with one another during the process. They then can calculate an *index of agreement* by examining each item, one by one, to see if the observers agreed or disagreed. They then count the number of times the scores agreed (As) or disagreed (Ds). The proportion of the time the observers agreed is determined by dividing the number of times that they agreed by the total number of times they scored, regardless of whether they agreed (A) or disagreed (D). To express the estimate of *reliability* as a percentage, multiply by 100 - just move the decimal points two to the right. The formula, found over and over in the research literature (where they are very fussy about reliability and validity) is:

Figure 11-1

$$\text{Percentage of agreement} = \frac{A}{A + D} \times 100$$

An appropriate goal is to achieve a reliability index above 0.90 (or 90%). If it is substantially below 0.80, there are too many disagreements. In such cases, get the team (including supervisors) together to discuss the nature of the problem and work out further refinements.

What Learner Data to Collect

On a day-to-day basis, the two most important areas for evaluation involve information about functional skill development, and information about the effectiveness of strategies aimed at reducing CIBs. Other information will help teachers continue to do the best job possible by helping to identify factors that may control both skills and CIBs.

Even when all of your attention seems to be focused on problem behaviors, recall that the *Pyramid Approach* emphasizes teaching functional skills and functionally equivalent alternative behaviors to CIBs. Therefore, although it might be tempting to limit data collection to problem behaviors, a teacher should concentrate most heavily on promoting learners' skill development.

Types of Data to Collect

Just as we use a ruler to measure the length of an object, a scale to assess weight, and a thermometer for temperature, depending on our purposes, a number of different behavioral assessment instruments are available. Examples include the form, shape, or *topography* of a response, or its results, its frequency, rate, and intensity.

Form of the Behavior

Often we count behavior by its form, shape, or *topography*: what it looks like when a learner is doing something like clapping his hands; how he holds his pencil; or how closely the product of his effort conforms to a set of standards (e.g., how round the circles or straight the lines are when writing). Response topography is illustrated by the contents of checklists, and those based on task analyses. We also can collect topographical data on problem behaviors, such as the form or location of a head hit, the place on his hand that the youngster bites, how severe the bruises are, the objects a learner with pica ingests, or the people he knocks off balance.

Form versus Function

Two or more behaviors may have different topographies but the same function. Technically, we can say that all behaviors that serve a common function are members of the same *operant response class*, a very important concept in behavior analysis. An entire array of problematic behaviors, including hitting, spitting, pushing, rocking, screeching, and others may all form part of a single response class because one is functionally the same as the next. Collecting data in such cases can be simplified if you collapse all those behaviors into one category, such as "aggression." Within skill acquisition, a learner may display several 'ways' to request toys - talking, writing, or using PECS. Each may involve a different form or modality, but all serve the same function. On the other hand, a single behavioral topography may have two or more different functions. In such cases, it is important to separate behaviors with the same form but a different function, as when a learner is spitting out food that is spoiled rather than spitting it at another learner, or when a learner slaps another learner on the back as encouragement versus a similar slap while angry.

Frequency

Sometimes we are concerned with how often a particular behavior happens. Giving the right answer to a multiplication problem once or twice is not the same as giving the right answer thirty times, nor is sorting the laundry properly once the same as repeating it a dozen times. Similarly, there is a big difference between knocking one's baby brother down a time or two versus twenty or thirty times. Frequency is measured by counting.

It's easy to count when a behavior has a tangible outcome, such as the written answer to a multiplication problem, or the piles of soiled laundry. When a behavior does not leave a lasting result, we need to measure it while it is happening (i.e., concurrently), or right afterwards. You can tally the number of different words spoken, or pictures used, by keeping an inventory by date and adding to the list each time the learner uses a new word appropriately. Provided they have a distinctive beginning and end, you can record the number of a learner's temper tantrums. You also can take frequency measures on your own performance, by recording the number of times you conduct a particular type of lesson.

Simply counting the *frequency* of presenting pictures or hitting actually gives us only the most basic information, though. What would be the meaning of a report that the learner used ten pictures correctly or hit himself ten times? That is impossible to answer. We need to know more, such as over what period of time these events happened (i.e., their *rate*), how long they lasted (i.e., their *duration*), or how powerful or *intense* the behaviors were.

Rate

This measure adds the important time dimension to frequency. Rate can be defined as the frequency of the behavior per a given amount of time. Using ten pictures or hitting oneself in the head once a week would be very different from once a minute. If you think about it, we often separate successful from unsuccessful learners by noting their learning rates. Levels of mastery or fluency may only be noted by recording a behavior's rate. Quickly calculating the correct answers to multiplication problems is quite different from doing so slowly and hesitantly.

Remember, though, that if you use a rate measure, you must keep the time duration and other circumstances constant. Otherwise, you will not know if a change in the measure was a function of the behavior, the number of times it occurred, or the conditions under which it occurred. A learner may say "Hello" 10 times during the first 10 minutes of the day, but not again until the end of the day. If we compared the rate of saying "Hello" without regard to the time and place, then the rate during the first 10 minutes would be dramatically different than the rate obtained across the first 4 hours of the day.

Many educators find rate to be the single most important type of information about a behavior. To be certain that your recordings of rate changes most closely represent what truly is going on, include details such as the place, dates, and times when you begin and end data collection whenever you take behavioral frequency data.

Duration

A behavior's duration, or the length of time over which it persists, may be the main issue. Crying briefly after scraping a knee would not be regarded as something extraordinary, but continuing to weep for hours would be. The length of time an individual continues to perform a job task can be critically important. Working for a minute and stopping for ten would be regarded as far more problematic than the other way around. Many lessons include expanding the duration of a behavior as their goal. Time on task, waiting, or remaining seated are examples. The objective is simply to stretch the length of time over which the behavior persists.

Similarly, shortening the duration of a behavior may be the goal when dealing with CIBs. Crying when hurt, or imitating a TV commercial for a few moments is reasonable. When our main purpose is to shorten the length of time a behavior persists, assessing duration becomes our sole data requirement.

Intensity

Sometimes your concern is with the forcefulness of a behavior. For instance, we may be satisfied with the rate and duration of a learner's speech, but unable to get the full message because the volume is too low. A different youngster may operate equipment correctly, but pushes the buttons and switches with such force that he breaks them. A learner who jumps up and down, loudly shouting out answers, is disruptive to the rest of the group. In each case, assessing the *intensity* of the response will aid our efforts to change the behavior.

Latency

A teacher asks Joan to come to the front of the room. Joan responds, but after 15 seconds. When she does respond, it is sufficiently intense, all the components are correct, she always responds - but usually after a long *latency* between the instruction and the response. In such cases, latency is an important aspect of the overall performance. In some situations (e.g., "Stop!"), the latency has to be very short for everyone. However, there may be situations in which you recognize that your learner typically takes a few more seconds to respond and you may prefer that over introducing a strategy to reduce that interval. You may measure latency in absolute terms (e.g., five seconds), or within a range (e.g., less than 5 seconds).

Behavioral Recording Procedures

Many procedures are available when it comes to collecting behavioral data. Some are relatively simple; others more complicated. The choice depends on the behavior observed, and the effort required to collect adequate information about it. Two fundamentals, though, are crucial to deciding what system to use:

1. That the data collected are meaningful.

2. That the data collected are used.

Getting Started

Do not try to do it all at once. Be selective, because data are only useful if you use them. Forms piled on desks or jammed unread into cabinets just take up space. Record only what you are reasonably certain will be used, and be sure to set priorities. This process is a team decision, dictated by IEP considerations. Mutually set priorities indicate what information is most pressing. Avoid beginning with minute process measures, those nit-picking details about who did what, when, and how, unless the more gross ones fail to tell you what you want to know. Begin with those data that are easiest to obtain reliably, like the steps mastered in a training program, or lists of new words spoken.

Should you encounter a road block and cannot figure out what is getting in the way, then you might begin to collect more complicated data, such as something about the instructional process or behaviors of the learner that interfere with learning. When using a delayed prompting procedure, suppose you are wondering if you are providing the cues too soon. You could have a peer count the seconds you actually wait between presenting a toy the learner likes to play with and saying its name.

Other instances might be observing how closely teachers adhere to the protocol for displaying and using the learner's daily schedule in the classroom; or determining the steps parents are conducting correctly in a PECS routine in the learner's home. Is the timing of trials, placement of materials, nature and frequency of prompts, or other antecedents or consequences arranged optimally? Perhaps a learner's temper tantrums seem to have increased during discrete trial training. You could get some valuable information about how to improve the way you organize those sessions by measuring the nature of the tantrums and the conditions that appear to set them off or keep them going. Another excellent choice would be to examine more closely those antecedents and consequences that tend to support the smoothest, most efficient progress.

So rather than plunging into taking data for data's sake, always ask yourself in what way the data will be meaningful and useful. If critical information is missing, or inappropriate methods selected, the data will lose its value. Instead, we need to be as certain as possible that these elements are covered.

Crucial Identifying Information

Regardless of the system, the following information needs to be included when data are collected:

- date
- time
- location
- name of the observer(s)
- name of the person or group being observed
- any atypical physical and social conditions in effect, such as other activities going on, unusual furniture arrangements, others present, and so on

Next we describe the two most common methods for recording behavior. One is based on its ongoing process; the other on its immediate results or products.

Observational Recording

When the behavior of concern leaves no enduring immediate product, like a work sheet, completed sandwich, or neatly organized toy shelf, we have no choice but to capture it while it is going on. That means that someone has to be present and watch either all the time or according to a schedule that permits the behavior to be accurately represented.

Continuous Observation

When faced with a particular challenge that requires us to know exactly how often, when, and where a behavior occurs, or some other measure of it, we need to count and record it every time it happens. We must be careful not to overlook or double-count instances. If a learner hurts himself or someone else, or damages property only rarely, we should prepare an incident report and total such episodes quite reliably.

If, on the other hand, a boy rapidly and continuously hits himself or others, we may find it difficult to get an accurate count. Subtle but important changes might then easily be overlooked. As described below, a better alternative in such cases is to use a representative sampling system, checking the presence or absence of the behavior within a given period of time.

Certain kinds of classroom learning activities lend themselves especially well to continuous observation because they are discrete events with easily identified beginnings and ends. Included are:

- The total number of items performed correctly during discrete-trial training.

- Progress through a task-analysis, like one for bed making. You have a checklist containing each item broken down into its individual elements. Either the item is performed correctly or incorrectly, or it is missing or in the wrong order.

- Items completed correctly per number of opportunities provided.

- Number of correct and incorrect responses by prompt level during carefully programmed instructional programs, or in classrooms arranged to heighten incidental teaching opportunities.

- Number of correct or incorrect spontaneous (unprompted) responses, during formal instruction, or when the classroom is designed to heighten incidental teaching episodes.

When teachers control the pace of the lesson, counting and totaling is easy. At the end of the session they can calculate a percentage correct, allowing them to see degrees of progress made over time.

Sometimes you might want to tally a behavior but can't take the time from your ongoing activity to do that. Use an audio or video tape recorder, or some other way of preserving the event until you have the time - perhaps after school.

Behavior Sampling

Is it necessary to record every response during every single teaching session? The answer depends on how essential or useful the information is. If you use it to make a decision about how to adjust aspects of your instruction, the more information you have, the better. But if you want simply to use it as a basis for judging progress over time, probably a periodic probe will be sufficient. Remember that if the data are neither meaningful nor useful, the time spent taking them probably can be spent to greater advantage elsewhere.

When a behavior happens so often that it's impractical to record it every time, ask yourself if it is really necessary to count every single response in a lesson or occasion the learner gets up from the table. Maybe instead, you could take *representative samples*[1], choosing as a reference a standard block of time, such as an hour, half hour, five minutes or a minute, and record whether the response of concern happens at all within each particular time block[2]. All you need to monitor for, then, is the first instance of the behavior, ignoring repetitions within that time interval. Alternatively, you can set a timer or use a sound, light flash, or vibratory signal to cue you to monitor, score, and record at that moment[3]. Although these samples can over- or under-estimate reality, eventually they can give you valuable information. You will become increasingly confident your tactics are succeeding when results show more and more blocks scored for the absence of a behavior you hope to see diminish, say 5 ten-minute periods without any self-hitting; or for the *presence* of a behavior you are encouraging, like playing interactively with a peer.

When resources are limited, even results of discrete trial instruction can be sampled, say by scheduling someone to record every X sessions or time blocks. Most important is that the data represent what actually is happening as accurately as possible, a decision best made by a team including someone with expertise in this area.

Recording Results of Behavior

When the behavior we are attempting to teach leads directly to a prod-

---

1   Beware of sampling based solely on convenience because you may find yourself cued to observe by something the learner is doing. Instead, decide ahead of time when the behavior is to be sampled and stick to the schedule.

2   This system may be referred to as a *partial interval time sampling system* or an interval *spoilage system*. See Sulzer-Azaroff & Mayer (1991) for a thorough description of various behavior sampling methods.

3   The name for this variation is *momentary time sample*. Pyramid Educational Consultants markets auditory signaling tapes for educators who elect not to prepare their own.

uct or other result, it may be possible to by-pass *observational* recording of ongoing behavioral data. In fact, sometimes, it matters little how a person does a job; just that the job is completed to standards of satisfaction. Once a learner has learned the steps in a task analysis involving filling envelopes, or cleaning rooms, our interest is in the number of envelopes filled, or rooms cleaned - not in the motions that produced the results. In a classroom, behavioral products can include the numbers of workbook pages or problems the learner completed, pictures in a communication book used appropriately, or the total number of pieces of furniture broken, or facial bruises seen. Computerized instructional programs may be designed to provide the number right, wrong, percentage correct, rate, and other important elements of the learning process. All we have to do is record that information.

The obvious advantage of using data based on products is that we need not engage in the time-consuming, or possibly distracting, process of observing the learner while the behavior is ongoing. The presence of observers also can cue, or otherwise influence, various aspects of the behavior. Cleaning one's room or dressing for work while someone stands there with a checklist is very different from producing a clean room or being appropriately attired while no one is there to observe. If the ultimate objective is for the person to perform a task independently, it is best to assess under natural conditions, those that match as closely as possible the typical environmental circumstances.

We can record information about the products of our own efforts just as well, such as counting how many learner schedules we have posted, or observational forms we have submitted. We could look at the way the physical environment is arranged for instruction - placement of chairs, table, pictures, and so on. We can count the number of times the supervisor initialed and dated classroom charts. Written compliments could be tallied just as readily. Data like these can supply valuable information about our actions as teachers or supervisors as they relate to learner progress.

Making Use of Data

Meaningful data can be used in a number of important ways, among others, to investigate the relation between the behavior and its consequences, immediate antecedents, and other contextual factors; to monitor and report learner progress; to evaluate the utility of instructional methods, and their costs and benefits. Here we detail some of those[4].

4   Two other important uses, beyond the scope of this book, are experimental research and staff management. Numerous examples of these can be found in scientific and professional journals, such as the *Journal of Applied Behavior Analysis* and the *Journal of Organizational Behavior Management*.

Assessing the Function of a Behavior

To determine the functional relation between a behavior and the environment, data must be collected on each element of our three-term contingency: specific behaviors and their antecedents and consequences. We want to know if the learner who presents a picture of a ball actually "knows" what it means. We say, "It's time to go outside and play"- the *antecedent*. The learner chooses a picture of a "ball" from an array of pictures and gives it to the teacher - the *behavior*. The teacher says, "Go get it," and the learner gets a ball before going outside to play with it - the *consequence* (Figure 11-2). Because the learner selected both the picture and the ball, we are more confident that he understands the meaning of the selected picture. Now, if we record a dozen or more instances in which that relationship is consistently maintained, we can feel more confident of the learner's "understanding" of the relation between the card and the ball.

Figure 11-2

The Function of a Behavior

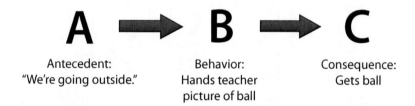

Antecedent:	Behavior:	Consequence:
"We're going outside."	Hands teacher	Gets ball
	picture of ball	

As mentioned earlier, if you have determined that a number of behaviors tend to happen together, like the group mentioned earlier under the heading of "aggression," you can handle them as a single set when assessing their function. When the same behavior has different functions, though, you will need to separate them from one another, depending on the antecedents or consequences. Presenting the picture of the ball just before recess would be very different from presenting the same picture at lunch. Head-hits following a teacher's reprimand vs. head hits while running a fever (perhaps elicited by the pain of an ear infection) are quite distinct and should be counted separately.

We need to measure all behaviors targeted for reduction in the behavior intervention plan from a functional perspective. Along with its rate, or some other measurable attribute of the problem, we also systematically measure any variations in broad environmental conditions that might relate (Figure 11-3):

- The presence or behaviors of teachers, supervisors, parents, other learners.
- Suspected physical variables such as the particular room, its arrangement, temperature, noise level, crowding, etc.
- Internal conditions of the learner including physical ailments, time since the last meal or break.

Figure 11-3
Possible Sources of Data to Collect from the Learner's Wider Learning Context

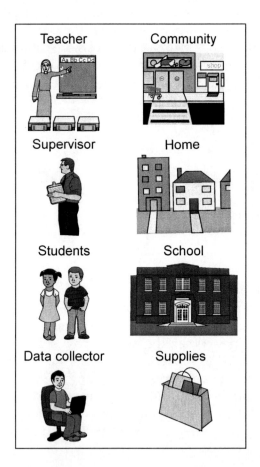

In terms of specific antecedents, examples might include teachers' instructions or gestures, or their presentation of written material, objects or pictures, time of occurrence, location, specific activity, and similar items or events. Possible consequences might be scolding, ignoring, giving tangible objects, praising, hugging, complaining, presence of an extinction burst, or other emotional responses and so on.

Assessing Learner Progress

Report cards represent a long tradition of recording information on learner progress and communicating it to parents and others. Just how valid and reliable report card data might be in any given case is open to question. Besides, standard report card measures represent major chunks of progress. Fine details are missing. Broad-brush measures of the relatively slower progress of learners with special needs may mean very little. More sensible, as described in the chapter on functional objectives, is breaking skills down into their parts and determining in advance just what standards constitute mastery of the skill. Now there is a more reasonable and accurate basis for measuring and reporting progress. These data then can be inserted in the learners' records, and communicated to the learners themselves, parents, supervisors, future teachers, and relevant groups.

Data on *learner progress* also can inform educators about the appropriateness of the categories, difficulty level, and size of learning steps. When progress is very slow, objectives are probably too challenging or not relevant to the learner's functioning, or reinforcement has been too sparse. The program needs to change. If, on the other hand, the learner is acquiring minor objectives by the bucket-full, there is a good chance that objectives can be made more challenging.

The *feedback* inherent in reporting progress data also may serve a powerful reinforcing function for its recipients, especially when objectives and instructional methods are carefully adapted to the individual learner. Many take advantage of this fact by issuing progress reports more often than the typical quarterly report card: monthly, weekly, or even daily. When objectives are listed in advance, inventorying progress becomes a simple matter of just checking them off.

Another related situation is when you want to monitor *learners' progress through a curriculum* chosen to support their broader IEP objectives. Here, especially in the early stages, you want to determine what, if any, headway the curriculum appears to be promoting. Figure 11-4 displays the number of pictures mastered by a learner being instructed in PECS. Here the purpose was to assess whether the decision to use PECS was justified and, if so, to determine just how well it was working. Notice that as time progressed and the learner began to master new pictures, data were collected less often. Probing once in a while, thereafter, could reassure us that the progress we think we see taking place actually is.

Analyzing Instructional Methods

Concern with tracking accomplishments and progress of individual learners is one thing. Another is to analyze instructional effectiveness by using data to help us plan the details of our teaching routines, to diagnose problems, and to prescribe promising solutions. We know, for instance, that while the learner is attempting to learn something new and difficult, like following her daily schedule, it is crucial for the *teacher* to provide lots of reinforcement. After the objective is mastered (when the youngster checks and follows the schedule regularly), reinforcement is supposed to be delivered less and less frequently because intermittent reinforcement is best for maintaining a well established skill. In that case, we may want to monitor the teacher's frequency of reinforcement to assure that the intended *thinning* of the schedule actually is taking place. We could count the number of praise statements delivered at the point of mastery, then probe at irregular intervals to determine if indeed the reinforcement rate were diminishing while the learner's progress remained consistent. Figure 11-5 shows this relationship.

Figure 11-4

Assessing a Learner's Progress through PECS

Number of Pictures Mastered

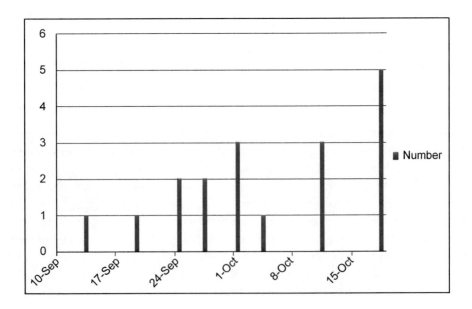

Figure 11-5
Ratio of Praise Statements to Number Correct

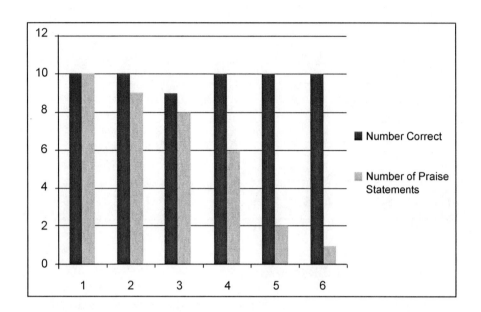

Making a Case for Special Placement or Supplemental Resources

Clear objective data are essential in order to justify recommending placing learners in a special setting, or requesting supplemental resources. Review the kinds of evidence demanded by law or standard practice, and supply it. One item of interest could be the learners' rates of progress through their academic curriculum; another might be information about their social or emotional skills and deficiencies. It is one thing to say that the learner has difficulty reading, and another to count the number of new words he has learned to decode within a given week. Even more powerful would be those data showing rates of progress (or of maladaptive behaviors) per day or week over a number of weeks or months. If these are very different from those of the members of a criterion group, your chances of reaching a reasonable resolution are increased. See Figure 11-6 for an example.

Figure 11-6
Number of New Sight Words Learned

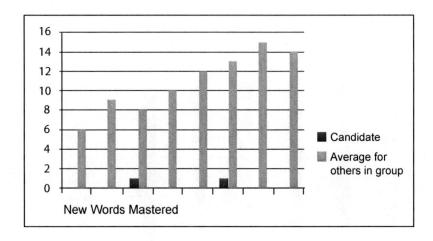

Dealing with Limited Resources

If you are limited by scarce resources, and have to sacrifice collecting data on some aspects of your program, maintain collecting and summarizing the most important elements of a learner's IEP. These could include individual objectives or combinations of objectives closely linked (see Figure 11-7).

Figure 11-7

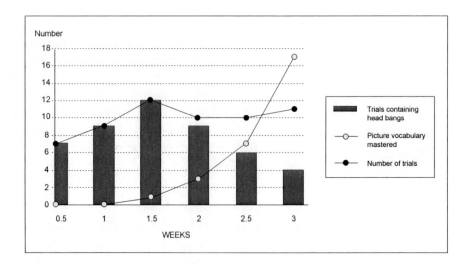

Who Else's Behavior is Assessed?

Typically, it is the learner whose performance is being assessed, and that has been the main focus of this chapter. Nevertheless, if we are to take a broad view of the learning environment, we might also take data on the performance of instructional or supervisory staff, data collectors, parents, peers, and others. To illustrate, quantitative information could be used to track:

- *Progress* of an educator's mastering the skills involved in using the *Pyramid Approach to Education*, or a district's number of personnel certified in PECS implementation per semester.

- Teacher *accomplishments*, such as the type of certifications a teacher has obtained.

- *Improvements* in staff satisfaction, staff absenteeism, turnover and so on.

- *Adhering to planned* teaching routines.

Assessing Costs and Benefits Associated with Taking Data

Getting good reliable, valid data consumes valuable resources. When deciding whether or not, or how, to collect any particular data set, always begin by asking "How much will these data contribute to the learner's educational objectives now and in the future? Will they accelerate rates of learner's goals achievement? Do those benefits outweigh the costs your system will need to invest? Is there a simpler way to obtain almost the same results?" Consider too, whether the learner currently is in the process of acquiring the skill, or just maintaining it at a steady rate. In the latter case, less frequent, more random samples are justified. Collecting data on seriously dangerous behaviors is crucial, but on mildly annoying behaviors probably is not.

> **The best educational decisions are based on sound, relevent data**

Here is an actual example of the misuse of data collection. A number of years ago, two observers were employed to see what they could do to stop the self-injury of a boy by recording every single time he his head. It took them a long time to differentiate between a bang, a tap, and a scratch. Thousands of data points were recorded but they never were made use of. One would be hard put to justify the cost of obtaining those data even if they were used, especially because information that probably would have been just as valid could have been gathered by using a sampling method. Also they could have combined all those behaviors into a single response class labeled "self-abusive acts." The main point is to use data to ask if what, and how much, you spend it is worth what you get in return.

Getting the Most from Your Data

We use data to make decisions. That is why it occupies such a central a position in the Pyramid, filling the whole inner space. But data are only of value if we use them wisely, to provide us with important information by which to guide our actions. That is why graphing and sharing data can be so profitable. We need to guard against making data collection, or its application, punishing, though, because then its purposes no longer will be served.

Graphing Data

Looking at rows of numbers is one thing, but when we see the patterns the numbers form, we can derive more value from them. In an instant, a clear graph can show progress or its absence, and much more, as you've seen elsewhere in this chapter. For example, using data as a basis for setting interim goals is a good strategy. You decide what level you ultimately want to achieve - a long-term goal such as a learner's mastering a basic picture vocabulary. Then you record progress over time, as shown in Figure 11-8. Those data about what the learner has accomplished then are used to set new goals for the next time period, such as a series of weeks. On the figure we show those interim goals as dashed horizontal lines on the graph.

Figure 11-8

Using Data to Set Interim Goals: New Vocabulary Learned

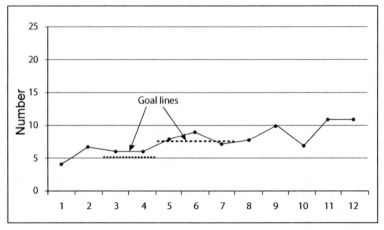

Additionally, graphs posted in a prominent spot can prompt participants to give themselves, or one another, feedback and reinforcement for progress. Reaching challenging goals is cause for celebration; so at that point some powerful reinforcers can be made available to those involved, learners and even sometimes staff (e.g., notes of recognition, commendation for teachers or parents, rewards for learners).

Data showing steady progress in the desired direction can be highly reinforcing to those responsible, energizing them toward promoting even greater gains. By contrast, data showing lack of progress, or deterioration in performance, tends to be punishing and may reasonably impel the teacher to change direction. We must be sure to give a new effort a reasonable try, though, before abandoning it. Some educational practices, such as ignoring troubling behaviors, testing new instructional styles, and so on, take a while to grab hold. Guard against giving up too soon by setting a reasonable trial period up front.

Data as a Reinforcing Tool

Now that you can see the value of using data to reinforce maintaining and accelerating positive change, as a final point, let us caution you against designing a data collection system that turns out to be punishing. That can happen when progress fails to occur, when collecting, plotting or interpreting data takes too long, requires excessively major changes in routines, or extra personnel, or when others use the data as a basis for assigning blame. These pitfalls can be avoided by keeping the system easy, by avoiding attempting too much at once, by randomly sampling, and by using the data constructively in ways described earlier.

Shape data collection by setting priorities and beginning with the data that will give you information that is both easy to obtain and with the greatest potential for rewarding the data collection activity. That could mean delaying auditing other important facts, but it is best to have a dependable system than one that breaks down due to overload. Also, it is okay to discontinue collecting some kinds of data after a while, say when an individual has firmly mastered a given skill; or as we said earlier, you might begin to space out observations separated more and more widely in time. And don't forget the importance of feedback and recognition for your data collectors (even if you are the one doing it yourself). Stop from time to time and let the person know (or remind yourself of) the value of these efforts, and even think about rewarding that activity from time to time in more tangible ways say, with a luncheon invitation, a soft drink, a note, or some equivalent.

The Data Collection Plan

We have talked about the importance of validity, reliability, and practicality. Assuming you are satisfied that these factors have been dealt with adequately, a few further issues remain. You need to plan *who* will gather *what data, how, where, when,* and *how often,* along with *how much* of it will be needed. Remind yourself of the purpose of collecting it in the first place - to make a sound educational decision. The exact nature of the particular decision being made, though, should influence how you design your specific data-collection plan.

Summary

To do their best, teachers need to make informed decisions about how to enable their learners to gain important skills and overcome problems. Clear, objective, reliable, and valid data provide the best basis on which to design and change lesson strategies. Data also can provide clues about what might be promoting and supporting problematic behaviors, and how to change that state of affairs.

Various people, trained and supervised to remain objective and consistent, cooperate in collecting data on the current status of individual learners, to track their progress, supply evidence of their accomplishments and improvements, assess and diagnose the origin of problems, provide a solid basis for making decisions, and as sources of feedback and bases for setting short and long-range goals. Different behavioral yardsticks may include the form, frequency, rate, duration, or intensity of the behavior, depending on the nature of the issue. Regardless of the measure selected, the information it provides will be valuable only to the extent it fairly and consistently represents what it is supposed to.

Data are not collected simply for their own sake. They need to be meaningful and be used. Among the ways of insuring this is to advance slowly, beginning with the simpler forms and moving gradually on to the more complicated forms. After crucial identifying information is noted down, either the direct immediate results or products of behavior can be assessed, or ongoing acts recorded. Counting is possible when those acts are clearly distinct, having clear beginnings and ends. As long as the method produces truly representative information, sampling is better suited for those behaviors tending to persist over time.

Functional assessments include tracking the behavior(s) of concern and systematically measuring related variations in the learner's (internal and external) environment. Findings then are used to re-design the individual learner's program of instruction. Recording the nature of a learner's progress under various new conditions, such as changing when they provide how many of what kinds of reinforcers, reveals the best mix for the learner. The outcome of cost-benefit assessments guides choices about the kinds of data that pay off sufficiently to justify continuing them.

Most educators want to know how their learners are progressing over time. Graphing their data will help them get the most out of the data they have collected.

Because data collection has so many advantages, it is important for teams to systematically plan to gather and review the data. Developing and adhering to a meaningful, doable, systematic plan is the best way to make data collection work for you and your learners.

Chapter 11 Resources

Collecting and Analyzing Data

To	Read
Become familiar with various ways to assess behavior and be accountable.	Sulzer-Azaroff, B. & Mayer, G.R. (1994). Achieving *educational excellence: Behavior analysis for school personnel.* (pp. 19-59). San Marcos, CA: Western Image.
Learn how to measure, record, graph, and analyze the results of behavioral interventions (t, bar)	Charlop-Christy, M.H. & Kelso, S.E. (1997). *How to treat the learner with autism.* (Chapter 17) Claremont CA: Claremont McKenna College.
	Cooper, J.O., Heron, T.E., & Heward, W.L. (2007). *Applied Behavior Analysis, 2nd Edition.* Columbus, OH: Merrill.
	Sulzer-Azaroff, B. & Mayer, G.R. (1991). Behavior *analysis for lasting change.* (Chapters 6, 14, 22). Atlanta, GA: Wadsworth Group: Thompson
To	Do
Practice assessing, recording, graphing data.	Maurice, C., Green, G. & Luce, S., (Eds.) *Behavioral intervention for young children with autism.* (Chapters 5, 7). Austin, TX, Pro-Ed
	Partington, J.W. & Sundberg, M.L. (1998). *The assessment of basic language and learning skills* (The ABLLS). (Appendix 1) Pleasant Hill, CA: Behavior Analysts, Inc.
	Quill, K.A. (2000). *Do-watch-listen-say.* **(297-322; 396-398)**. Baltimore, MD: Paul H. Brookes.
	Sundberg, M.L. & Partington, J.W. **(1998).** *Teaching language to children with autism or other developmental disabilities.* (pp. 163-170). Pleasant Hill, CA: Behavior Analysts, Inc.
Practice reading and analyzing the research literature; planning to use your own experimental analyses	Exercises in Sulzer-Azaroff, B. & Reese, E.P. (1982). *Applying behavior analysis.* (Chapter 6) New York, NY: Holt, Rinehart & Winston

12
A Day in the Life: Practical Application of the Pyramid Approach to Education

by Anne Overcash, MEd

Congratulations reader! You have worked your way through the *Pyramid Approach to Education* book and no doubt learned a lot. I am certain that you are energized about some new possibilities for your children or learners. However, you may be wondering how all of these pieces actually fit together in real environments. While a myriad of examples have already been given to illustrate each concept, it is often difficult to visualize these techniques and strategies when implemented during school, community and home based routines. In this chapter, we visit three classrooms and two families to see how many of these extremely important concepts are seamlessly incorporated throughout the day with many individuals.

Before we look in on these individuals, let's review! Remember that the *Pyramid Approach* is firmly based upon the science of learning - it is orderly and lawful. This foundation has allowed for rigorous research in the field of learning theory (Applied Behavior Analysis). The nine elements of the *Pyramid Approach to Education* are all important areas within Applied Behavior Analysis (ABA). Dr. Bondy recognized long ago that there are some elements of ABA that are so important they must be addressed first.

These serve as the foundation, or base elements, of the Pyramid. If these elements have not been properly addressed, then it may not matter how much thought has gone into the actual lesson design. The lesson may not be as effective as it could have been had these areas been first addressed. These elements are:

Functional Activities

Powerful Reinforcers

Functional Communication

Contextually Inappropriate Behavior

Once the base elements have been addressed, then proper lesson design is critical. These are the instructional elements and they comprise the top of the Pyramid. Whether you have an elaborate lesson plan or a less formal one, these areas must be addressed to maximize learning for your learner:

Generalization

Lesson Formats

Teaching Strategies

Error Correction Strategies

Data collection and analysis are the glue that holds everything together. It is through the careful collection and analysis of information about progress, or lack thereof, that we make the best educational decisions.

After some learner and setting information is provided, the remainder of this chapter is divided into different time periods. We look inside a preschool, middle school and high school setting. In each, two learners will be highlighted, but other people (learners and staff) are certainly a part of ongoing activities within each setting. The chapter will conclude by spending time in a two different home settings. You will see the *Pyramid Approach* in action in a variety of settings with individuals engaged in a variety of activities at many levels. I am sure you will see some similarities to your own setting, and perhaps gain even more insight into ways that you can begin to incorporate the *Pyramid Approach* into your work or home life.

Miss Mindy's Preschool Class

All of Miss Mindy's learners have a diagnosis of autism and are taught in a separate classroom within a neighborhood elementary school. Opportunities for integration with peers who do not have a diagnosis of autism are provided as appropriate for each individual learner, both within small and large group activities. The classroom itself is visually divided into different areas, including a table for breakfast and snack time that is located near a kitchen area where both staff and learners work on food preparation as well as cleaning up after these types of activities. Centered along one wall is a large area with a brightly colored rug where many large group activities take place such as language group, motor group and morning circle. A small free play area is tucked away by the windows complete with toy shelves, bean bags and a book rack. Just inside the door each learner has a cubby where coats and book bags are stored. Learners who use PECS or other alternative/augmentative communication devices will find those waiting for them upon entry into the classroom. Miss Mindy took the advice of her mentors and did not create separate spaces in her classroom for each learner to work either independently or within 1:1 lessons. Even though the children in her class have special needs, she is preparing them to learn alongside their same age peers and none of the general education preschool environments have cubicles. Individual instruction will certainly occur in this environment, just not in isolated areas.

A quick look around the room reveals strategically placed data sheets either on clipboards or taped to the wall. One thing Miss Mindy has learned over the years is that if the data sheets are not readily accessible throughout the day, no one will collect data. Of course, this does not mean that meaningful teaching has not occurred, but it does mean that it would be impossible to make sound teaching decisions about lessons without this important information. Visitors to this classroom also note large colorful posters. These posters contain pertinent information about each learner in the class. This information may include just about anything the team feels is important at this time, but at a minimum should include current preferences, current status of communication goals, including all nine of the critical communication skills, current non-preferred items (especially if the learner is learning to communicate, "No, thank you" or working on Phase IIIA of PECS), minimum rate of R+ to be provided throughout the day, and any contextually inappropriate behaviors the team is currently targeting. This information is critical to the overall smooth functioning of any classroom setting.

When teaching staff have the information they need about any given learner at a glance, they will be as prepared as possible throughout the day. In addition to these very large public postings, other information is strategically displayed throughout the environment so it can be accessed at any point throughout the day when needed. For example, lists of pre-ferred items for each learner have been placed on the lids of the small di-vided trays that contain small toys/edibles. This strategy allows for staff to "know" at every given moment who likes what inside the box. While it may seem like an insignificant strategy, it decreases any time teachers have to stop and think about each learner's preferences and allows them to continue with the lesson/goal at hand. Currently, there are six learners in this classroom, two of whom will be highlighted within this chapter.

Ezra is four years old and currently has no vocal communication skills. He communicates via the Picture Exchange Communication System (PECS) at Phase V. In addition to a visually based communication system, Ezra uses a visual schedule for transitions throughout the day, and within cer-tain activities such as gym class and occupational therapy. Currently, Ezra uses a token based visual reinforcement system. His tokens have been individualized to reflect his favorite characters, the Dalmatian dogs from 101 Dalmatians. Miss Mindy has laminated stickers and placed Velcro® on them so she and the other team members can deliver these stickers to Ezra as needed throughout the day.

Ezra

Likes	Dislikes	Communication	Reinforcement
Dalmation dogs feathers glue colored pencils cheese pretzels juice milk	puppets loud music pudding	PECS Phase V attributes visual schedule yes/no with head gestures	Variable Interval (VI) 3 minute *also working during transitions and less struc-tured time of the day

Behavior Target	Functionally Equivalent Alternative Behavior (FEAB)
hitting	Request to turn music off/down Indicate "no, thanks" when offered non-preferred items

Janelle is five years old and uses speech as her functional communication system. In fact, her vocal communication skills are quite advanced for her age, but she struggles with the social aspects of language. Janelle's team uses quite a few visual supports for her receptive understanding of language. Daily, Janelle uses a visual schedule as well as a visually based reinforcement system. Janelle earns letters that spell out the name of a popular televised word game. Upon completion, she chooses either a peer or staff member and plays an electronic version of that game for a few minutes.

Janelle

Likes	Dislikes	Communication	Reinforcement
all things Disney small figurines butter ketchup puzzles computer games word games word puzles	not winning not being correct cheese popcorn	speech for all requests "help" request with visual spoken yes/no word-based schedule	VI 5 minute during transitions and less structured time of the day

Behavior Target	Functionally Equivalent Alternative Behavior (FEAB)
Shut-down (functions to gain additional attention)	Share disappointment with staff member *also earns additional staff 1:1 time for the absence of this behavior
Yelling out (when help is needed)	Request "help" using a visual card

Ms. Beal's Middle School Class

Ms. Beal is a Resource Teacher in a neighborhood middle school. She is responsible for nineteen learners; however, most of them are in and out of her classroom as appropriate throughout the school day. Ten individual desks are located in the central part of the classroom. An area for group activities that can accommodate 5 to 10 learners is located in the back corner of the classroom. This area is used for language activities, morning meeting and other group activities. A row of computers is located along one of the walls. Learners enter and exit her classroom many times throughout the day. Team members are scheduled, either in the resource room or around the school building, with either one learner or groups of learners at various times of the day.

Due to the complex nature of the weekly schedule, Ms. Beal developed an elaborate color-coded visual schedule for the week that is situated above the chalkboard so that all team members are aware of where, and with whom, they are working at any given point throughout the day. All team members carry a laminated version of this schedule with them so changes to the schedule can be marked with a wet erase marker. Everyone rotates among all learners and groups. This helps with generalization and decreases the likelihood of any one learner becoming too dependent upon any one team member. One page summaries of each learner's preferences and all other pertinent information are affixed to the clipboard that follows each learner throughout the day. This provides quick access to this information for the person working with that learner at any given point throughout the day. In addition to all of the data sheets, each clipboard has a printed daily schedule with space to jot down notes that will go home with that learner at the end of each day. This enables Ms. Beal to quickly review how things are going with the learner and also allows school to home correspondence on a daily basis. Parents are encouraged to initial this sheet daily and provide any information they deem important to the team on the reverse side of the form.

Learners in the middle school have lockers located near their homeroom. Ms. Beal is the homeroom teacher for all of her learners. Each morning and afternoon she organizes all school/home correspondence and collects all relevant data sheets. For all transitions throughout the day, her learners transition alongside their peers when the bells ring to signal class change. Although space is at a premium in her class, Ms. Beal has designated a relaxation station for free time. This area is complete with bean bags, magazines, a community puzzle in progress, and a variety of other activities/items that change as her learners' preferences change across the school year. A separate area is designated for breaks. This area consists of a chair and no other items/activities. If learners request a break from a task, they will go to this area for a specified amount of time and then return to the task when an auditory signal sounds. This chapter will highlight Marquis and Joshua at various points throughout a typical day.

Marquis uses a sophisticated Speech Generating Device (SGD) for communication throughout the day. He is proficient with the device and, if he cannot find the correct icon, he may type the word into the device since it is programmed with picture retrieval. Alternatively, he can write the word. Marquis works on grade level for most subjects and needs occasional monitoring in his general education classrooms. A group of peer tutors/helpers naturally and informally developed. The behavior analyst at the school has initiated some structured sessions with Marquis and this group of learners where they work on specific social skills. Within the general education setting, these learners provide both reinforcement and reminders as needed.

Marquis

Likes	Dislikes	Communication	Reinforcement
High School Musical	close proximity	SGD for expressive	VI 5 minutes
vampire books	onions		
salty, crunchy snack foods	noisy environments		
Lemon Heads			
mini marshmallows			
flavored seltzer water			
intricate puzzles			
busy patterns			

Behavior Target	Functionally Equivalent Alternative Behavior (FEAB)
Pinching (functions to move away and to escape noisy environments	Request person to move away Request a break in a quiet area Use earplugs or iPod with ear buds
Body rocking and humming (elicited by uncertainty or abrupt change in schedule	Help create and follow a variety of schedules Tolerate "change" in routine Request a break in a quiet area

Joshua enjoys all things music-related. He is an easy going young man and over the years he has developed several close friends at school. Speech developed late for Joshua. During the period when he was completely non vocal, his early intervention, preschool and kindergarten teams implemented PECS. Even though Joshua no longer needs visual supports for expressive communication, he is quite independent throughout his school day in part due to visual supports for receptive communication, specifically his daily schedule which he either types or writes as a beginning activity each day. Most learners have long since memorized their schedules for A and B days, but Joshua is much more confident with transitions if he has the schedule to reference when needed. Joshua's daily schedule is printed into a grid where he has additional columns to accommodate his visual reinforcement system. He has learned many money concepts and is able to monitor his own on-task and work behavior, so he and the team agreed that his reinforcement system could certainly involve earning money and be self-monitored. Each point he receives is worth $1.00. Joshua's iPod has an app that vibrates on a 15 minute variable interval schedule. Upon either hearing or feeling the device vibrate, Joshua assesses his behavior and if he is on-task, gives himself a point. Upon delivery of the 5th point, he has an opportunity to either take a 10 minute break, where he can listen to songs on his iPod, engage in a variety of other preferred activities, or he can "bank" the money. When he "banks" the money he records this in his checkbook register. The team, along with Joshua and his parents, developed a shopping mall of sorts where Joshua can write checks for specific items. Most of these items consist of music CDs, games, and candy bar/ dessert selections. In addition to the points Joshua earns throughout the day, his parents and team members may provide "bonus" points for excellence in work or instances of using a new social skill.

Joshua

Likes	Dislikes	Communication	Reinforcement
music (specific CDs) mini candy bars music magazines writing rhymes and songs treadmill and exercise	olives mushrooms	speech for most expressive skills written/typed daily and activitiy schedules	Self-monitored VI 15 minute money-based visual reinforcement system wich is combined with daily schedule

Behavior Target	Functionally Equivalent Alternative Behavior (FEAB)
None at this time	

Mr. Manuel's High School Class

Mr. Manuel's classroom is located in a large high school. Currently, Mr. Manuel coordinates services for 12 learners. Some of his learners are in this classroom for the entire school day with the exception of physical education (PE), art, and tech classes as appropriate for each learner. In addition to the weekly structured PE class, nearly all of his learners spend time in the fitness studio for daily cardio and other fitness experiences. Mr. Manuel recognizes that many adults with disabilities struggle with weight gain, just like individuals without disabilities, and strives to make fitness a fun and integral part of each day for his learners. He also recognizes that many adults engage in a variety of fitness activities as part of their recreation and leisure experiences for the rest of their lives. He wants his learners to be exposed to a variety of activities so that if preferences emerge, these may be carried over into their lives after school. Some of his former learners have participated alongside their classmates in swim meets, track events and weightlifting competitions.

Rose's new fascination with jewelry and hair accessories has opened up some exciting new possibilities for her both at home and school. She is non-vocal but uses PECS to communicate quite effectively throughout the day. She has recently moved into a group home part time. Everyone in the group home is quite impressed with her communication skills via PECS, as well as how independent she is with a variety of routines throughout the day when she has her photo schedule in place. They plan to teach some new routines, especially grocery shopping, meal preparation, yard work and gardening, since all of the residents are quite busy on a daily basis with the general running of their home. She has had a token based visual reinforcement system in place for years. Since she has become interested in jewelry and enjoys decorating things, she made a new set of glitzy tokens for herself and the other girls in her classroom. Rose's occupational therapist was impressed with how well she did with this task since it required her to don a pair of gloves, due to the use of super glue, and persist for quite some time with this fine motor task. This is a testament to the power of preferences indeed!

Rose

Likes	Dislikes	Communication	Reinforcement
pudding ice cream cookies magazines	fine motor tasks trying new foods	PECS Phase VI (photos) photo schedule uses visuals to request "help" and "break" Responds to "wait" card Responds "yes" and "no" with head nod and shake	VI 20 minute visual reinforcement system

Behavior Target	Functionally Equivalent Alternative Behavior (FEAB)
Pinching self when frustrated	Request "break" Use putty/small items for relaxation/calming
Pinching others	Request 'help"

Darrin is a very diligent worker. He can also be quite single minded when it comes to task completion. He's happiest when he has a "To Do" list and can mark off items as he completes them. His mom reports that from an early age he was always her helper and he seemed most content when he was able to assist her with tasks around the house. She remembers an early fascination with her vacuum cleaner, so she bought him a toy vacuum for his birthday. He was excited to have his very own vacuum cleaner until he realized that it didn't "work" like his mom's! All of Darrin's teachers throughout his school years have incorporated his preference for helping with all kinds of tasks. When in middle school, he was the preschool "helper." In this role, he assisted the preschool teachers by loading the dishwasher, washing dishes by hand, packing book bags, vacuuming, etc. Each year during the IEP, Darrin stated that he wants to have a job in a hotel or office building where he can help ensure the environment remains clean and organized. Darrin understands money concepts and is excited to have his first paying job. He now works at a local hotel as an assistant to the chief engineer. He works 5 mornings a week and enjoys changing into his uniform before going to work each day. Even though he is certainly aware that he receives a paycheck every 2 weeks, he also looks forward to breaks during the day where he generally chooses to surf the web on his iPhone to check out the latest NASCAR stats, peruse the websites of his favorite cleaning supply and organizational tool distributors, or chat with coworkers. He is a little forgetful when it comes to time, so he uses the alarm function on his iPhone to remind him when his break is complete!

Darrin

Likes	Dislikes	Communication	Reinforcement
organizing things and spaces high fives/social approval computer games talking about NASCAR talking about cleaning equipment and supplies	clutter	speech for expressive	paycheck (Fixed Interval 2-week) self-monitored performance evaluation twice a day

Behavior Target	Functionally Equivalent Alternative Behavior (FEAB)
Cleaning personal space of others without permission	Differential reinforcement of refraining from this behavior (DRO)

Arrival – Miss Mindy

Miss Mindy strongly believes that preparation each day prior to the arrival of her learners is critical to their success. It is well worth the effort when transitions run as smoothly as possible and materials are prepared and placed in predictable locations. All team members are responsible for different tasks. These tasks rotate, so that no one team member burns out on a specific task. Some of these tasks include: arranging single picture directions or visual schedules, preparing breakfast and snack items, filling the reinforcer trays, setting up the group and individual clipboards with appropriate daily or weekly data forms, vacuuming, washing dishes and sanitizing toys/surfaces.

Each learner has a cubby located near the door. If a learner uses an alternative or augmentative communication system, those are placed inside the cubby alongside token boards or other reinforcement systems. Ezra is having some difficulty saying goodbye to mom in the morning, so the team signals the first possible reinforcer just as they approach the classroom door. Signaling the availability of Dalmatian dogs has certainly smoothed his transition into the classroom. Once inside the classroom Ezra finds his cubby easily because his is the one with the bright purple tape outline that matches the tape on his book bag straps. This strategy was utilized with some of the learners at the beginning of the year and gradually eliminated as they learned to locate their cubbies by their name or their name and a couple of stickers of preferred characters. Of course, Ezra's cubby features Dalmatians!

Miss Mindy plans to change the position of the cubbies every 3-4 weeks. When the learners consistently locate their cubbies, even when the location changes, she will be confident that each learner is locating his/her cubby by name or decoration and not location. Ezra earns stickers toward some preferred Dalmatian figurines as he completes the arrival routine: take off book bag, unload book bag, place notebook on Miss Mindy's desk, check schedule, complete the toileting routine, check schedule and join the rest of the class at a table with the first activity of the day. Generally, the first activity of the day involves some type of small manipulative. On this day, a variety of puzzles are available. Ezra is keen to join the other learners at the puzzle table as soon as he sees a variety of Dalmatian puzzles available alongside many others. Ezra is so keen to get started on his puzzle that he immediately constructs a Sentence Strip and makes a request via PECS, "I want + puzzle." Miss Marsha shows him the two puzzles she has available (Dalmatian puppies and Mickey Mouse). She makes a space on his Sentence Strip and places pictures of Dalmatian and Mickey on the front cover of his communication book. He immediately drops the picture of Dalmatian onto the Sentence Strip and exchanges the strip with Miss Marsha. She "reads" back the Sentence Strip as he points to each picture and then she provides access to the chosen puzzle. Ezra gets right to work on the puzzle.

After all of the other learners are settled around the puzzle table, Miss Marsha picks up a big puzzle piece and a small puzzle piece. The larger one is the one that will fit Ezra's current puzzle choice. She asks Ezra which one he wants. He begins to construct the Sentence Strip by dropping the Sentence Starter "I want." Just as he begins to reach for the picture for puzzle piece; she gestures to the picture for "big." Ezra drops that picture to the Sentence Strip and completes it by dropping the last picture. Miss Marsha will try to capture several more attribute requests during this motivating activity.

Even though today's activity itself is quite motivating for Ezra, he still earns Dalmatian stickers for staying on task. The team knows that when it's time to clean up the puzzles they will be glad that a deal is already in place! Since all of the learners are busy putting puzzles together, Miss Mindy and Miss Marsha decide that they can get in a couple of yes/no opportunities with Ezra. This is a relatively new skill for Ezra. While holding up either a preferred or non-preferred item they ask, "Do you want this?" Depending upon his reaction, Ezra will be prompted from behind to nod his head, "Yes" or shake his head, "No." At this point, the person situated just behind him needs only to provide the slightest physical prompt and he finishes either gesture quite independently. They have full confidence that by the end of this reporting period he will have mastered both of these gestures! In the beginning, they were worried that they would not be able to manage since two trainers are necessary to properly teach this skill. However, once they started embedding opportunities throughout lessons just like this one, they were surprised to note that on some days they had as many as 20 to 25 data points for this skill!

As with each activity throughout the day, many IEP objectives are targeted for each learner. Miss Mindy feels that this is the best way to address individual learner objectives. In some ways, it might seem easier to isolate each skill and teach it to mastery, but experience has taught her that when skills are taught in this manner, it takes more time to teach for generalization after mastery. Building in for generalization right from the start will go a long way toward ensuring that these learners have the skills they need throughout their daily lives, both while they are in school and out. During this lesson, some learners are working on fine motor skills, time on task, asking for help, making simple requests, making complex requests, responding "yes" and "no," as well as peer requests. Peer requests are encouraged when the pieces for 2 puzzles are "accidentally" mixed up. In order to complete the puzzle, learners are taught to request specific puzzle pieces from a classmate. Initially, Miss Mindy and Miss Marsha had to provide quite a bit of prompting for both the request and the honoring of the request, but they have been quite pleased to see an increase in peer-to-peer requests since they encouraged this during structured activities!

At the beginning of the school year, Janelle was not at all pleased to say goodbye to mom and enter the classroom. On the first day, both she and her mother were in tears. Both of Janelle's parents reported that transitions were difficult for her and this turned out to be true for her transition into the classroom as well. However, after about a week, Janelle was more than pleased to enter the classroom. Both Miss Mindy and Miss Marsha made an effort to fill the classroom with as many preferred items as possible for all of their learners. That first week was spent moving the learners from activity to activity, but the focus was on doling out as many reinforcers as possible and constant informal reinforcer assessments. Specially designed data forms were put on each strategically placed clipboard. These data sheets were simply large blank boxes with each learner's name. Throughout the day, if a team member noted a preference or possible preference, it was listed. For example, while in the dress up area Janelle played with the wand, black top hat and Minnie Mouse ears. That information was noted in the space provided for her on the data sheet. Miss Mindy knew that if she relied upon her memory about what each learner preferred, she would miss too much!

Even though these morning transitions have greatly improved, Miss Mindy will keep Janelle's visual reinforcement system, and all other visuals for receptive communication, in place. She has learned that even when behavior difficulties improve, or disappear altogether, it is a mistake to remove the supports that have played a significant role in these remarkable gains! Miss Mindy asks Janelle if she would like to work for an opportunity to play the word game with someone in the class. Janelle's reply is quick and positive, so the "deal" begins. On average, every 5 minutes a tone sounds. If Janelle is engaged in the planned activity or lesson, she will earn a token. Her tokens will either be given to her, or the team member working with her will give her the canister with all of the letters that spell out the name of her most favorite game show. She enjoys looking for the letters so, depending upon everything else that is going on, she looks for the next letter and places it on her token board. The name of her favorite game show has 14 letters in it. Technically, it could take her 70 minutes to earn access to some time to play the game with the peer or staff member of her choosing. However, it rarely takes that long for her to accrue all the letters since the team is diligent with differential reinforcement and may give out more than one letter at a time. They also switch to giving her letters for specific performance criteria instead of at the tone only. For example, if she is completing a math lesson that is more difficult for her, she will likely earn one token for each correct response. Typically, it takes Janelle 35 to 40 minutes to earn access to her favorite game.

Janelle is just as excited about this morning's activity as Ezra, so she works diligently to unpack her belongings, use the toilet, check her word based schedule and join her classmates at the table. She is incredibly independent with her arrival routine and generally she can complete all of this in less than three minutes. Today, however, something is blocking her cubby. The large foam board is part of an art project for later in the day; Miss Marsha placed it in front of her cubby on purpose because this is something that generally elicits yelling from Janelle. Both Miss Mindy and Miss Marsha are ready as Janelle makes her way toward her cubby. Just after Janelle drops her book bag, but before she has a chance to yell, Miss Marsha prompts her to give the "help" card to Miss Mindy, who immediately removes the obstacle for Janelle. Miss Marsha notes on the data sheet that Janelle needed full physical prompts to exchange the "help" card. With her way freed of the obstacle, Janelle completes the morning entry routine that concludes with her independently going to her visual schedule, moving the typed words "table top activity" to the "current activity" box located at the top of her schedule, and joining the rest of the class at the table with the puzzles. The team has struggled to find naturally occurring opportunities to teach her to request help via a visual card (a blue card for help in the shape of a hand), so they try to create as many additional opportunities across each day. The baseline data for Janelle's "yelling out" behavior indicates that on average she engaged in this behavior about 3 times per hour across each school day. So, the team has decided to capture or create between 4 and 5 opportunities per hour to teach this new Functionally Equivalent Alternative Behavior (FEAB). Depending upon the activities, sometimes this is difficult to achieve. However, without a specific goal in mind, they may not achieve as many opportunities as they would like. During the puzzle activity this morning, Miss Mindy plans to give some of Janelle's puzzle pieces to her in a small canister that she cannot open to create some additional opportunities to teach this skill.

Even though Janelle can use speech to communicate, she is sometimes so independent that she really doesn't use her speech as much as she could, so the team will often create opportunities for her to use her communication skills. Today, they have "forgotten" to put out her all time favorite Disney Princess puzzles. Upon noticing, she taps Miss Marsha on the arm and requests the Disney Princess puzzle. Sometimes, a piece is missing, and this too provides another request opportunity. Janelle's favorite chair is the green one. At the beginning of the year, she would slowly wriggle her way into the green chair until the other learner was left standing at the table instead of sitting. The team taught Janelle another strategy for acquiring her favorite chair. This involved the use of partial physical prompts to tap the learner on the shoulder/arm and a picture/written reminder that represented, "May I sit in the green chair?" The visual prompt was enough to elicit speech for this request. Of course, the learner that surrendered the green chair was reinforced for sharing.

Over the course of the first reporting period, both the physical prompt for gaining attention and the visual reminder for what to say have been eliminated from this lesson. Janelle now has a more socially appropriate method for gaining access to her favorite chair. At various points during this 20 minute activity, Miss Mindy and Miss Marsha asked Janelle a yes/no question in the form of, "Do you want/need this?" while holding up either a puzzle piece that she needs or a piece from a different game. This is a relatively new skill, so both team members had to be ready prior to the question being asked. One would ask while the other paid close attention to Janelle's body language. If she reached out to simply grab for the item, the other teacher provided a vocal model "Yes!" or "Yes, please!" Since Janelle's vocal imitation skills are superb, she has a high probability of repeating words and phrases. When she imitates, she is provided access to the item within ½ a second. If, on the other hand, she began to push away the item or turn from it, a vocal model for "No!" or "No thanks!" would have been provided and that item would have been immediately put away.

Arrival - Ms. Beal

All of Ms. Beal's learners ride to school on school buses and are independent with the transition from the bus to her classroom. Both Marquis and Joshua ride the same bus. Marquis' SGD is programmed not only with all of the things he loves to request and comment about, but also greetings and

other social exchanges. The team asked a group of peers to help generate the list of possible greetings and common social phrases for their age group. Ms. Beal and the rest of the team were delighted at the interest of all these learners in helping to put the list together. This process was a learning experience for everyone, and a source of enlightenment when the team realized how differently peers of this age interact compared to when they all attended Middle School. In the end, a set of phrases was added and Marquis quickly learned how to access these greetings and phrases.

Marquis greets the bus driver and some of his peers each day as he gets on the bus and is always ready with a greeting when he steps off the bus in the morning. Of course, he seeks out specific staff members and seems pleased to see Miss Garza, the building Principal, outside monitoring the unloading process. He greets her and then fills her in on a current favorite scene from High School Musical. Joshua is just as enthusiastic about greeting the bus driver and a few friends each morning, but he is not as interested in conversation. After first visiting their lockers, both Marquis and Joshua make their way to Ms. Beal's classroom. Upon arrival, all learners move their names to the "checked in" column on a magnetic chart. Some learners have additional picture support so they can correctly identify their name from the field of 19, but most of them are quite accurate. Just to mix things up a bit, Ms. Beal has typed all of the names in a variety of fonts on the computer so they continually build their generalization skills with written name recognition. In the future, some of them will wear name tags on the job and everyone from time to time will need this skill to find an item with their written name to identify something they have made in art class, or to find an assigned location, etc.

Both Marquis and Joshua write or type their daily schedules. Other learners in this classroom use picture based schedules. Regardless of the format of each individual schedule, all of them carry their schedules with them throughout the school building because they frequently change classes. These schedules all have a visual way to indicate when an activity is complete. For written or typed schedules, learners generally opt to cross off items as they are completed. For others, the pictures have a bit of Velcro® on both sides, so they can flip the card over where the word "finished" has been printed over a green check mark. Ms. Beal likes to cross things off of her "To Do" lists and she has noted that when some variation of this feature is included, learners tend to transition more independently. Of course, this was not a "magical" occurrence, the team worked diligently to ensure that none of her learners developed prompt dependence on the phrases, "Check your schedule." or "See what's next." Ms. Beal's team recognizes that these types of vocal prompts when added to lessons can be quite difficult to eliminate, so they opted to teach the mechanics of schedule following using either gestures or physical prompts. Ms. Beal is convinced that the process of collecting data on schedule following skills also served as a constant reminder about the types of prompts that should be utilized with each learner, and decreased the tendency to over prompt, since team members regularly looked at, and recorded, data for each learner. For example, they saw on the data sheet that only a gesture was utilized for the past several transitions, so they used less of a gesture for the current transition and in so doing were able to quickly eliminate all prompts from this lesson.

While Marquis is adept at finding his conversation phrases, he seems to use them mainly in response to peer greetings and their attempts to engage him in conversation. The team continues to teach him how to initiate both greetings and conversation starters using his visual reinforcement system to boost his interest. He is starting to initiate some conversations that focus on High School Musical movies. Once he is more comfortable initiating, maintaining and ending conversations about High School Musical, the team will teach lessons on how to stay with a conversation even when the topic shifts.

Morning arrival into any school can be a bit chaotic and noisy, so this is a particularly challenging time of day for Marquis. In the past, he has engaged in pinching with the highest average frequency during arrival and dismissal. Ms. Beal and the team feel strongly that when a learner is able to transition independently throughout the day, this should be encouraged and reinforced. However, Marquis' pinching created a situation where he had to be met at the bus and escorted to the classroom. As the year has progressed, Marquis is learning to request that others move away from him if they are too close, to request a break to a more quiet space, and to use either ear plugs or listen to music on his iPod. Since the episodes of pinching were so frequent, the team immediately went to work on teaching him several Functionally Equivalent Alternative Behaviors (FEABs). They found that offering Marquis a choice of either his iPod or earplugs worked best during the arrival and dismissal routines. Initially, team members boarded the bus as soon as it entered the line-up and offered these choices to Marquis so that he could be prepared before exiting the bus and entering the busy hallways. Some team members wanted to teach Marquis to exit the bus before the rest of his peers and enter the school building via an alternate entryway. Of course, the team carefully considered this option because if the route was not chaotic, he would probably not engage in pinching. However, the team reasoned that sometimes in a person's daily life outside of school, there will be chaotic situations and people simply have to learn to deal with these situations. They view this as an excellent opportunity to teach Marquis an important life skill. Over time, a variety of earplugs and his iPod were placed in his book bag.

Staff members have stopped boarding the bus and the bus driver now provides a simple reminder if he notices that Marquis has not prepared for the transition. Some of these statements include: "It sure looks crowded in the courtyard." "Listen to all of that noise!" and "Man, look at all of the people!" The bus driver was asked to refrain from using a direct vocal prompt such as, "Marquis, put in your earplugs/iPod." The purpose of working with the bus driver to avoid direct vocal prompts is to teach Marquis to assess situations and make adjustments in his behavior. If he is prompted to remember everything, he will not need to attend to the natural cues (i.e., lots of people and/or noise) in the environment.

Joshua is generally very quiet on the bus ride to school. He either reads the current issue of Rolling Stone or Spin, or reads the song lyrics he has recently printed from one of his favorite websites. Upon arriving at school, he has no problems navigating his way to Ms. Beal's room where he greets some peers with a high five and staff members with either a wave or a snappy new gesture (chin lift) that all the "cool" middle school learners are using! He "checks in," unloads his book bag and settles in to write out his daily schedule in his planner. All of the learners in this school have the same daily planner. When he types out his daily schedule, he prints it out and tapes it inside his planner. Prior to getting started on this task, he looks at his checkbook register and notes that he has less than $5.00 left to earn before he has enough "money" to purchase the new High School Musical soundtrack. Joshua used to identify his reinforcer prior to starting each new "deal." He would write in his preference to earn something specific or his intention to "bank" that set of points. As he has become more and more independent with this point system, he generally earns the points and then decides what to do with the points at the end of each "deal." When he banks the points, he writes in the date and time in the cash register and totals his points. When he wants to "cash in" his points, he lets a team member know his preference at that point and then takes a 10 minute break. By the time he has finished with his daily schedule, his iPod has vibrated once and he has given himself a point!

Some team members were worried that this type of self-monitored system would distract Joshua away from all of his tasks and work; however, they have not found this to be the case. His iPod vibrates for 5 seconds and automatically begins the next interval. He simply accesses his planner (which is generally open and on the table or desk where he is working) and gives himself a point if he is on-task. In the beginning, both Joshua and a team member or peer would mark the points at the same time to ensure he was marking his point card accurately. To help Joshua properly self-monitor, the team created a small checklist and attached it to his schedule. Listed on that checklist are the behaviors he should check for that would indicate that he was on-task. Once he consistently achieved 90% agreement with all monitors for 2 weeks, he was allowed to mark his own points and a team member checks his accuracy for 1 class period each week. As long as his accuracy remains at, or above, 90%, he will continue with this self monitoring system.

Arrival - Mr. Manuel

Darrin and Rose arrive at school in a van that transports several adults to different places in the community on a regular schedule. Due to limited space inside the van, all book bags and other items are placed in the cargo space in the back. Prior to placing her book bag in the cargo space, Rose removes her transition notebook. Rose uses PECS for expressive communication. Complete communication books are located in her classroom, at home, school and her group home. The transition notebook is a nearly complete replica of her other communication books, but this one is used solely for transitions. If the transition book is lost in transit, at least she will not be without a way to communicate upon arrival at any location.

Once at school, Rose disembarks, gathers her book bag, places the transition communication book back inside and tries to zip the bag. The zipper snags on a loose thread. This is the type of fine motor task that has always been a challenge for Rose. She pushes back her sleeve to reveal a wristband with some miniature "help" and "break" cards attached with Velcro®. She removes a "help" card and tries to give it to Darrin, but he is already walking away. She turns toward the van driver and presents the small "help" card to him while gesturing toward her book bag. He quickly indicates his intention to help and moves in that direction. He pulls the loose thread free and closes the zipper. He hands back the "help" card and she places it back on the wrist band before putting on her book bag and making her way to Mr. Manuel's class. If only her middle school teacher and SLP could see her now. In the past, similar scenarios resulted in shrieks and pinching behavior. To see her calmly request help and wait patiently for assistance would certainly be quite satisfying. The behavior plan which incorporated the request for "help" as the FEAB has certainly benefited Rose.

Mr. Manuel has placed a time clock in his classroom and requires each learner to "swipe" his/her own magnetic card upon arrival. He found this time clock in a wholesale business equipment store. He reasoned that if he intends for each of his learners to spend time in the community working, then they would need a skill of this type and it was certainly not too early to begin making this a focus. Rose has had difficulty identifying her magnetic card among the others. Mr. Manuel added a sticker of a long stemmed red rose directly on her card to make it easier for her to identify. This strategy has worked quite nicely, so yesterday he removed a small sliver of the sticker. He is pleased to see that this gradual change in the lesson did not cause her the slightest bit of difficulty this morning. He makes a mental note to remove another small sliver of the sticker at the end of the school day. Fearing he will not remember, he places a yellow sticky note reminder in his lesson plan book for the next morning. Rose has no further difficulty with the book bag zipper and completes the morning routine of unloading her materials and checking her schedule. The first photo on her schedule is one of her favorite activities - taking a break in the recreation area of the classroom. During this activity, learners are allowed to spend time with self-chosen activities. Mr. Manuel embedded this activity on the days when some learners need more time/supervision in the morning to get ready for the day than others. Even though the learners are independent with the available choices in this area and need very little supervision, a team member has been assigned to oversee this activity. Mr. Manuel learned long ago that if someone is not given the responsibility for each and every lesson, every member of the team would assume it was someone else's responsibility and this could lead to decreased rates of reinforcement and an increase in behavior difficulties.

Before making her way to the recreation area, Rose goes to her desk and makes a choice of something to work for from the choice board that was set up on the previous afternoon. Since it takes her about an hour and 40 minutes to earn the five tokens she needs before she cashes in for the chosen item, she occasionally changes her mind at the point when she has earned her last token. The team agrees that this is probably due to the passage of time and they certainly allow her to choose something different at that point. Last year, they tried to use a "choice" card to indicate that she could make the choice at the end, but this seemed to confuse Rose, so they went back to this strategy. Decision made, she takes the token card, grabs her communication book by the strap that she enhanced with rhinestones and beads, and makes her way to the recreation area. Rose is delighted to find that all of her favorite magazines have new issues so she is more than content to busy herself with a magazine while reclining in a comfortable chair.

Just as it is about time to transition to the next activity, a tone sounds and Mr. Manuel makes his way to the recreation area where several learners are busy with their chosen activities. He digs through the tub of tokens for one of Rose's new glitzy ones. He lets her know that she's a star and presents his fist for a "fist bump." Rose always giggles when he does this, but returns the greeting, takes the token and places it on her token card that is affixed with Velcro® to the back of her communication book. A bell rings to signal the end of "chill time." Most of the learners put away their materials right away. For Rose, this transition is a bit more challenging because the magazines are new! A team member sees that she has not begun to put away the magazine, so she walks over to Rose, sees that she is working for hair accessories, and provides her with a reminder about this. Rose sighs deeply as she begins the transition process.

Darrin always seems more excited to get to school now that he goes to work at the nearby hotel each day. His first paying job has not been without challenges, but it seems to be working out well for both Darrin and his employer. Since Darrin has been especially keen to get ready for work, Mr. Manuel has decided to sabotage his morning routine a bit. Mr. Manuel placed some chairs in the hallway along with a pile of papers that appear to be bound for the trash. This is something that can potentially cause Darrin some distress. He strives to ensure that everything is neat, properly aligned and in its place. However, he has gotten into trouble over the years for re-arranging things "his" way when they were set up in a specific manner by another person. Darrin has learned to ask if he can re-organize or clean up something if it is not a task that he was specifically assigned. Darrin immediately notices the chairs and the papers. He asks Carmen if he can take care of this mess. Carmen replies that someone else will get to it soon, and reminds him that he needs to prepare for work. Now focused on getting ready for work, he continues with his morning routine which includes changing into his work uniform. He has no problem finding his magnetic card to swipe and then immediately busies himself with getting his freshly cleaned uniform from the closet and makes his way to the boys' locker room where he has room to change.

Some of the high school boys in the locker room comment about how lucky he is to have a paying job and Darrin beams with satisfaction. They ask him about the NASCAR race results and make comments about their favorite drivers. Darrin joins in the conversation and states that his favorite driver is bound to have a better race the next weekend! Before leaving the locker room, Darrin removes a small card from his wallet. This card has a work readiness checklist. He checks to ensure he has his name tag pinned to his shirt, his lanyard with his work ID badge, wristwatch on, and his iPhone. The last item on the checklist reminds him to look in the mirror and tidy his hair if necessary. On the way out of the locker room, he checks himself in the mirror. Satisfied and ready for work, he returns to the classroom where another learner and team member are waiting. The three of them make their way out of the school building to the bus stop. When all three have everything gathered and ready, they leave the classroom. They must sign out in the main office before leaving school. Darrin lets folks in the office know that he is off to work and they give him the thumbs up sign from across the room. The Principal enters the office, greets both learners and admires how they look in their uniforms. After a quick high five, they are off!

The local transit authority has recently changed from tokens to a fare card. Darrin's team decided to use modeling to teach Darrin the new payment routine. So far, Darrin completes the routine independently as long as he boards the bus after someone else. Today, Carmen decides to test the waters to see how independent Darrin is when he is the first to board the bus. She breathes a sigh of relief when she sees that they are the only ones awaiting the arrival of this particular bus. She is also pleased to see the regular driver. He's been picking them up for this trip three times per week for the entire school year, so he knows a little about their backgrounds. Carmen is confident that Darrin will remember all of the steps, but also realizes that she might have to conduct error correction if he does not complete all of the steps in the correct order. Since it is the regular driver, he will likely be more patient if she has to use the Backstep error correction procedure than would an unfamiliar driver. Excellent work! Both learners board the bus independently and they are on their way. During the quick ride to the hotel, Carmen writes a brief note on the home/school sheet describing this success! This is an excellent start to the school week indeed.

Midday - Miss Mindy

Today's large group language lesson involves some favorite books: *The Very Hungry Caterpillar* and *It Looked Like Spilt Milk.* The challenge with any group of learners is juggling everyone's objectives. Miss Angie, the speech-language pathologist (SLP), is so pleased that Miss Mindy uses many visual supports for the team around her classroom. The large posters of information designed for each learner help her keep track of each individual learner's preferences. Individual preferences change rapidly so she would have no way of remembering all of this information week to week or even day to day! Each learner already has a "deal" in place and token cards are strategically placed so that Miss Angie can deliver tokens as needed throughout the lesson. One learner is also on a very rich rein- forcement system (30 second DRI) for staying seated during large group instruction. It would be impossible for Miss Angie to maintain her lesson and this DRI, so one of the other team members will be responsible for this particular aspect of the group lesson, in addition to helping "back up" the group. Since so many IEP objectives will be the focus of this large group activity, both Miss Mindy and Miss Marsha assist Miss Angie. In addi- tion to providing any needed prompts from behind the learners, they are responsible for collecting data. Each person backing up the group has a clipboard with relevant data sheets.

Before getting started with the book, Miss Angie begins the group either by enticing with some preferred items to elicit spontaneous requests or by asking the question, "What would you like?" Each learner is allowed an opportunity to request via their expressive communication modality. This is an excellent way to re-establish herself as "Grandma," since she does not see these learners on a daily basis. Everyone has now had an opportunity to request a preferred item, so the lesson begins with requests for specific props. Since this is a familiar story and activity, learners enjoy requesting the props that help Miss Angie tell the story. She learned long ago that ac- tivity boards and pictures for lessons should be prepared in advance. Mak- ing multiple boards for each lesson is another strategy that helps decrease the chaos during a large group activity. For example, PECS users will need access to pictures and possibly Sentence Strips. In addition, PECS users in any large group will likely be working at different phases. Pictures for rel- evant lessons may not always be housed inside each communication book. One side of the activity board will be for learners working on Phase I or II of PECS. This side will have only Velcro® strips so a single picture can be exchanged. Add additional non-preferred or preferred pictures and, voila, the activity board is ready for Phase IIIA or IIIB. A separate activity board will have Sentence Strips on both sides. One side features the "I want" symbol for the PECS user at Phase IV. The other features a variety of Sen- tence Starters and attributes. Being prepared enables Miss Angie to move quickly from one learner to another.

With the language lesson, Phase IV with attributes is the primary goal for Ezra. For example, "I want + 2 + green + leaves." Janelle's goals in- clude responsive commenting via speech and requests for props. Janelle will occasionally use attributes within her requests and comments, but this depends upon her motivation for the specific item. Ezra is working on attributes within PECS, so the team has worked diligently to embed many attribute opportunities. So far, this has been a challenge since attribute requests require a specific interest. During the language activity with the two books, Ezra requested big pretzel when big and little pretzel twists were offered at the beginning of the lesson. During *The Very Hungry Caterpillar* book, he requested strawberry, orange and ice cream cone in response to the question, "Which one do you want?" Miss Angie reads the final book, *It Looked like Spilt Milk* and asks some learners commenting questions. For Ezra and other learners, she asked them to point to specific things on some of the pages or asked them to count. In between the two books, she once again enticed the group with a variety of items. While Janelle is quite proficient with speech when it comes to requests, she does better with commenting and higher level language lessons when visual supports are available. So, even though she is not a PECS user, Miss Angie will often allow Janelle to use the activity boards and pictures when she is asked a commenting type question. One question she asked today was, "Does this look like a pig?" while pointing to the cloud that resembled a rabbit. Janelle said the word "No" right away, but then assembled pictures on the Sentence Strip to indicate, "It does not look like a pig. It looks like a rabbit." Miss Angie is pleased to see this level of complexity. In addition to exchanging the Sentence Strip, Janelle says each word as she points! If Janelle had not said all of these words, Miss Angie would have still been pleased, but since she did, she immediately gave Janelle two letters to add to her token board. This is a quick and powerful example of differential reinforcement and Janelle is delighted to have earned 2 letters!

As a conclusion to this language lesson, all of the learners gather around the art table to make some sponge paint or chalk clouds on blue paper. Even though the sample has white paint, Miss Mindy has decided to give the learners as many choices as possible, so many different colors of paint and chalk are available. Ezra only has two Dalmatian stickers left to earn, so he is keen to complete this task. Miss Marsha notices that Ezra has gotten ready for the activity by putting on his art smock. She is hopeful that he will request something and get started right away, but she is ready with some additional materials (glue and colored pencils) if he is not motivated to request paint or chalk. To their delight; all of the learners, including Ezra, make requests to get started with this project. Some learners are given instructions to follow that align with their IEP objectives (e.g., following written or oral directions). Midway through this activity, Ezra earns his final Dalmatian sticker. Miss Marsha is closest to the small tray of edible reinforcers. She grabs a couple of broken pieces of mini pretzels and gives those to Ezra after he gives her all of his stickers. It takes no time for him to consume those pretzel bits. Just as he is going back to work on his art cloud design, Miss Marsha presents the choice board to him once again so he can make another choice to continue with his visual reinforcement system. This time he chooses milk.

At the beginning of the year, Miss Mindy felt overwhelmed with the number of objectives she needed to teach each learner. In part, this was because she felt like each lesson should focus on only one skill at a time. She quickly realized, however, that when she teaches using motivating materials within functional contexts, a little planning goes a long way. As long as she is prepared to teach multiple goals to multiple learners within each lesson, she has had less difficulty than she ever imagined! She is grateful to her mentor teacher and other staff members who have provided her with invaluable guidance. It has taken the entire team working together to make this year as successful as it has been.

The transition away from the art lesson begins with the class instruction to "Tidy up!" Each team member has been working diligently to avoid direct vocal prompts for these learners to check their schedules. They have seen too many learners become prompt dependent on the direct vocal prompt, "Check your schedule." In addition, they feel that this is just another oral direction for them to follow and if they are going to provide that direction for each transition, then perhaps they should simply give the instruction about where to go next instead. The visual schedules are supposed to increase independence, so they have vowed to provide other types of prompts (e.g., gestures or physical prompts) if necessary, and rapidly eliminate those until the learners are responding to natural cues.

Ezra tries to place his artwork on the drying rack but has difficulty aligning the sheet into the small slot. Miss Mindy sees Ezra struggle and asks him if he needs help. Ezra responds with the head nod for "Yes" and Miss Mindy immediately steps in to provide assistance. Having stowed his artwork, Ezra removes his smock and places it back on the hook near the cubbies (this is the natural cue for him to check his schedule). At this point, Miss Marsha points to the wall where his visual schedule is located near three others. His schedule has his name and some Dalmatian stickers, and he finds it easily. He quickly removes the picture for language group and places it in the "finished" pocket located at the bottom of the schedule. He then places the next picture (ladybug center) up to the current activity box. As he makes his way to the correct center, Miss Marsha starts a small timer for 15 minutes and marks the data sheet near his schedule with a "G" for starting the schedule following routine. The team taught Ezra how to manipulate his visual schedule using backward chaining. This is an excellent strategy to use when the learner is eager to move to the next activity. Before teaching this routine, the team established the steps for teaching this skill and came up with the following:

Staff	Transition	Prompt level needed to begin transition			
	Morning activitiy	FP	PP	G	+
	Bathroom	FP	PP	G	+
	Breakfast	FP	PP	G	+
	Morning Group	FP	PP	G	+
	Center 1	FP	PP	G	+
	Center 2	FP	PP	G	+
	Center 3	FP	PP	G	+
Key	+ = independent	G = gesture			
	PP = partial physical	FP = full physical			

The data could be recorded as shown above for this specific transition. To simplify data collection, Miss Mindy generally highlights the important bit of data to be collected, so no time is spent scoring aspects of the lesson that have already been mastered, or creates a new data sheet.

So, the charting could also look like this:

Staff	Steps	Performance
MG	Approach visual schedule	FP PP G +
	Remove picture from current activity box	FP PP G +
	Drop picture in "finished" box	FP PP G +
	Remove top most picturePlace picture in current activity box	FP PP G +
	Go to location indicated by picture	FP PP G +
Key	+ = independent	G = gesture
	PP = partial physical	FP = full physical

Note: Ezra has mastered all of the pictures on his visual schedule. Miss Mindy and her team began by teaching this skill (what each picture represents) prior to the introduction of the full visual schedule.

Today, the ladybug center is set for dress up! Ezra is thrilled to see an assortment of feather boas in this center. He dearly loves feathers and could spend the rest of the day in this center. Miss Marsha and Miss Mindy know that while Ezra is in the dress up area they can focus on teaching some attribute lessons, both expressive and receptive, and that they can probably stretch the time between tokens because this center is likely to be quite naturally reinforcing. While Ezra is busy picking up a stray feather, Miss Marsha gathers all of the feather boas. When Ezra constructs and exchanges his Sentence Strip, it reads: "I want + boa." He found the picture for boa inside his communication book on the dress up page. Duplicates of many of these pictures can also be found on an activity board filled with pictures related to the dress up.

Instead of simply offering one boa, or allowing him to choose by taking one, she asks, "Which one?" He studies the boas and his communication book and chooses the picture for "black" and places it at the end of the sentence so it reads, "I want + boa + black." Miss Marsha calmly says, "Hummm," while deconstructing the Sentence Strip. She points to the Sentence Starter, "I want." Ezra quickly drops that picture as she points to the picture for "black," which he places on the Sentence Strip. He then independently drops the picture for the boa, rips off the Sentence Strip and exchanges it with Miss Marsha. He points to the pictures as she "reads" it back to him. She pauses for 5 seconds before she says the word "boa." He doesn't say anything during the pause; however he does give her some excellent eye contact! He's quite pleased when she gives him the black feather boa. He grabs the white top hat and a cane to complete the ensemble. Before Miss Marsha has a chance to record the data, another learner is grabbing the feather boa from Ezra who begins to protest loudly. She must step in to referee but makes a mental note about Ezra's improper sentence construction when using an attribute. She marks the data sheet after the learners have settled back to playing.

Staffing assignments for center rotations feature one person assigned to the center that will require the most supervision. This is the center where they focus on teaching skills that are in early acquisition. It is at this point in the learning process where the ½ second rule is most important. Today, the Mr. and Mrs. Potato Head center is the one that will require the most supervision. Miss Mindy is stationed there and Miss Marsha floats between the dress up center and the workshop that features a work bench and a variety of construction materials and tools.

Janelle has independently transitioned to the caterpillar center which is set up with Mr. and Mrs. Potato Head game pieces. Janelle's occupational therapist is pleased that Miss Mindy routinely provides activities that require fine motor skills. Janelle is much more likely to persist with difficult fine motor skills if she is motivated by the activity and materials, and she really needs the extra practice! Because Janelle is really motivated by this activity, Janelle practices fine motor skills and Miss Mindy is able to incorporate many receptive directions throughout this lesson. For example, Miss Mindy asked Janelle for certain body and wardrobe parts to complete her own Mrs. Potato Head. Janelle is not accurate with every direction, so Miss Mindy has to conduct the 4-Step Error Correction Procedure (4-Step) when Janelle makes an error. The error correction procedure is not Janelle's favorite part of the lesson, so she occasionally exhibits mild protest behavior within the 4-Step. Both Miss Marsha and Miss Mindy ignore the protests and proceed through the steps very matter-of-factly. Since Janelle loves as much attention as possible, they are aware that paying extra attention at a time like this could lead to the increased probability that this behavior will occur again in the future.

In addition to the receptive directions, Miss Mindy targets time on task within this lesson. Janelle is preparing to spend more and more time in a general education preschool classroom, so Miss Mindy has observed several potential classrooms and taken note of all of the skills she will need to be as successful as possible in that environment and has incorporated those skills into her IEP. During this activity, Janelle earns her last Disney sticker for her DRO. This system is in place to continually reinforce Janelle for the absence of "shut down" behavior. She earns a Disney sticker for every 10 minute period that goes by with no instances of this behavior. Once she has earned all five stickers, she cashes in for 1:1 time with a staff member. In the beginning, she would choose which staff member, but over time the team agreed that Janelle loves to spend 1:1 time with all of the team members, so whoever has time for this when she earns the fifth sticker is the one who hangs out with Janelle. The important aspect of this time is the 1:1 time just with Janelle. They may take her for a walk to the office or to run another necessary errand, play a short word game with her, or look up the weather on her favorite internet site.

Ezra earns his last Dalmatian sticker and immediately begins to remove the five stickers and hands them to Miss Marsha. She accepts the tokens, provides social praise, and immediately goes to his special bin of preferred items to find the stuffed Dalmatian that Ezra has so diligently worked to earn! She sets a small timer attached to one of the clipboards for 3 minutes. Ezra and most of his classmates have learned that the ringing of a timer ends the specified reinforcement period. Another learner also trades in her five tokens at about the same time. Miss Marsha resets the timer for 3 minutes so that both reinforcement periods will end simultaneously. Since these two learners are occupied with their chosen reinforcers for a couple minutes, Miss Marsha takes a moment to catch up on any data points that she did not have time to write down, and checks with Miss Mindy to see if she can be of assistance with any of the learners in her group. When there are only two team members in the classroom each day, and some skills require two trainers, everyone must be on the lookout for teachable moments and in some cases create opportunities to teach skills at a moment's notice. It happens that Janelle has earned her final letter for her visual reinforcement system and has asked another learner to join her in a round of her favorite word game. The hand held electronic game is perfectly portable. The other learner is one who also enjoys word games, so this is an excellent opportunity for Miss Marsha and Miss Mindy to work together with the remaining two learners on skills that require two trainers (i.e., yes/no in response to the question, "Do you want this?" and initiation of requests).

After the timer rings to indicate the end of the reinforcement period, Miss Marsha ensures that all of the learners either return to their tasks or start new deals by making another choice. Miss Marsha is grateful for the Audio Reinforcement Reminder Tones (ARRT). This is a set of CDs with each track featuring a different variable interval. Each interval features unique tones. This is important because in any given class, learners will likely need different rates of reinforcement. Miss Marsha remembers scrambling around to remember to reset timers. It was so busy this morning that she forgot to tell Miss Mindy about a new app that she just found online. This one is called *R+ Remind* and it functions just like the ARRT CDs, but is downloaded onto an iPhone which is certainly more portable than a CD player or laptop. Use of the *R+ Remind* app will help ensure maximum rates of reinforcement across the day.

The end of each center is also signaled by a bell, but this one you pick up and ring. This bell belonged to Miss Mindy's mother who also spent her career as a teacher of learners with special needs. Just prior to the transition, Miss Mindy gives the honor of ringing the bell to a learner. Upon hearing this bell, learners straighten their areas and proceed to their visual schedules to see what's next. Miss Mindy tries to remember to provide a vocal warning when there are three minutes left for each center, but sometimes she is caught up in teaching and forgets to give this warning. This typical phenomenon has actually helped many of the learners adjust to just listening for the bell instead of *always* needing some type of warning before a change in activity.

Ezra does not begin to put away the dress up items and he does not seem pleased that his time in this center with the feather boas has come to an end. Instead of reminding him that he should be cleaning up the dress up items, Miss Marsha reminds him that he is working toward his chosen reinforcer. Ezra protests vocally and does not begin to put items away. She assists the other learner in the center with the transition and returns to begin putting Ezra's things away. Since he is not engaging in the expected behavior at this point when the tone signals the end of the 3-minute interval for his visual reinforcement system, she does not give him a token. His refusal to follow the routine and directions simply delays his access to the reinforcer. She does not lecture and she is not punitive. After all of the items have been put away and the other learners are busy checking their schedules, Miss Marsha gestures toward his visual schedule. Ezra reluctantly leaves the area to see what is next. He completes the transition and settles into the next activity, at which point the tone sounds once again and Miss Marsha delivers a Dalmatian sticker along with a positive statement about how nicely he has gotten to work with the next task.

Midday - Ms. Beal

Each year, Marquis' general education teachers are nervous about having him in their classroom. They are unsure about how much time it might take to adapt materials and accommodate his needs in this setting. However, after the first week or so, they are impressed with his skill level and enthusiastic about having him in their class. Marquis has been with the same peer group for quite some time and has developed many friendships. Marquis does not require any significant modifications to lessons. He reads on grade level and can follow both individual and group directions. He is proficient with his SGD and can write and type with the same level of proficiency as his peers. Marquis' main difficulties in this mainstream setting are: dealing with abrupt changes, close proximity, and social interactions with his peers during less structured times of the day. Twice a week, Marquis meets with his behavior analyst, Mr. Ryan, and a small group of peers for a "rap session." These are brief meetings where they discuss anything that may be going on, both in and out of school, and work on specific social skills. Mr. Ryan generally chooses one skill to address for each reporting period. This reporting period they have been working on conversation skills which include: beginning, maintaining and ending a conversation with an individual and a group.

The peer group that meets along with Marquis has chosen to join them twice a week during lunch. All of the learners either bring their own lunch or first go through the lunch line and then meet in the resource room. Mr. Ryan provides some additional lunch/snack items and everyone looks forward to these as well as their time together. Today, they consider everyone's preferences and discuss how people may have some common interests, but also may like completely different things. Over the next several sessions, they will focus on how conversations can evolve and shift and that every conversation cannot center on one person's interests. In addition to live role play, Mr. Ryan incorporates video modeling and lecture accompanied by a PowerPoint presentation to teach these important life skills. He also plans to meet with Marquis' SLP, Mrs. Matteo, to ensure that Marquis' SGD can accommodate communication about a variety of different topics of interest, as well as some generic ways to participate in a conversation. For example, Marquis will need a fairly broad way to ask for more information such as, "Can you tell me more about that?" and "What else do you like about that?" It will also be useful for him to have statements like "WOW, that's cool." Mr. Ryan's conversation with Mrs. Matteo will include ensuring these statements are programmed and that Marquis can efficiently access them when needed throughout the day. He will also ask what steps he and the classroom staff can take to incorporate these conversation skills throughout the day.

This period, Marquis is in science class with Miss Myers. Now that he is in Middle School, most peer interactions occur during class change and during group activities. Today, Marquis arrives early enough to greet Alexis. She returns the greeting and proceeds to tell him about a movie she saw over the weekend. She asks if he has seen this one and he replies, "Nope," but goes on to ask her about her favorite part. She begins to reply, but Miss Myers calls the class to order before she can finish.

Marquis is quite adept at using his SGD to answer questions throughout lessons, ask for clarification of information, and request help as needed. He has learned to raise his hand before responding via his device. In years past, he would "call out" answers using his device before the teacher had a chance to call on a specific learner. Learning to wait until called upon, and that he may get to respond only once or twice per class period, was initially difficult. All of his teachers agree that Marquis still needs his visual reinforcement system in place because it has allowed them to reinforce at a certain rate even when he is not the one called upon to answer questions. At this point, Marquis earns 5 to 7 minutes of time with a preferred snack or activity about every 50 minutes. Initially, some teaching staff were concerned that this would detract from his focus on tasks and interfere with his class time to complete assignments. However, they all agree that Marquis remains on task and completes perhaps more work in the time that he is working than many of his peers who do not have similar systems. His "cash in" times do not always coincide with a time that is convenient for the teacher and this was also an issue at the beginning of the year. However, the team agreed that as soon as Marquis earns his last token, he should be given access to his chosen item/activity, and time to enjoy it. In reality, these intervals do not interfere with the flow of classroom activities as they had feared. All of his peers are quite familiar with Marquis as they have been his classmates for many years, so they are used to his "reinforcement breaks."

Today Miss Myers has planned a "game show" competition that will involve learners shouting out responses as quickly as possible. She knows that this level of noise and activity might be difficult for Marquis, so prior to introducing the lesson, she approaches Marquis to privately let him know that they are about to play a new game and that it may get loud in the classroom. She also reminds him that he can ask for breaks at any point and he also has his earplugs if needed. After her conversation with Marquis, she describes the game to the class and the learners are divided into teams. Marquis does not immediately ask for a break as he is on a team with many of his closest friends and he knows the material quite well. They let him know they are pleased to be on a team with him because he really knows the material so they are hopeful they will win the game.

As the game begins, the noise is not too bad, so Marquis participates by calling out with his device. A team member is keeping a close watch on the device and helps him "call out" answers because the volume on the device is not loud enough to be heard over all of the other guesses being called out. Between rounds of the game, Miss Myers approaches Marquis and gives him a token even though it isn't quite time. She wants to focus on the fact that he participated in an activity that can be quite challenging for him. As the rounds continue, the score is close and the activity and noise level increase. Marquis places his fingers into his ears. In the past, this specific behavior occurs just prior to pinching episodes. One of his friends sees this behavior and immediately reminds Marquis that he should ask for a break. This is something that Mr. Ryan suggested at a "rap session" last year. Marquis leaves the team and approaches Miss Myers to deliver his request for a break. She suggests he take a trip to the library to either relax for a bit or find a book on the subject they have been studying. As he leaves, his team mates give him high fives and thank him for helping with the questions up to that point. Miss Myers is proud that Marquis participated in this activity for as long as he did before he asked for a break. At the beginning of the year he would ask for a break even before giving any noisy lesson/game a chance. She makes a note on his behavior data sheet that he appropriately asked for a break as she continues to monitor the game.

Joshua transitions to his math class alongside his classmates. He responds to greetings from peers and occasionally initiates a greeting. The pace of these hallway transitions does not provide too many opportunities for Joshua to interact with peers. If he makes it to class before the bell rings, however, he may interact with peers but typically prefers to look at a magazine instead. His iPod vibrates during the transition so, upon arrival in his math class, he gives himself a point. The only modification Joshua receives in this class is the choice to complete the assignment via paper/pencil or the computer. The mathematics curriculum has already been adapted for both, so this does not require extra preparation from the math teacher, Miss Palmer. During this class period, Joshua earns his last point for this trade-in or bank period. He chooses to cash in for some time to listen to some of his newly downloaded music. He lets Miss Palmer know that he has chosen to earn some listening time and moves to a separate area in the classroom. Before choosing a song, he sets a timer (also included as an app on his iPod) for 10 minutes. He quietly listens to the music until the timer signals the end of this reinforcement period. Upon returning to his desk, he completes the assignment and writes his homework assignment in his planner. When learners complete class work before the end of the period, they are allowed to sit quietly at their desks completing math related enrichment activities or to form small groups and work on computer games that target math related skills.

Even though Joshua had a break during this class, he still has some time before the end of the period. He makes his way to a computer and chooses a game that can be played by one or more people. He starts the game in 1-player mode. Once he completes the first level, Rashi is watching him play. Joshua stops the game and asks Rashi if he would like to play. They reset the game in 2-player mode. Even though their time with the game is brief, they enjoy it! When the bell rings to signal class change, they shut down the program, grab their belongings and move on to the next class. Just prior to the end of this class period, Joshua has earned another point.

Midday - Mr. Manuel

Rose has been busy completing each of the activities of the day. She is currently enjoying her time in the classroom with Mr. Manuel and several other learners. Each day, Mr. Manuel tries to embed one or two preferred activities. These could last 10 to 30 minutes, depending upon the rest of the daily schedule. During these activities he tries to incorporate many communication opportunities. He recognizes that his learners will be more likely to initiate communication during preferred tasks. Today, Rose has an opportunity to continue working on her beaded jewelry. Her parents and the rest of the team were thrilled to see this interest emerge because fine motor skills have often been a challenge for Rose. This interest has been powerful enough for Rose to persist with an extremely fine motor activity. Rose's parents have taken her to a local bead shop for supplies on several occasions. These outings have been enjoyable for Rose and she has also gotten to practice using her debit card. The most difficult part of that routine for her was remembering to hit "enter" after punching in her PIN. Rose's mom can certainly relate to this as it seems that the cashier sometimes has to remind her to hit the "enter" key as well! Rose's interest in this activity has also inspired Mr. Manuel to consider teaching her some additional attributes within her requests. He makes a note in his lesson plan book to ask her SLP about this and perhaps begin teaching this new skill as soon as possible. Some of Rose's previous teams tried to teach her a variety of attributes via PECS, but her interest in the materials was never quite powerful enough, so those lessons did not go as well as they planned.

Mr. Manuel notices that Rose only has one more token to earn and he decides to stretch this interval a bit. When the tone sounds to remind him to deliver tokens, he lets her know that her work is beautiful and he loves how she is persisting, but does not give her the token just yet. He points to Rose's token board and comments that she only needs one more token before she will earn cookies (these are cookies she made yesterday during a cooking lesson). He signals the end of this particular activity by saying, "Hey look at the time, it's nearly 12:30! Let's clean up our materials." Rose wastes no time in organizing her jewelry making materials, putting them away, and going to her schedule where she sees that the next task is "coffee mug cleaning service." This task is represented by a photograph of the cart that she uses to gather the coffee mugs. She places the photo of "make jewelry" in the "finished" pocket, moves the picture for the coffee mug activity to the current activity box, and proceeds to the kitchen area to get the cart. At this point, Mr. Manuel approaches Rose with her final token. Rose accepts the fancy new token and places it on her visual reinforcement card to complete the deal. She immediately begins to remove all five tokens and gives them to Mr. Manuel. He tells her how impressed he has been with her work today and indicates that she can help herself to two cookies from the green container on his desk. She stops by the kitchen for a napkin and a cup of water then makes her way to Mr. Manuel's desk where she takes two cookies out of the green container and returns to her desk to enjoy them. Just as Rose is finishing cleaning up her quick snack, Mr. Manuel asks her what she would like to work for and she responds by choosing the photo of "magazines" from her choice board. She places the photograph on her token board and heads for the kitchen to gather the materials she will need for the coffee mug activity.

Staff members at this high school have the opportunity to sign up for a coffee mug washing service provided by Mr. Manuel's class. Monies they raise for this, and a variety of other goods and services, go toward the purchase of grocery items for cooking lessons, reinforcers/snacks for the learners, and materials for art projects. Each day before noon, those staff members who have paid for daily coffee mug washing leave their coffee mugs in a plastic bin located near their doorway. Rose uses a printed list to guide her to the correct classrooms. Her number matching skills are good, so she is quite accurate at finding the correct classrooms. Once she has gathered the mugs from a classroom, she marks that number off on the laminated list with a write-on/wipe-off marker. She has learned to quietly enter the classroom and gather all of the coffee mugs from the bin.

When Rose first began this job, Mr. Manuel found that he and the other team members were unable to eliminate the gestural prompts for her to look at the classroom numbers on the doors. After several weeks, the team found they were providing the same level of prompting. Attempts to delay the gestural prompt proved ineffective. Mr. Manuel decided that perhaps a visual prompt might be more beneficial for Rose within this task. The strategy was two-fold. He placed sticky notes that had a sticker or picture of jewelry that he had cut out of a catalog next to the relevant classroom numbers. Upon finding a classroom with one of these sticky notes, she would collect the sticky note and attach it a blank piece of paper on the clipboard, enter the classroom and complete the routine. At the completion of the routine, she would mark off the room number on her list and receive a token for each and every classroom. Of course, this new strategy took some pre-planning because a team member had to place the sticky notes prior to the routine and the person working with Rose had to be prepared with the items Rose might wish to work for within the visual reinforcement system. In order to speed the delivery of these reinforcers, a special choice board was developed. The choices available to Rose were items that would be quickly consumed so she could continue with the activity. This new strategy of increasing rates of reinforcement along with the decorated sticky notes helped Rose acquire the skill of independently looking at the classroom numbers. Over the next several weeks, Mr. Manuel began to place the sticky notes only on certain classrooms, so she would intermittently find sticky notes. Tokens were delivered in a less predictable manner until they were delivered on her typical variable interval 20-minute schedule. Rose treated her collected sticky notes like little treasures. She liked to keep the page on her desk for the rest of the school day. It did not seem to bother her that on some days she discovered 3 or 4 and on others only 1 - she simply seemed delighted each time she discovered one.

Once back in the classroom, the coffee mugs are placed in the dishwasher. When the cycle is complete, the mugs are dried and returned to the cart on freshly sanitized trays. Rose is careful to place each mug upside down to reveal the room number written on the bottom. She then aligns all of the mugs in ascending order so returning them to the appropriate classroom will be as efficient as possible. Depending upon her afternoon schedule, Rose will either deliver the clean mugs immediately or continue with her schedule which would end with her returning the mugs to the classrooms as the last task of her school day. Today, she has another task to complete and then an outing, so she will return the mugs at the end of the day. If something happens and the van is delayed in returning to the school, one of the team members will return the coffee mugs.

While the coffee mugs are in the dishwasher, Rose moves to another activity. She will work on this activity until the dishwasher cycle is complete. Once the dishwasher cycle has begun, she moves to her schedule, removes the photo that shows the cart with dirty coffee mugs, places it in the "finished" pocket and places the photo of the shredder in the current activity box. Rose's mother feels that shredding sensitive documents could be a perfect job for Rose. She cannot read, so it would be unlikely that she would try to gain information from sensitive documents. The entire shredding process includes several routines and on some days these routines are divided among learners. Today, Rose's part of this process consists of going to the guidance office, setting up the shredder and shredding paper documents that have been gathered into boxes. Rose will either shred everything in the boxes or continue shredding until someone in the guidance office lets her know it is time to return to class. Mr. Manuel or another team member will watch the clock and listen out for the dishwasher cycle to end. If Rose has not returned to class, they will call the office and ask them to let Rose know she can finish up with the shredding task. Regardless of which way this task ends, Rose completes it by emptying the shredder one last time into special bags, returning the shredder to the space under the counter, and vacuuming the area. Rose's return to the classroom generally results in the delivery of a token either just as she enters or just after. Mr. Manuel is careful not to be too ritualistic in the delivery of the token at this point so that, if he is occupied with something else, Rose simply continues with her daily schedule until he or another team member can deliver the token.

Darrin arrives at his worksite. He says a rote goodbye to the van driver and remembers to pause for the driver's "turn" to say goodbye. He enters the hotel through the employee entrance and immediately swipes his ID card and punches in his birthday to clock in for this shift. He goes to his locker, opens it with the key on his lanyard, and puts away his belongings. Today, he will be at work through lunch, so he places his lunch bag in the refrigerator. Once everything is put away, he sets off in search of the chief engineer. This generally requires that he ask a variety of people if they know where Mr. Becker is at this time because he could be anywhere in the building. Initially, Darrin needed a reminder card that provided instructions about finding a person and what to ask because he would simply wait in the employee area until someone noticed that he had not yet checked in with Mr. Becker. Darrin rarely uses this card now and only resorts to it if something has upset him, or his schedule, on that particular morning. Carmen makes a note on her clipboard to ask Mr. Manuel to check with Mr. Becker about teaching Darrin to use a walkie-talkie to locate him so he can be more independent and find him as efficiently as possible.

As soon as Darrin learns that Mr. Becker is in the ballroom, he takes his clipboard and sets out to find him. The ballroom is buzzing with activity. Mr. Becker is pleased to see Darrin and greets him with a handshake. He wastes little time and lets Darrin know that the first order of business is to set the ballroom for 750 guests. He takes Darrin to a table that has already been set for 8 people and tells him that all of the tables on the main ballroom floor need to be set exactly the same. He writes on Darrin's clipboard: #1 vacuum and #2 set tables. He draws a line across the paper and writes: "only if you have time" at the top and writes in two additional items. Many other people are busy moving the round tables into the ballroom and placing stacks of 8 chairs near each one. Darrin gets right to work. His attention to detail is incredible and he is a diligent worker. He rarely stops to chat with other workers unless they are in the break room, but if someone greets him or asks a question, he will respond. Darrin has learned that his break begins at 10:45 and ends at 11:15. He has adjusted to this early time for lunch and generally packs something light. He has set one of his alarms on his iPhone for 10:45am. He would happily keep on working through his breaks, but he learned that taking a break is part of going to work and it is important that he take his break at his assigned time. During his break, Darrin completes his performance evaluation that is also located on his clipboard. He checks off the following:

- Arrive on time

- Unpack and organize quickly

- Locate Mr. Becker

- Begin on assigned tasks

- Work accurately

- Work quickly

- Ask for clarification/help as needed

- Take break at scheduled time

At the bottom he has an area to write in any issues or comments he may have for that day. Mr. Becker and Mr. Manuel review these documents on a daily basis and make notes as needed. While Darrin eats lunch, he checks the stats for his favorite driver and quizzes some coworkers who also like NASCAR. They add information about Formula 1 drivers, and Darrin listens politely but ends the conversation by saying that NASCAR is #1 as he hears a favorite country music song begin to play. This is the alarm for him to return to work.

Back on the job, Darrin completes the last table setting. A coworker gives him a slap on the back and congratulates the team for a job well done. He joins Mr. Becker to assist with the last touches on the head tables and setting up the plants around the podium. Even before Mr. Becker can tell him what a fabulous job he has done, Darrin launches into a description of some cleaning supplies that he discovered are on sale on one of his favorite websites. Mr. Becker thanks him for the information and lets him know he will check on how their supplies look and whether or not that particular company is listed as an approved vendor for the hotel as they leave the immaculate ballroom. On their way back to the employee area, another alarm chimes and Darrin checks his iPhone. It's time to prepare for the bus ride back to school. He gathers his belongings and meets Carmen and the other learner by the employee entrance. She asks how his day at work was and he gives her his standard reply, "Awesome!" then adds, "Only four more days until payday!"

Afternoon - Miss Mindy

In years past, most of the learners in Miss Mindy's classes loved going to gym so their visual reinforcement systems were sufficient. Gym class this year has been quite a bit more difficult for many of her learners. One learner, Frederick, is particularly sensitive to the noise level and echoes created by this large space. At the beginning of the year, he rolled around on the floor and refused to participate for the entire gym period. Frederick's team last year inadvertently promoted this behavior by waiting for him to drop to the floor and roll around and then taking him on 5 to 10 minute walks around the school building. Upon returning to gym, the scenario would repeat until the end of gym.

When this school year began, Frederick's team conducted an A-B-C assessment to determine possible functions for this set of behaviors and developed a comprehensive behavior plan because Frederick had essentially not participated in gym class at all the previous year. Once the team determined that the primary function of this group of behaviors was escape, they developed a plan to teach Frederick that he could calmly escape this environment by requesting a break. His specified break area during gym class is in the hallway just outside the gymnasium entrance. In addition to teaching the Functionally Equivalent Alternative Behavior (FEAB), the team decided to use a fixed interval 1-minute DRO. Fortunately, Frederick loves the ball pit and to climb on a fixed climbing structure. The gym teachers agreed to have these available in the gym at all times, particularly in the beginning of this new behavior plan. The team was confident that increasing his rate of reinforcement for participating and giving him a calm way to escape by asking for a break would prove beneficial for Frederick.

Since Frederick is a PECS user, he is learning to request a break via the exchange of a "break" card. Teaching this skill as a spontaneous request requires two trainers. This could present a bit of a staffing challenge for the team because either Miss Mindy or Miss Marsha takes a break during this class period. However, Miss Mindy's class attends gym with another class. Each class sends one staff member to gym, so there are four staff members during this activity because the gym teacher has an assistant. All team members agreed that one person was essentially working with Frederick 1:1 the entire class anyway, so they would utilize this as an opportunity to teach the FEAB of requesting a break. The baseline rate of this particular set of behaviors was about 15 per hour. This class is 30 minutes in length, so at the beginning of the year, Frederick was dropping to the floor and refusing to participate 7 or 8 times per class.

The school psychologist, Mrs. Horton, was asked to assist with this plan for the first several weeks, to model appropriate implementation of the plan and provide feedback to the rest of the team and the other staff members working with Frederick. Frederick was taught to exchange a bright yellow card printed with the word "break." Staff utilized the two-person prompting procedure to teach Frederick to exchange the "break" card. The team member working specifically with Frederick would look for some initial signs that he was about to drop to the floor. Generally, these included refusal to participate or ceasing to participate, standing very still, and/or putting his hands to his face/ears. Upon observation of these behaviors, he was prompted to exchange the "break" card with one of the gym teachers. At that point, he was excused to the hallway to take a 1 minute break. Breaks were unlimited at the beginning of this intervention and there were days that Frederick took 10 breaks. Frederick learned this skill rapidly and was initiating breaks after only 2 classes. After several weeks he was still requesting about 10 breaks per class. At this point, the team tried to decrease the number of available breaks. They began to visually present the number of available breaks with a board and 12 "break" cards. Now, when a "break" card was exchanged, it was not replaced so he could see the number of cards decrease as he requested breaks. Decreasing the breaks proved unsuccessful. If he used all of the "break" cards, he would simply revert back to dropping to the floor as a means of avoidance. Of course, when this happened, the team did not take Frederick for a walk, instead they followed the new reactive strategy described within his behavior plan. It was clear that the behavior plan needed some changes.

After these unsuccessful attempts to decrease the number of break cards available, Mrs. Horton suggested that the noise in the gym class may still be quite overwhelming for Frederick and scheduled a meeting with his occupational therapist to discuss other options. Meanwhile, the team continued with the plan and collected data. The occupational therapist concluded that Frederick was demonstrating behaviors consistent with an aversion to loud noises (covering his hears, humming, etc.). She also determined that he could tolerate wearing a variety of noise canceling headsets as well as earplugs. The earplugs may be the preferred method for noise reduction since these will be much more discreet than wearing a bulky headset. She had to wait for permission from the family to order a kit to create a custom set of earplugs that are molded specifically for his ears. Using this type of earplug greatly diminishes the possibility of the earplug getting lodged in the ear canal and allows Frederick to hear if someone is speaking directly to him. Once the custom earplugs arrive, they will place them in Frederick's ears prior to the transition to gym. More importantly, they will continue with the Fixed Interval DRO as well as honoring his requests for breaks during this challenging time of day. If a marked improvement is noted, they will continue with the use of the earplugs, gradually increase the amount of time of the DRO, and gradually reduce the number of breaks he is allowed to take per gym class. All of these strategies are currently necessary to help Frederick participate in gym. Miss Mindy and the rest of Frederick's team realize that this has involved a great deal of work, but it is certainly worth the effort as they see him participating in this class.

The entire school is preparing for an exercise challenge as part of a national competition. Both gym teachers agree that they want all of the learners in the school to compete if the families return the permission form. The competition will occur on a Saturday. During the competition, the organizers will play music for motivation and there will be lots of activity as several schools come together to compete. In preparation, they will play upbeat music during gym classes for the next several weeks.

Typically, Ezra is happy to participate in gym so everyone is taken off guard when Ezra hits a teacher during warm up exercises. Ezra has a behavior plan in place for hitting, so the person he hits responds by following through with the plan. At this point, the gym teacher realizes that he is likely responding to the loud music and indicates that he will turn it down. Miss Marsha catches the attention of the gym teacher and asks him to keep the music at that level as she will step in to teach Ezra to make the request to turn the music down. Of course, Ezra transitioned to gym class with his communication book. He has learned to place his book on the blue line near the basketball net when he arrives in the gym. Miss Marsha and the teacher working with Ezra switch so that she can teach Ezra this specific request. Realizing this might be a more difficult time for Ezra because of the music, she decides to increase the rate of delivery of tokens.

Generally, prior to hitting, Ezra will stop whatever he is doing and begin to hum, so these are the behaviors that Miss Marsha is looking for as they continue with warm up exercises. Just before the next set of crunches, Ezra stops. Miss Marsha immediately points toward his communication book. Ezra opens his communication book and constructs, "I want + music + down." He takes the completed Sentence Strip to one of the gym teachers and, even though he is teaching, the teacher makes his way to the audio system and turns it down quite a bit. After about 5 minutes, someone turns the music back up and, after several minutes, this gives Ezra another opportunity to request the music be turned down. By the end of the class, he spontaneously goes to his communication book to request the music be turned down. Miss Marsha records the hitting episode and also records his performance on requesting the music to be turned down. She also makes a mental note that during class time they should turn on loud music from time to time to provide additional opportunities for him to practice this request because they want him to participate as successfully as possible during the competition. Throughout the remainder of gym class, Ezra makes several more requests to lower the volume of the music. He also requests his favorite orange jump rope, the soccer ball and a peer when they need to pair up for the relay. In addition, he requests several items to begin his "deals" for his visual reinforcement system.

Janelle enjoys gym class when she is working on individual skills. However, when the activities involve competition and someone else or another team wins, this can be a challenge for her. While she excels academically, her gross motor skills are not always a match for her peers. Gym class has been a time of day when Janelle might shut down as a result of her not winning. Today, during the relay, her team came in last. Janelle sat down, folded her arms and refused to participate in the next relay. Her behavior plan specifies that when she engages in this behavior all adults are to ignore her and continue the lesson with all of the other learners. It is important that no one lectures her about this behavior because that would provide reinforcement for the behavior. In addition, she will not earn for any of the DRO or her visual reinforcement intervals while she is not participating. Janelle's partner on the relay team is temporarily paired with one of the teachers. This gets her attention, because the function of these behaviors is to gain adult attention. After about 4 minutes, she rejoins the relay races and begins to earn again. Miss Marsha marks Janelle's behavior data sheet, which includes the duration of the episode. At the beginning of the year, these episodes occurred quite frequently and could last 10 to 15 minutes, so definite gains have been made. Before the end of gym class, Janelle earns some 1:1 time with the staff member of her choosing. She chooses the gym teacher. He continues to work with other learners with Janelle in the role of his assistant. She loves this!

Every gym class ends the same way, with a brief cool down. The gym teachers let the learners know it is time to gather for the cool down by clapping a pattern. Learners and staff all clap the same pattern back while making their way to their assigned spots around the gym. After stretching, Janelle quickly makes her way to line up and nicely deals with the fact that she is 3rd in line. Miss Marsha notices this and stands near her and gives her some extra attention by asking her about the weather today. Janelle just beams because she loves all things weather related! Ezra does not immediately line up at the end of stretching. Instead he first goes to the blue line to get his communication book and then joins everyone else in line.

This year, gym class has been quite a challenge for Miss Mindy and her team, but they are starting to see huge benefits. All of the learners, including Frederick, are now participating in gym class more than they were, and she knows with continued diligence and teaching that everyone will participate even more fully with the passing of each reporting period. Miss Mindy considers the many gains and is also happy with her decision to call in for the support of Mrs. Horton during gym class for the first several weeks after all of the intervention decisions had been made. In addition, it was wise for the team to rotate which team member would assist in gym. She knows that this strategy decreased the probability of staff burnout.

Afternoon - Ms. Beal

Transitions between classes in this middle school are a bit noisy and chaotic, but it seems that the transition to the lunch period is the most boisterous. Marquis prepares for this transition by putting in his earplugs as he is packing up his materials. He will need his SGD, so he carries this instead of placing it in his book bag. His earplugs block out a fair amount of noise, but he can hear well enough if someone is directly addressing him. Upon arrival in the lunch room, learners choose where to sit. Most choose to claim a spot before entering one of the many lines. Today, Marquis enters the line serving hamburgers and hotdogs, chooses a tray and gets in line behind another learner, leaving adequate space so he does not feel too crowded. When another learner accidentally bumps into him, he turns around, but does not "say" anything at this point. Apparently, the learner understands and makes an effort not to bump into Marquis again. Ms. Beal is monitoring the situation from a short distance away and is pleased to see that Marquis does not attempt to pinch this learner.

Marquis orders a hamburger with lettuce, pickle, tomato and mayonnaise via his device. The person serving asks, "Will you have fries with that?" and Marquis shakes his head "No." After receiving the hamburger, he joins the salad bar line. Just as many of the learners in this school, Marquis enjoys assembling his own salad and does so on most days. When another learner bumps into him in line, he quickly constructs a message on his device and presents it to the learner before hitting the "speak" button. The device says, "Please move away. When people are too close, I get nervous." The learner mumbles a quick apology and makes an effort to give Marquis more room. After paying for his lunch items, Marquis is pleased to see some of his friends have already gathered at the same table. He enjoys this time of day because he has some time to converse with friends about the latest vampire book that everyone is reading, or High School Musical. Today, most of them are busy chatting about the upcoming school dance. Melissa asks Marquis if he will be attending the dance, and he lets her know he has not yet decided. She provides encouragement saying that everyone would be there and she hoped he would decide to attend. Marquis digs into his bag to find his iPod and switches his earplugs with the ear buds and clears his area. Marquis learned that taking care of this before the bell rings is much easier for him. He settles in to listen when the bell rings.

After lunch, Marquis goes to his next class where he is met by his teacher who informs learners as they arrive that there has been a change in the daily schedule and everyone should return to their homeroom class. She asks Marquis to see his daily planner so she can note the change because she knows that he may transition more easily if the change is made directly on his daily schedule. She asks him if he wants to write in the change and he shakes his head "No." She asks if she can note the change, and he nods his head "Yes." She quickly asks another learner from her homeroom class to help her inform learners of the change while she takes a moment to note the change in Marquis' planner. Marquis begins to slightly rock back and forth and places one hand near his ear and presses a finger into that ear. His teacher lets him know that the sudden change has certainly come as a surprise, but she will see him again soon. Just before he walks away, she provides him with a token and a reminder that if he needs a break at any point, he can always ask.

Ms. Beal is relieved to see Marquis enter her classroom with the rest of the learners filing in the room. This probably means that he tolerated the change fairly well so far and has not requested a break. Marquis sits at his desk with his SGD perfectly aligned with the right edge of his desk. He is busy looking at his planner which now has a line through one class and "assembly in gym" carefully written underneath.

As the last learners arrive, Joshua makes his way to his desk. His iPod vibrates as his R+ Remind app continues to run. He opens up his planner and gives himself a point to find that it completes that set. He decides to "bank" those points, so he removes his checkbook from his book bag and adds in $5.00 for the points he has received. He also writes in "bank" on his daily schedule. After adding this to the balance, he sees that he now has enough to "buy" the High School Musical Soundtrack. He rushes to the front of the class to let Ms. Beal know. She is busy with several things, but acknowledges his excitement and then says, "I'm sure this will be the first thing you tell your dad when he gets home this evening!"

Once all of the learners have settled into her classroom, Ms. Beal announces that there will be a short surprise assembly in the auditorium. She glances around the classroom and notes that Marquis looks especially anxious. As soon as she was informed of the change in schedule, she altered the visual schedules for the learners that were already in the room. With the announcement made, she and the rest of the team work their way around the room to alter the written and picture schedules of the rest of the learners. She double checks Marquis' schedule and is pleased to note that the change has already been made. She gives Marquis a token and a favorite puzzle to work on during this downtime. Joshua is already busy writing out song lyrics. Other learners access leisure activities either independently or when offered choices.

The transition to the assembly is uneventful and Ms. Beal is hopeful that Marquis will use his communication skills during the assembly and not resort to pinching or body rocking. She notes a couple of his closest friends were making their way to sit on the bleachers near him and is confident that they will provide reminders if needed. As soon as the Principal begins with the announcements, the audio system makes a terrible noise. Marquis winces and puts his hands to his ears, just like most of the other learners. He then uses his SGD to excuse himself from the row. He approaches Ms. Beal and asks for a break. She says this is fine and he leaves the auditorium. He checks his watch. After three minutes pass, he returns to the auditorium, a bit less agitated but still not thrilled. He asks Ms. Beal if she has anything he can do for her. She thanks him, but says, "No," and offers him her seat on the end of the row. After a moment, she asks him if he remembered his earplugs. His eyes light up as he reaches for his book bag and finds them. A visibly more relaxed Marquis remains in the auditorium with his class for the rest of the assembly.

Afternoon - Mr. Manuel

Some of Mr. Manuel's learners did not leave campus today. They are busy with a fun weekly activity - putting together a grocery list. Mr. Manuel guides his learners to make choices of needed items based upon the dishes they plan to make later in the week. Some of the learners can read traditional recipes and others need picture recipes, so both are provided. When Darrin and other learners return from their job sites, Darrin types the grocery list and Rose checks the pantry for ingredients as Mr. Manuel asks, "Rose, do we have any _____?" After checking, she returns from the pantry and gestures "Yes" or "No." Mr. Manuel grabs a recipe box filled with both photos and pictures of common grocery items as other learners return. Some of the learners make the trip to the grocery store which is a short van ride away.

The grocery store trip is now much less work than it was when these learners were new to Mr. Manuel's class. He remembers teaching each of the many routines required for a successful and independent trip to the grocery store. Some of these routines included: entering and accessing cart(s), following visual lists, weighing produce, following oral directions (this is especially useful when items are forgotten along the way), waiting in line, bagging groceries, and paying with cash or debit cards. Of course, not every learner has mastered every routine, but he is impressed with the independence and confidence his learners have gained. He and the rest of the team agreed upon specific task analyses for each routine and taught them utilizing teaching strategies that were specific to each learner. For example, Darrin learned to pay with the class debit card by following the written instructions on the key pad, but he had to be taught *when* to swipe the card and he had to memorize the PIN. Darrin was taught to swipe his card using a forward chaining teaching strategy within two short sequences.

1. After the cart was positioned at front of the line, Darrin knew to

stand near the keypad. As soon as he stopped at the keypad, a staff member showed him a reminder card (orange sticky note) that stated, "Get your debit card ready."

2. At the point when the cashier looked at Darrin and said, "Your total is ____" a staff member would gesture to the keypad for him to begin the sequence. Vocal social praise was offered as needed and the team tried to vary the praise statements used.

Over time, both the orange sticky note and the gesture to swipe the card were eliminated from this lesson.

Each week several copies of Darrin's list are printed. Each learner is responsible for finding different items, so these are highlighted and distributed to each learner on a clipboard with a pencil attached. Once in the grocery store, the learners each grab their own carts and set off in different directions. Depending upon staffing for that day, they may be in groups of 2 or 3 with a staff member assisting either in close proximity or at a distance. Rose cannot read the printed words on the grocery list, so the person assisting her group shows her a photograph of each item she needs to find. Rose is given the picture when they turn down the appropriate aisle. When time permits, they tape the photos next to items on the list for Rose and she places a check mark by the photo after she places the item in the cart. The learner that Rose is paired with on this day is able to find aisles by number matching. On his list, Mr. Manuel has included the aisle number next to each item (this is an example of the usefulness of number matching in everyday life). Of course, it may be simpler to tell this learner that bread is on aisle 7, but this team strives to promote independence whenever possible.

Several learners request different items while in the store. Mr. Manuel says yes to some, but not all, of these requests. His learners have come to understand that sometimes they get to add a specific item to the cart and at other times they do not. Again, depending upon the amount of time they have, some learners will make separate purchases, either with cash or debit cards. Darrin generally takes a detour down the aisle of cleaning supplies and will happily announce the benefits of certain products over others to anyone who will listen.

While in the grocery store, Rose earns her last token. Mr. Manuel is relieved when he realizes he did not forget the tokens, but then discovers that he has not remembered the bag of reinforcers or the small plastic reinforcer tray. Rose has been doing quite well with the "wait" card and, at this point, it is truly Mr. Manuel's only option. After Rose exchanges all of her fancy tokens he places the photo for pudding on the "wait" card and apologizes for not having her pudding available right away. Rose sees that her favorite pudding is in the cart, so she tries to take it. Mr. Manuel blocks her access to the pudding and points to the "wait" card. He asks one of the assistants to accompany three of the learners to the bench by the exit and reminds them about the real estate brochures. Rose enjoys looking at all types of magazines. She waits with the group and looks at a brochure.

Even though the class has several carts while shopping, they consolidate the contents of the carts before going through the line when they are running short on time, as they are today. By the time all of the items are consolidated, Rose and several learners are already waiting on the bench. Darrin completes the transaction with the cashier, says "Thank you, have a nice weekend and I hope you enjoy the NASCAR race on Sunday." The cashier says "Good bye!" Mr. Manuel notes that, this time, she looks at Darrin when she says goodbye instead of at one of the teachers! All of the learners help place the groceries in the van and pile in for the trip back to school. Mr. Manuel remembers that Rose is waiting for pudding. He would like to give it to her at this point because she has been waiting so well, however, he doesn't have a spoon for her so he will arrange for her to enjoy the pudding, and perhaps an extra 5 minutes with an activity of her choosing, when they arrive back at school.

An "unscheduled" stop has been planned because one learner has difficulty when his parents make stops that are not indicated on his family outing travel schedule. This makes running errands quite difficult and the behaviors exhibited by this learner are potentially quite dangerous. He removes his seatbelt and grabs his mother around the neck. His mother says that he calms right down if she does not make the unplanned stop and continues with the stops in the order they are listed on her son's visual schedule. Over time, she has stopped taking her son on trips by herself and has asked neighbors to run errands for her instead of surprising her son with an unscheduled stop. Mr. Manuel and the rest of the team agree that this must be a priority for this learner and they have developed a plan. This "unexpected" stop is part of the plan today. All of the reinforcers were left behind, however, so they decide it would not be in anyone's best interest to begin this lesson today. Upon arriving back at school, everyone helps unload the van and all of the bags are taken back to class. One staff member stops by the office to sign the class back in to school. Rose receives her pudding and loads of praise for waiting so very nicely for this earned reinforcer. She is also given an opportunity to request something in addition. She requests a jewelry catalog and flips through the pages as she enjoys her pudding. One team member oversees the putting away of the groceries as Mr. Manuel makes some final notes in the home/school communication notebooks. Darrin completes his end of the day self evaluation and uses the last five minutes of the school day to surf the web on his iPhone.

Evening - Ezra's Home

Ezra lives at home with his parents and siblings. He has an older sister, Eliza, and an older brother, Elijah. Ezra's mom and dad recall that life used to be quite a bit more hectic, especially at night. They have worked in concert with Ezra's team to prioritize and address goals in the home environment. Initially, they felt completely overwhelmed with Ezra's behavior and, in many ways, simply did all they could to eradicate everything that might potentially "trigger" a tantrum from the home. They quickly realized that the entire family was stressed and that it was unrealistic to alter everything at home, because they simply could not anticipate or alter everything outside of the home. They want their son to accompany the family on outings and participate in neighborhood and religious events because these are important to the family.

After Ezra started school and settled in a bit, they observed, and were absolutely thrilled with, his progress. Of course, he still has challenging moments and some lessons are more preferred than others, but this is true for any preschooler. They met with Miss Mindy and the behavior analyst, Dr. Tony, and asked to schedule a home visit so they could get a fresh perspective and begin to develop a plan of action. They decided to address communication skills and develop some consistent routines. They also decided to collect some data on tantrums to begin the process of determining the function(s) they may serve. Even though they were eager to get started, they realized that putting in the time to organize, prioritize and start with only a few goals would certainly pay off.

Once Ezra began to make gains with communication via PECS at school, they began to teach PECS in the home environment. They found that Ezra generalized these skills quickly. He has a communication book at home and he takes this book on outings and transitions to school. He has a separate communication book in the school setting, so this one stays with him while he is with his family.

It has been several months since the initial home visit. We join the family to observe some of their evening routines. After eating dinner, Ezra's family plays a board or card game every other night. On most other nights, they play outside or watch a TV show together. Tonight, they are playing Candy Land. It has been adapted in two ways so that Ezra has an easier time playing along. First, they have taken the "doubles" cards out of the stack so it is an easier matching task for him when it is his turn. Miss Mindy suggested ways for the family to adapt other popular family games so that Ezra is not only participating but also applying skills he is learning at school. For this game, Ezra will work on turn taking and matching along with the fine motor skills to manipulate his game piece and the cards. His game piece has been modified as the second adaptation. Ezra does not particularly care which game piece he uses, but sometimes has trouble identifying his after the game begins. A Dalmatian sticker is placed on the game piece he chooses. This has certainly helped him within this game and others that involve game pieces.

Bath time can be quite hectic in any household, especially when there are multiple children! Ezra has no problems getting undressed when it is bath time; he loves this time of day. His parents have been diligent in finding opportunities for Ezra to request via PECS. Granted, it might be easier to simply interpret his behavior and/or assume they know what he wants at any given moment. However, they understand that giving their son the power of communication is a wonderful gift. Of course, they would love it if one day he woke up and started talking. They are encouraged because they have learned that several other PECS users in his class have begun to use some vocal approximations or speech. They realize that there is no way to predict if Ezra will have this outcome, so they are pressing forward with functional communication training via PECS. Miss Angie, his SLP, continues to work on oral motor goals as well as sound imitation. Tonight, Ezra's mom, Elise, has "forgotten" to place his favorite blue washcloth and his 101 Dalmatians figures into the tub. Last night, she "forgot" to provide his bubblegum scented body wash. Some nights are too hectic, especially the nights when Eliza and Elijah have karate practice. On those nights, she simply ensures that all of his favorite tub toys and gear are available. Miss Angie has provided the family with many pictures as Ezra has gained PECS skills in the home environment. The pictures that are used at bath time are affixed with Velcro® to an activity board that hangs on little hooks on suction cups. These pictures are triple laminated and everyone was thrilled to learn that Velcro® still works when wet. Miss Angie let Elise know that these pictures may not last as long as all of his other pictures, but that they will last longer than she thinks. He also has a Sentence Starter "I want" and a Sentence Strip available so he can communicate via PECS at the same phase he uses the rest of the day.

During the bath, Ezra requests his Cruella figurine via PECS, "I want + Cruella (a photo) + figurine." He has a variety of 101 Dalmatians characters and uses attributes to specify which one he wants (e.g., stuffed animals, figurines, puzzles, etc.). He also requests his washcloth, "I want + washcloth." Elise is relieved that Ezra's visual discrimination skills are quite good. She learned how to conduct the 4-Step Error Correction Procedure, but thus far has not had to correct any errors within PECS. Elise set a timer at the beginning of bath time because if it were up to Ezra bath time would last and last! The timer beeps and Elise shows Ezra his favorite Dalmatian Pillow Pet™. Ezra vocalizes in protest as she pulls the plug and the tub begins to drain. The loud protest increases in intensity and the tears begin to flow. Elise places the towel around her son and gives him a big hug and murmurs a few words of consolation. She does not give in. She steels her resolve not to give in to her son's protest. In discussions with his Miss Mindy and Dr. Tony, she learned that giving in taught Ezra that engaging in those behaviors would result in getting his way. She was ready for the increase in intensity and was grateful that they let her know to expect this. Elise still wasn't clear why they called this an "extinction burst," but she knew that changing her mind or giving in would only exacerbate the problem. Once he is all dry, Ezra is no longer crying and Elise gives him his beloved Dalmatian Pillow Pet™. He squeals with joy and hugs the pillow. Elise reaches for his pajamas and sees the pudding cup. She had planned to get at least one "No" opportunity during bath time by offering the pudding. Alas, she will try to remember tomorrow!

After Ezra is dressed in his pajamas, Elise tells him that it is nearly time for stories and then shows him his toothbrush. Using this reinforcer first strategy has helped Ezra tolerate less preferred transitions. He backs away from the sink. Elise makes a mental note to ask Miss Mindy if she thinks that a mini visual schedule might help with the evening routine as she turns to the task of helping her youngest son brush his teeth while her other two children are buzzing about also getting ready for bed. A laminated card has been taped to the mirror. This card has the steps for teaching Ezra to brush his teeth. She and her husband helped develop the list of steps on this card. The last three steps on the list have been highlighted. This visual aid helps remind the family not to provide help for these steps because Ezra has mastered them. Elise notes the time - it is getting late. Sometimes she asks Ezra which flavor toothpaste he would like. He generally prefers the bubblegum flavor and will use the picture for bubblegum as an attribute within his request.

Tonight, she opts to ask a yes/no question and this works perfectly because she did not have time for a yes/no opportunity while he was in the bathtub. She signals her other son to be sure he can provide a prompt if needed. She holds up the mint flavored toothpaste (Ezra does not like this one) and asks, "Do you want mint tonight?" Ezra begins to push away the toothpaste and clearly shakes his head "No!" Elise says, "No thank you!" and puts away the mint and asks him about the bubblegum flavor. He grabs for the toothpaste, but does not nod his head to indicate "Yes." Elijah helps him with the head nod by providing a slight physical prompt. Ezra is given the toothpaste and he seems quite pleased. Elise provides physical prompts for each of the steps indicated on the card and gives him some vocal praise when she feels that he is more fully participating in a step. Once he reaches the step to rinse the toothbrush, she stops helping altogether and allows him to complete the routine. She is delighted and provides loads more vocal praise as she hands him his Pillow Pet™. They both exit the bathroom and head toward his room. It is time for stories with all three children. Elise is exhausted and she's not sure how long it will take Ezra to get to sleep tonight, but since they started this routine, he is beginning to settle down and get to sleep more quickly. She reminds herself that the family has worked diligently to set up routines as much as possible, but no one is perfect. Change takes time and just because the family has had to make some adjustments does not mean that their old ways of doing things were wrong, they just did not work well for Ezra. Initiating the home visit with Miss Mindy and Dr. Tony was an excellent first step. Elise and her husband will continue to learn ways to help Ezra in the home environment.

Late Afternoon and Evening - Rose's Group Home

Since Rose does not live at the group home full time, her group home team created a special photo calendar that depicts which place she will be on specific days. They have multiple copies of a photo of the group home and a photo of her home. These are attached to a calendar in her room so she can see the entire month. This has helped Rose tremendously in the mornings. When she first moved into her group home she would get very nervous and agitated in the morning as she waited with her book bag. If the transport van pulled up, she would often have a tantrum. The staff at the group home created the photo calendar and they made sure that on the days when she was going home, she had her duffle bag in addition to her book bag. They also began to use a visual reinforcement system with her that stayed at the group home. They have tried their best to match the rate of reinforcement she was getting in the school setting. All of these strategies are helping because it has been a long time since Rose demonstrated any tantrum behavior in the mornings.

Rose is excited as the van pulls up to the group home. She takes her travel communication folder with her as she heads toward the back of the van to get her things. After placing her folder into her book bag, she races toward the door. She approaches the front door and waits. Miss Jill is busy with something in the yard, but she keeps a close eye on Rose. She is learning to unlock the front door with her key. She has mastered all of the steps except for the first one (i.e., take out the key). Everyone agreed that if a member of the team stood next to her on the porch each and every day, it was likely serving as a prompt. Not to mention, along with such close proximity, most people are more likely to provide some type of subtle prompt but a prompt nonetheless. They decided to utilize the progressive time delayed prompting procedure and yesterday, Miss Jill had to step in to provide a prompt after pausing nine seconds. Today they have arranged for Miss Jill to "shadow" Rose at a distance. Miss Jill begins to count to herself, "one, two, three..." Everyone practiced counting at a very slow rate until they were counting at about the same pace. Miss Jill is not to step in or provide any type of prompting until she has counted to ten. She continues to count, "...five, six, seven..." and Rose reaches into her book bag and takes out her keys. She did it! Miss Jill is thrilled but she contains her excitement and continues clipping flowers. As soon as Rose enters the foyer, Mr. Kris greets her with a hearty hello. He is also pleased with Rose's independence with this new routine and he wants to provide even more social praise, but Rose is generally not thrilled with that type of social display. Her team has learned that giving her more time with preferred activities functions better as differential reinforcement than additional socially based reinforcement, even when it comes from her most favorite staff members. As Rose makes her way to her room, Mr. Kris marks her data sheet for using a key to unlock door. He cannot resist drawing a star beside the date.

Rose puts down her book bag and takes off her shoes. She likes to wear slippers while she is in the house, so she changes into those. After picking up her communication book, she walks to the family room where several residents are watching a home shopping channel. She goes to the desk and takes out her purple folder. This purple folder contains her photo schedule for this setting. The first photo depicts choice time. This is a yellow card with the word "choice," along with photos that depict many things she can choose and an open dot of Velcro®. Rose has a corresponding yellow sheet in the folder pocket. This yellow sheet contains photos of available choices. She also has a blue and green sheet for other types of choices. The choice photos on the yellow page are: make jewelry, magazines, Wii® and television. She wastes no time selecting the picture for "make jewelry" and placing it on the Velcro® spot on the choice card.

Rose heads right for the utility room where she has an entire shelf dedicated to her jewelry making supplies. She makes three trips and stacks all of the plastic bead boxes on a large table in the recreation room. This room also has a television, but it is currently not being watched. Mr. Kris stops by and lets her know he is setting the timer because there are chores to complete and a meal to prepare. He sets the digital timer for 40 minutes. This is 10 minutes longer than Rose would normally have for recreation time. He added time due to her flawless execution of the sequence when unlocking the door and entering the house. He tells her that he has given her more time and why. He tries to use simple, yet age appropriate language. Rose's receptive understanding of language is inconsistent; how-ever, most people address her as they would any other 19 year old except perhaps using fewer words and less "flowery" language because too much language tends to confuse her.

Rose has chosen to use some very small turquoise beads for this set of earrings. After several attempts to get three of them on the wire, she becomes frustrated and pinches herself. Mr. Kris has been monitoring at a distance as he completes some forms on the computer. He observes her pinching episode. Rose's behavior plan specifies ignoring this behavior if it has already begun. As unobtrusively as possible, he takes a clipboard from the desk. This clipboard contains all of Rose's behavior data sheets. He notes the time and approximate duration, 15 seconds. Once Rose is no longer actively engaging in this behavior, he approaches her and admires her work. He sees the small beads she has been working with and com-ments about the beautiful turquoise she chose for this set. Just as she be-gins to pick up the earring and try again, Mr. Kris notes that she seems a bit agitated and that she is humming and beginning to rock a bit. Both of these behaviors can be indicators that a pinching episode is about to begin. He offers her a choice between a squishy tennis ball and a very soft koosh. She carefully places the earring back on the gray towel, and takes the squishy tennis ball. After a moment of intense squishes, she sets it aside and goes back to her beading. Mr. Kris and the rest of the team are teaching Rose that when she is frustrated she can use items such as these to reduce some of the stress and, if needed, ask for help. So far, these procedures seem to be working. The team has noted a decrease in self pinching behavior and they are hopeful that this trend will continue.

Rose's mother has purchased some earring and necklace cards with Rose's name and a logo. She hopes that Rose will have enough jewelry complete in time for the next community festival so they can display and sell some of her creations. Rose has quite a bit of difficulty placing the jew-elry onto these special cards. If she asks for help while making jewelry, it is usually with this task. Mr. Kris gives Rose only 1 token for this task be-cause it is one of her preferred activities - the rate of reinforcement certainly does not need to be as rich as it is for more difficult or less preferred tasks. However, he still had Rose choose something to work toward just as she prepared to follow her visual schedule for the afternoon. When the digi-tal timer sounds, Rose does not immediately begin the process of putting away her materials. Mr. Kris is still busy at the desk and he waits to see if Rose will stop the timer and begin the process on her own. His patience is rewarded when Rose silences the timer, and begins to organize her materi-als. Once she has nearly all of the materials back in the plastic trays, Mr. Kris approaches with a token and lets her know she is a "rock star!" This is

Rose's second token. She places it on her visual reinforcement card which is located near her communication book. Her book is discreetly hidden inside a trendy purse. Her mom made this for her. When the outer flap of the purse is lifted, it reveals her communication book.

While putting away her materials Rose has a difficult time balancing some of the boxes on the shelf because she has placed the smallest one on the bottom of the stack. After two attempts, she places them on a lower shelf and goes to her communication book. She constructs, "I want + help + boxes." and hands the Sentence Strip to Mr. Kris. He sees the boxes on the shelf and helps her by placing the largest one on the bottom. She finishes by stacking the rest. Once all of the materials are properly stored, she goes back to her purple folder to find another choice card; this one is green and indicates choices of outdoor chores. There are two Velcro® dots next to the "choice" photo. This indicates that she will complete two different activities. The choices included on the corresponding green sheet are: water plants, rake leaves, pull weeds, and pick up magnolia leaves. Rose places her two choices, "water plants" and "rake leaves," on the green choice card and moves it to the current activity box. She picks up her materials and is making her way to the back yard when Mr. Kris asks her where her home/school notebook is. He shows her another resident's book to provide some additional information. She makes her way back to her bedroom to find her book bag. She quickly locates it and tugs at the zipper. It is jammed once again. Rose takes her purse off of her shoulder, flips open the front closure to reveal her communication book and constructs, "I want + help + zipper." and takes this to Mr. Kris along with the book bag. He frees the loose string and opens the zipper for Rose. Once she has removed the home/school notebook, he asks her if he can keep the bag for a few minutes to attempt a repair. She leaves him with the bag and begins to make her way to the backyard. She steps out the doorway to the patio. Ms. Jaime sees that Rose has forgotten to put on her work boots. She casually approaches Rose and says, "Uh oh, forgot something pretty important." She provides a slight physical prompt for her to go back up the steps and back into the recreation room. She points to Rose's work boots. Rose slides out of her slippers and puts on her work before going back outside.

Now properly attired for yard work, Rose places her communication book, visual schedule and visual reinforcement system on the picnic table and saunters over toward the garden hose. She's quite proficient with this routine, so she grabs the sprayer, turns on the water at the tap, and begins to unwind the hose by pulling it in the direction of the flowerbed at the back of the lot. The "shower" mode on the nozzle has a bright blue star that serves as a visual reminder for the residents about which mode should be utilized. She turns the nozzle to the appropriate spot and begins to water the flowerbed. The team working with Rose has had several discussions about how they can promote even more independence for Rose within this task. They have decided to incorporate a timer that can either be worn around her neck or clipped on her clothing. Today Ms. Jaime will introduce this new part of the routine. Rose is sometimes resistant to changes in routines, so the team has decided to first incorporate the use of the timer and over time incorporate her wearing and setting the timer independently. Over the years, Rose has had experience with many timers in the school and home settings, so when the timer begins to beep, Ms. Jaime simply points to the other garden plot. Rose stops spraying the flower garden and moves in the direction of the vegetable garden. Ms. Jaime sets the timer once again. While Rose is watering, Ms. Jaime realizes that it is about time to give her another token. She will give Rose the token in between this task and raking leaves because a quick stop at the picnic table makes more sense at that time. The timer beeps and Ms. Jaime points at the place where Rose will stow the watering hose. Rose stops watering and begins the process of cleaning up as Ms. Jaime checks on the progress of the rest of the residents who are just as busy as Rose with other outdoor chores.

Once Rose has put everything away and placed the token on her visual reinforcement card, she makes her way to the shed to get a rake. She is independent with this part of the task, but has difficulty staying with it for a very long period of time. Rose has learned all of the steps in this task, so the team works on increasing another quality of the task, duration. They use shaping to achieve this goal. Rose knows how to hold and orient the rake, but only pulls the rake toward her body 4 times on average. The lesson plan clearly states the process for increasing this particular skill. The person working with her should withhold social praise and the delivery of a token until she pulls the rake toward her body 5 times and quickly deliver a token. Ms. Jaime knew that the rate of token delivery would likely increase during this task so she holds Rose's visual reinforcement card during this task. Ms. Jaime counts and waits. She is tempted to jump in with a prompt, but she understands that pure shaping requires no prompts and utilizes increasing the amount of work required before gaining access to the reinforcer (in this case a token, the conditioned reinforcer). As soon as Rose pulls the rake toward her body the 5th time, Ms. Jaime provides both social praise and the token. Rose places the token on the card that Ms. Jaime is holding. It's the last one! She takes the tokens off of the board and exchanges them with Ms. Jaime who immediately provides Rose with a ring that has a large pink stone. Rose seems delighted and places the ring on her finger.

Ms. Jaime starts a new deal with Rose (the photos for her to choose between are attached to the back of the card with Velcro®). Once again, Rose chooses jewelry. This is a fairly consistent choice for Rose at this time of day, so Ms. Jaime is prepared with other baubles. Ms. Jaime says, "Alright, you are working for more jewelry, let's get back to work." Rose picks up her rake and gets back to work. Within the rest of this lesson, Ms. Jaime will continue to increase her expectations as long as Rose is independent. This type of within-lesson shaping is very important so Rose does not think that raking involves moving the rake only a certain number of times. This type of "ritualistic" behavior can develop if staff members are ritualistic about their delivery of reinforcement. Once Rose is able to stay with this task for longer periods of time, they will begin to work on another quality of the task such as raking until all of the largest leaves are in piles. Rose quickly earns another five tokens and is delighted when Ms. Jaime presents the set of pearls with a flourish!

The staff members that have assisted in this group home for more than a year are all impressed with the amount of work the residents complete each day. They have been committed to ensuring that the residents in this group home take part in the everyday operation of their home. It seems as if the staff members have less and less to do with each passing week. They are pleased that their adherence to the *Pyramid Approach to Education* has enabled them to teach so many skills over this past year. Even the data collection that Miss Anne told them about has been more manageable than they ever expected. They were all convinced that taking data would some-how detract from the skills they wanted to teach. They learned that once you start taking data it simply becomes part of the lesson and the process has become more efficient over time. They are also pleased to see all of the progress the residents were making on so many goals. The group home manager, Ms. Catherine, analyzes the data for all residents on a weekly basis and she shares this information, often in the form of graphs, with the entire team at weekly staff meetings. This meeting time is important for so many reasons. It provides a time to discuss success stories as well as challenges. This is also a time when they practice new teaching techniques or specific behavior procedures. All of the staff members enjoy these meet-ings, in part because Ms. Catherine is a huge source of reinforcement for each of them. In many ways, she has become a conditioned reinforcer be-cause of all the ways she has devised to reinforce every person that works in this group home. She is delighted that her company hosted the *Pyramid Approach to Education* training last year. She knew it would be a perfect fit for her, her staff and, most importantly, the residents in this group home.

Summary

Of course, there is no way to capture all of the energy within any set-ting. I hope, however, that these glimpses into the classroom and home environments of these individuals gives you, the reader, a sense of how the *Pyramid Approach* works together as an integrated whole. Examining the structure piece by piece is necessary and beneficial. However, the whole is so much more than the sum of its parts. Professionals and parents who are equipped with a working knowledge of Applied Behavior Analysis, as presented within the *Pyramid Approach*, will encounter each unique situation well prepared to answer critical questions. Dr. Bondy trusts that when the appropriate questions are asked, professionals and parents alike will indeed come up with the right answers. Use the *Pyramid Approach* to guide your formulation of these questions. Remember to concentrate on the structural issues first.

Functional Activities: Is this a functional lesson? Am I using materials that are meaningful from this learner's perspective?

Powerful Reinforcers: Is this learner adequately motivated by the natural reinforcers within this lesson? If not, can I add artificial reinforcement in a way that speeds up the process of shifting from these artificial reinforcers back to more natural ones?

Functional Communication: Does this learner have all of the expressive and receptive communication skills s/he needs to properly access this lesson?

Contextually Inappropriate Behavior

Preventative strategies: Have we determined to the best of our ability the function(s) of this behavior? Does the plan involve a heavy emphasis on teaching Functionally Equivalent Alternative Behaviors? Should we explore the usefulness of developing a reinforcement system for the absence of this behavior?

Reactive Strategies: Is everyone familiar and comfortable with the reactive part of this plan? Do we have adequate resources to successfully implement this plan? Is there a plan to review the data on a regular basis to ensure the plan is working?

Developing specific lesson plans for skills is a tremendously important part of education. However, if questions like the ones listed above have not been fully addressed, these lessons may not be as effective as they could be. The instructional part of the *Pyramid Approach* may lead to questions like these:

Generalization: Have we adequately planned for both stimulus and response generalization of this skill?

Lesson Plan Formats: Are we offering opportunities for both learner- and teacher-led lessons? Is everyone clear on the distinction between discrete and sequential lessons and which lesson format this particular skill requires?

Teaching Strategies: Has the best possible prompt for this learner within this lesson been selected? Is everyone clear that we will use one, and only one, type of prompt? Have we developed a plan to shift from prompts to natural cues?

Error Correction Strategies: Is each team member proficient with the error correction strategy associated with this lesson? Does everyone understand the importance of utilizing error correction instead of simply fixing errors when they occur?

Data Collection: Have data collection systems been developed for this lesson? Are they efficient and well understood by all team members? Has the team developed a minimum number of data points to collect each week for this lesson?

Of course, this is only a sampling of the types of questions that a team may come up with for creating an effective educational environment or lesson. Certainly you have gained insight throughout your reading of this entire book. No doubt many of your current ideas about teaching have been validated and others were challenged.

As you begin to create an environment based upon the *Pyramid Approach to Education,* remember to start small and address each element. Careful attention to the construction process will result in a solid educational foundation for your current learners and many learners to come. You will certainly achieve great things as you strive to enrich the lives of those you serve!